ENCYCLOPAEDIA OF INDIAN GOVERNMENT: PROGRAMMES AND POLICIES

ENCYCLOPAEDIA
OF
INDIAN GOVERNMENT:
PROGRAMMES AND POLICIES

Vol. 33

Commerce

Edited by

Satish Tiwari

ANMOL PUBLICATIONS PVT. LTD.
NEW DELHI - 110 002 (INDIA)

ANMOL PUBLICATIONS PVT. LTD.
4374/4B, Ansari Road, Daryaganj
New Delhi - 110 002

Encyclopaedia of Indian Government: Programmes and Policies

First Edition, 2000

ISBN 81-261-0515-1 (Set)

[Responsibility for the facts stated, opinions expressed, conclusions reached and plagiarism, if any, in these volumes is entirely that of the Editor. The Publisher bears no responsibility for them whatsoever.]

PRINTED IN INDIA

Published by J.L. Kumar for Anmol Publications Pvt. Ltd., New Delhi - 110 002 and Printed at Mehra Offset Press, Delhi.

Contents

Preface

Encyclopaedia of Indian Government: Programmes and Policies contains authoritative information on about fifty departmental policies and their future developmental programmes.

Organised to be completed in 40 volumes, this gigantic work covers Agriculture; Atomic Energy; Chemicals and Fertilizers; Coal; Commerce; Communication; Culture; Defence; Education; Environment and Forests; External Affairs; Finance; Food & Consumer Affairs; Food Processing Industries; Health and Family Welfare; Home Affairs and Internal Security; Human Resources; Industry; Information and Broadcasting; Labour; Law, Justice and Company Affairs; Non-conventional Energy Sources; Ocean Development; Parliamentary Affairs; Personnel, Public Grievances and Pensions; Petroleum and Natural Gas; Planning and Programme Implementation; Planning and Statistics; Posts and Telegraphs; Power; Rural Development; Science and Technology; Social Justice and Empowerment; Space; States Affairs; Steel; Steel and Mines; Sugar and Edible Oils; Surface Transport; Textiles; Tourism; Urban Development; Water Resources; Women and Child development etc.

Based on the information derived from authoritative sources, this work contains authentic facts and figures. I am deeply beholden to all the scholars whose writings are cited or substantially made use of in the present work. I am also thankful to Anmol Publications Pvt. Ltd. for undertaking publication of this encyclopaedia. I am solely responsible for shortcomings in presentation of matter.

Encyclopaedic in nature, this will prove a dependable reference work for scholars and academics besides those appearing for different competitive examinations.

—Satish Tiwari

1

Introduction

The Department of Supply in the Ministry of Commerce is the nodal Department for purchase and inspection of stores for the Ministries/Departments and offices of the, Central Government. It also arranges purchases and inspection of stores for the State Governments, Public Sector Undertakings, Autonomous Bodies and Quasi-Public Bodies at their request. Related functions like timely payment to suppliers, shipment and clearance of stores and disposal of certain categories of surplus stores belonging to Ministry of Defence are also looked after by the Department.

The Department caters to another important area with regard to the testing/evaluation of various types of materials, products and equipments. Cadre management and all other matters pertaining to two Group 'A' Central Services viz. Indian Supply Service and Indian Inspection Service, are looked after by the Department. Cadre management of Group-A Scientists of National Test House is also looked after by this Department. Department of Supply is a Department in the Ministry of Commerce. The Secretariat of the Department is headed by Secretary (Supply). The following Organisations form part of the Department of Supply:

(a) Directorate General of Supplies and Disposals (DGS&D) an attached office;

(b) National Test House (NTH) a Subordinate Office;

(c) Chief Controller of Accounts (CCA) a Subordinatae Office;

Directorate general of supplies and disposals

Directorate General of Supplies and Disposals, is the executive arm of the Department of Supply as far as matters concerning procurement of stores, inspection of stores, shipment and clearance and disposal of surplus stores are concerned.

Of late DGS&D has also entered into the areas of training with the establishment of a Training Institute. This step was taken to widen the service base of the organisation.

National Test House (NTH)

The National Test House (NTH) is the executive arm of the Department of Supply as far as matters concerning testing and evaluation of materials, products, equipments and systems are concerned. This work, alongwith the maintenance of test data and research and development in testing technology, is carried out by National Test House. The National Test House also assists Bureau of Indian Standards (BIS) in evolving national and international specifications and standards and carries out tests on behalf of the Bureau.

Keeping in view the present liberalised and export oriented industrial scenario in the country, stress is being given for improved quality products. For this purpose NTH has started offering Industrial Qualilty Consultancy Services. To begin with, a few areas have been identified for the consultancy purposes and the efforts are on to add more and more areas keeping in view the market needs. NTH is also imparting training to Scientists, technologists, technicians in test technology.

Chief Controller of Accounts (CCA)

The payment and accounting functions of the Department, including those of DGS&D and the National Test House, are performed by the Chief Controller of Accounts (CCA) under the Departmentalised Accounting System. The organisation is one of the largest in the country in so far as the payment of suppliers, bills is concerned.

Budget estimates and revised estimates

As compared to 1997-98 Actuals viz. Rs. 48.72 Crores the total provision in Budget. Estimates 1998-99 viz,. Rs. 55.76 Crores shows an increase by Rs. 7.0 Crores mainly to meet the increasl Pay Commission.

The Revised Estim provision Rs. 55.76 Crores shows an increase by Rs. 7.0 Crores mainly to meet the increased salaries/allowances of the employees due to iation of the recommendation of the Fifth Centra Pay Commission. The Revised Estimates for 1998-99 viz. Rs. 55.80 Crores has been retained at the level of Budget Estimates 1998-99 except for an increase of Rs. 4.0 lakhs on the plan side.

In Budget Estimate 1999-2000 a Non-plan provision of Rs. 55.28 Crores has been made, thereby showing an increase of Rs. 1.28 Crores due to salaries to meet normal increment and additional allowances during the year. The plan provision for the year 1999-2000 has been fixed at Rs. 5.0 Crores including Rs. 3.0' Crores for Lands and Building kept in the Demand of Ministry of Urban Affairs and Employment.

Staff strength of department of supply

Actual staff strength of Department of Supply including its attached and subordinate organisations, as on 31.12.1998 is as follows:-

		Gazetted	Non-Gazetted	Total
(i)	Deptt. of Supply (Sectt.)	34	137	171
(ii)	DGS&D	592	2282	2874
(iii)	NTH	177	465	642
(iv)	CCA	110	644	754
	Total	913	3528	4441

SIU has undertaken the work measurement study of DGS&D. In their preliminary assessment, they suggested steep reduction. In staff at different levels. Considering the sensitivity of the matter and to solicit the cooperation of the staff, a series of meetings were held with the staff associations.

The views of the Department are being projected to SIU for early finalisation of the report. On receipt of the final report, it will be placed before the Departmental Council as per the requirement. SIU has already-initiated a work measurement study of the office of CCA. They have also been requested to undertake similar exercise in respect of Department of Supply.

2

Directorate General of Supplies and Disposals

Directorate General of Supplies and Disposals is the Central Purchase Organisation of the Government of India. The concept of Central Purchase dates back to the year 1860 when India Stores Department was established by British Government in London for purchase of imported stores. Later, in 1917, Central purchasing in India began to take shape when the Indian Munitions Board was established for Government purchases.

The need for establishing an expert purchase agency equipped with a data base of the manufacturing resources throughout the country and competent to purchase efficiently in the domestic market as also to carry out inspection tot ensure quality of goods was felt and India Stores Department was established in July, 1929, in India for arranging purchases for Government Civil Departments.

The organisation underwent many changes thereafter and the DGS&D as the Central Purchase Organisation in its present form, came into being in 1951 for procurement Departments/Ministries. DGS&D extends its services, on request, to State Governments, Union Territories, Public Sector Undertakings, Autonomous Bodies and so on.

Decentralisation of DGS&D's Functions

Over the years, the DGS&D has under gone many changes. In 1974 some of the major Central Government Departments like Defence, Railways and Posts & Telegraphs were authorised to make their own purchases for items exclusive to them. All Scientific Departments were also exempted from the purview of DGS&D for their purchases.

Functions of DGS&D

Purchase

Government further reviewed the position in the year 1991 and decided to further decentralise the functions of DGS&D. According to this scheme of decentralisation, procurement against adhoc indents was transferred from DGS&D to the Indenting Ministries/ Departments. However, procurement on Rate/Running Contracts for common user items continues to be done by DGS&D except for P.O.L. (Petroleum, Oil and Lubricants) products for Ministries of Defence and Railways who procure these stores themselves.

In addition to Rate Contracts, DGS&D continues to render services on request, to State Governments, Union Territories, Public Sector Undertakings, Autonomous Bodies etc. provided they agree to make payments themselves against DGS&D contracts. If any Central Government Department experiences any difficulty in arranging its adhoc procurement, it can project its indent on DGS&D subject to fulfilment of certain conditions and also if the request has been recommended by the Head of the Department or the Secretary of the Department. DGS&D does not entertain indents for stores of a proprietary nature. As a result of instructions issued by Ministry of Finance, Deptts. other than Central Govts. and Union Territories are required to make the payments themselves against contracts concluded by DGS&D.

After decentralisation of payment, the State

Government/PSUs were delinked from the centralised payment system through Chief Controler of Accounts (CCA), Department of Supply, to ensure budgetary control and avoid Suspense Balance against State Governments. However, on the request of some of the State Governments, the matter has been reviewed in consultation with Ministry of Finance, and now the State Governments/PSUs are being allowed the facility of payment through CCA provided they deposit the requisite amount with the CCA in advance.

DGS&D also arranges disposal of surplus stores other than those for which powers have been delegated to various authorities by general or special order. The purchase procedure adopted by DGS&D are guided by the instructions laid down in the booklet titled 'Manual of Procedures for Supplies, Inspection and Disposals' (MOPSID) effective from 1.1.92.

The High Level Committee set up by the Deptt. of Supply in October '93 made number of suggestions to modify the existing policies and procedures and consequent thereto a large number of amendments were notified. Due to economic reforms since June '91, certain areas of policies and procedures also called for further modifications in the context of decentralisation- of adhoc purchases. Detailed discussions had taken place under the chairmanship of Secretary (Supply) to suggest a modified document. The modifications emanating from these discussions were circulated to the major Indenting Departments and comments obtained.

Consultancy and training

DGS&D has a fulfledged Training Directorate engaged in the training and HRD activities. It has recently established the Institute of Supply & Quality Management, to impart training and Quality Management to the Staff and officers of Govt.

Departments, Autonomous Bodies and Public Sector Undertakings and to render consultancy services to these organisations to the extent possible. Over a period of time, this facility is expected to be extended to Private sector also

Cargo clearance

DGS&D has set up facilities at Regional Supply offices at Mumbai, Chennai and Calcutta to arrange clearance of Imported cargo at all major Ports against orders placed by DGS&D and also by other Departments, Quasi Public Bodies, Government Undertakings and various State Governments, if called upon to do so.

Quality assurance

The Quality Assurance Wing is the technical arm of DGS&D providing technical support in its purchase functions. The technical support in purchase functions is rendered by laying down the procurement specifications, assessing the vendors and ensuring the quality of stores. The inspection functions continue with the DGS&D and its services are available to all Central Government Deptts./Offices, State Governments etc. both for contracts placed by DGS&D on their behalf or against direct orders placed by them. Q.A.

Wing of DGS&D carries out pre-despatch inspection of stores against contracts placed by DGS&D on behalf of the Central Government Departments, State Governments and Public Sector Undertakings and also accept inspection assignments against the contracts placed directly by them. The detailed functions of each Wing/ Branch/Directorate of DGS&D are as follows:-

Purchase wing

The Purchase wing is the mainstay of the procurement action for conclusion of rate Contracts and adhoc purchases. Stores of similar nature are grouped together and are dealt in different Purchase Directorates.

There are fourteen such Purchase Directorates, including one Directorate to deal with procurement of Stores for projects aided by World Bank and ADB etc. Each Purchase Directorate is under the charge of a Director (Supplies). Apart from the fourteen Purchase Directorates at Headquarters there are three Regional Supply Offices located at Mumbai, Chennai and Calcutta who deal with certain specified items allotted to them, which are peculiar to their Regions.

Conclusion of rate contracts

Conclusion of rate contracts is the main activity of Purchase Directorates. Rate contracts are concluded by DGS&D for common user items i.e. the items required by more than one Department/organisation and rather frequently. The system of buying through Rate Contracts facilitates procurement of quality goods from reliable source at most reasonable prices without the bother of inviting tenders by each Deptt. separately at every time the demand arises.

As an 1.1.99, there were 259 items on DGS&D Rate Contracts. In order to bring more items on Rate Contracts, a Standing Committee under the Chairmanship of DG (S&D) with representatives of major Indenting Departments and Apex Industrial Associations as Members has been set up.

The Committee periodically reviews the items on Rate Contract and considers fresh suggestions for inclusion of new items in the Rate Contract. The Committee identified 22 new items and also, suggested deletion of 15 items from the list of items for which Rate Contract are concluded. To generate greater competition and 'bring about more transperancy, DGS&D Tender Notices and R/C related information are published in some of leading National Dailies in respect of some of the major R/C items having large drawals and which are not of proprietary nature and their prices are not administered by the Government. Under this system composite information is inserted in the Dailies at regular intervals.

In the Rate Contract system, it is very essential that the new Rate Contract is in place immediately after the expiry of the existing Rate Contract so that there is no discontinuity. Discontinuity causes inconvenience to the DDOs and also the suppliers. Discontinuity in the case of number of Rate Contracts was reviewed and directions were issued to prepare pert chart identifying intermediate milestones in respect of each Rate Contract item to ensure timely conclusion.

This was followed up with monitoring. Consequently, the continuity has improved to 97% as against 85% of the previous year. Presently, 2.57 items are available on RC. The basic objective of DGS&D is to gravitate towards procurement of BIS marked goods. Presently, out of 257 items available on RC, the QA Wing of DGS&D carries out technical particulars checking in respect of 199 items. For the remaining 58 items, the responsibility of technical particulars of checking rests with the identors.

Out of 199 items, 99 items are procured as per BIS specification. For 50 items, the specifications being followed by DGS&D are superior to BIS specification. Remaining 50 items are procured conforming to Defence/ DGS&D/manufacturers' specification. DGS&D, at present, have been concluding RCs with BIS marking for 10 items which are exclusively covered under mandatory BIS certification. It is proposed to cover other items which are not under mandatory BIS marking in order to ensure quality. Towards this end, 16 additional items have been identified for procurement with BIS marking from the year 2000-2001.

The Rate Contract document is the most important document in the rate contract system. The Rate Contract document is also used by other Departments as a bench mark. A need was felt to have a simplified standard contract document for all the rate contracts concluded by DGS&D in order to ensure uniformity, transparency and also to facilitate speedy conclusion of Rate Contract. With these objectives in view the Rate Contract documents concluded between DGS&D and RC holders were examined during the year.

The document comprises of three parts. First part contains clauses which are standard and uniform irrespective of items/RC holders. These standard clauses were reviewed, amended/updated during the year. It is proposed to put this standard clauses in print in a priced publication. This will preclude the need for repeating these clauses in each and every contract typographically and would thus save stationery as well as time.

Only a reference to the printed booket would be sufficient for contractual purposes. It is also proposed to put these standard clauses in DGS&D website so that these are known to all Direct Demanding Officers (DDOs) who can access through NICNET.

In the event of any changes in the standard clauses, the DDOs will also automatically come to know about such changes. The second part of the contract document is item specific. Since DGS&D covers 257 items under RC, it is proposed to standardise the item specific contract clauses in respect of important items where the annual drawals are Rs. 5.00 crores and above.

An exercise on the issue has since been initiated and is expected to be completed during the current financial year. On conclusion, it is proposed to be placed on the website for reasons indicated earlier. The third part of the RC document contains schedule of item and prices, which are RC holders specific. On conclusion of rate contract, only this part would need to be finalised. To give wider choice to the indentor, information relating to all the RC holders fox, an item would be made available at one pace.

It is also proposed to issue amendment through 'website' of DGS&D in addition to informing them by post. The proposed changes would facilitate prompt updating of contract clauses, quick dissemination of information to DDOs and avoid delay.

DGS&D sends the rate contract documents to large number of Direct Demanding officers (DDOs) spread throughout the country. A need was felt that the mailing list of DDOs needed revision as number of DDOs are no longer acting as DDOs and new DDOs have also started utilising the service of DGS&D.

Procurement under world bank/Asian development bank aided projects

World Bank Directorate at DGS&D Hqrs is handling the procurement of stores required for following projects aided by World Bank /ADB:-

a) Technical Education Project (under Ministry of Human Resources Development) for various Polytechnics in different States throughout the country.

b) National Aids Control Organisation Project under Ministry of Health and Family Welfare.

c) State Road Projects under the Ministry of Surface Transport.

d) Vocational Training Project under the Directorate General of Employment and Training.

e) Maharashtra Emergency Earthquake Rehabilitation Project under India Meteorological Department.

f) Hydrology Project of Central Ground water Board and India Meteorological Department.

g) CATs project of NCT of Delhi.

h) Equipments for waste disposal of Hospitals in Delhi.

i) Malaria Control Project for NMEP, Delhi.

Value of orders placed by World Bank Directorate for the last five years is indicated in the following table:-

(Rs.in crores)

1994-95	1995-96	1996-97	1997-98	1998-99 (Upto Dec.98)
39	26	4	15	1.46

Analysis of purchases by DGS&D

No. of idents, contracts and value of contracts

The following table indicates the purchases effected in terms of indents, number of contracts and value of contracts placed by DGS&D over the last five years:

	94-95	95-96	96-97	97-98	98-99 (Upto Dec. 98)
i) No.of indents received	1735	1387	1298	1386	958
ii) No. of contracts placed	3316	2976	2884	3078	2610
iii) No. of contracts cancelled at the-risk & cost	1776	162	22	30	41
iv) Value of contr-acts (Rupees in crores)	2645	2412	2092	1836	855

Purchase made from hqrs. and regions

The major portion of purchases effected by the DGS&D are made from the Headquarters at New Delhi as may be seen from the following table:-

(Values in Rs. in crores)

	94-95	95-96	96-97	97-98	98-99 (Upto Dec. 98)
i). Headquarters, N. Delhi	2166	1792	1566	1082	361
ii) DS&D, Calcutta	434	589	511	749	492
iii) DS&D, Mumbai (incl. DS (Tex.) Mumbai.)	22	18	10	1	1
iv) DS&D Chennai	23	13	5	4	1
Total	2645	2412	2092	1836	855

Value of purchases-regionwise

The following table indicates the value of orders placed on the suppliers located in the four zones:-

(Values in Rs. crores)

	94-95	95-96	96-97	97-98	98-99 (Upto Dec. 98)
Northern Zone	803	865	1030	547	1601
Eastern Zone	629	829	764	931	547
Southern Zone	142	169	109	114	41
Western Zone	1047	538	189	242	107
Direct orders abroad	24	11	0.28	2	–
Total:	2645	2412	2092	1836	855

There is some unevenness with respect to the purchases effected from different Regions. Northern and Eastern Regions contribute:, to a larger portion of DGS&D purchases than Western and Southern Regions.

Value of purchase; indigenous, imported, large and small sector wise

The following table indicates the value of purchases sector wise:

	94-95	95-96	96-97	97-98	98-99 (Upto Dec. 98)
	1	**2**	**3**	**4**	**5**
A. Indigenous					
i) S.S.I	228	204	196	245	64
ii) L.S.I.	2372	2156	1858	1569	777
	1	**2**	**3**	**4**	**5**
Total	2600	2360	2054	1814	841
B. Imported	45	52	38	22	14
Grand total:	2645	2412	2092	1836	855

The above statement shows that imported stores account for just about 1% of the total purchases effected by DGS&D.

In the remaining purchases from indigenous sources, 92% is from large/medium scale industries and 7% from small scale industries.

Value of purchase, item wise

D.G.S.&D. purchases various kinds of stories. These can be broadly grouped into 15 categories as indicated below:

(Values in Rs. crores)

	94-95	95-96	96-97	97-98	98-99 (upto Dec.98)
1	2	3	4	5	6
1. Fuel Oil, Lubricants	256.72	194.86	346.57	129.35	18.67
2. Road Dresing & Roof covering Materials	893.41	555.27	232.12	40.11	0.12
3. Jute Goods	431.73	589.43	511.10	749.21	491.70
4. Automobiles	233.49	228.17	124.68	138.77	15.80
5. Paper & Paper products	47.40	28.09	51.65	23.09	15.73
6. Cement & Cement Products	263.58	283.43	286.42	295.04	202.96
7. Pipes & Fittings	101.90	67.19	134.47	24.17	2.25
1	2	3	4	5	6
8. Drugs & Medicines	1.42	15.25	2.61	–	–
9. Cotton Textiles & Khadi	1.35	5.06	4.57	4.13	0.31
10. Machine Tools & Accessories	24.78	10.14	4.44	8.68	7.76
11. Woollen items	6.47	6.85	3.66	3.54	0.01
12. Electronic Equipments	45.73	5.59	19.30	3.94	0.47
13. Rubber Tyre & Tube	9.65	141.06	83.16	65.92	5.01
14. Wood & Wood Products	21.47	3.87	14.71	17.17	0.90
15. Others	300.36	280.77	271.97	333.10	92.93
Total	2644.60	2411.85	2091.92	1836.22	854.62

Value of purchase indentor wise

The purchases made by the DGS&D is for Departments of the Central Government. However, State Governments, Public Sector Units/Autonomous Bodies also make use of DGS&D purchase system. The share of the various major users over the last five years as per the payment effected for them by the C.C.A. is as follows:-

	94-95	95-96	96-97	97-98	98-99 (upto Dec.98)
1	2	3	4	5	6
I. Central Ministries					
1. Defence	517	506.47	568.07	535.36	334.29
2. Railways	219	251.87	286.99	329.79	246.23
3. P&T	14	25.11	19.79	22.85	12.57
1	2	3	4	5	6
4. Home Affairs	164	128.94	150.95	184.28	116.34
5. Health & Family Welfare	78	48.69	33.60	32.74	11.69
6. Urban Dev.	125	94.87	125.05	107.22	63.52
7. Telecom	106	169.37	198.92	202.00	259.25
8. Others	126	157.30	137.09	171.61	52.39
II. State Governments	1571	1565.97	1310.56	161.30	15.94
III. Union Territories	129	120.96	183.32	193.42	95.06
IV. Public Sector Under takings/Autonomous Bodies	157	230.97	335.85	360.50	320.46
Total	3206	3300.52	3350.19	2245.79	1527.74

Shipping and clearance of cargos

DGS&D handles clearance of shipment against its own contracts and also against contracts placed by other agencies, if so desired by them. In addition, it also handles despatch of cargo to Andaman & Nicobar Islands. The shipping and clearance work is handled by the Regional offices located at Mumbai, Calcutta and Chennai.

Clearing Agents have been appointed for Ports located in Mumbai and Chennai Regions. For Calcutta Region, the work is handled departmentally. Presently, clearance arrangement is available at the following Ports:-

Sea Ports —Calcutta, Haldia, Chennai, Vizag, Mumbai Cochin.

Air Ports —Calcutta, Chennai, Bangalore, Mumbai.

The cargo (tonnage) handled by DGS&D during the last five years by the Regional Directorates at Mumbai, Calcutta and Chennai is given below:-

Tonnage handled (M/T)	94-95	95-96	96-97	97-98	98-99 **(upto Dec.98)**
1	2	3	4	5	6
Mumbai	1400	8860	9508	6855	3110
Calcutta	9308	9336	9421	4940	2161
Chennai	3308	5163	6622	4223	4013

The decline in cargo handling is mainly due to decentralisation of ad-hoc procurements. The Sharp decline at Calcutta Port is attributed to low exports to Andaman and Nicobar Islands. However, during the period under report concerned efforts were made by the above three Regional offices to get more -clientale, by contacting major Government Departments, Semi-Government Departments, Public Sector Undertakings etc., who are regularly importing stores. As a result four new importers have been added to the existing list of clients.

Quality assurance wing of D.G.S.&D.

Organisational set up:

The Quality Assurance Wing of DGS&D is the technical arm of DGS&D, providing technical support in its purchase functions. It is assigned primarily with the task of registration of firms capacity verification an pre despatch inspection of goods supplied by rate contract holders against the indents placed by the Direct Demanding officers.

In addition, it also undertakes third party pre despatch inspection on behalf of Govt. and other organisations as and when requested for even in respect of non rate contract related items. For the services rendered Quality Assurance Wing charge a nominal fee varying from 0.25% to 2% of the value of stores inspected.

Structure

The Quality Assurance Wing with its headquarters in Delhi is headed by an Additional Director General (Quality Assurance) who directly report to DG(S&D) and is assisted by a Deputy Director General (Quality Assurance). The field quality assurance work through out the country is segregated into zones viz. Northern (Delhi), Southern (Chennai), Eastern (Calcutta) and Western (Mumbai), each headed by a Deputy Director General (Quality Assurance).

Each zone has 2-3 Directorates with Director as head of Directorate and sub offices at major industrial centres, staffed as per requirement. At present there are 11 field

Directorates situated at New Delhi, Chandigarh, Kanpur, Calcutta, Jamshedpur, Mumbai, Ahmedabad, Bhilai, Chennai, Hyderabad and Bangalore. The Quality Assurance Wing has 34 centres with its offices at almost all the major industrial production centres with its presence in every major State of the country.

The presence of QA Wing office nearer to the production centres helps in dealing with the inspection work in an efficient manner with the advantage for the contractors to have direct communication for any guidance needed in operation of the contract.

Functions

The Quality Assurance work is of a specialised technical nature calling for assimilation and dissemination of knowledge and experience. In fact Quality 'Assurance Wing of DGS&D has been one of the poineer organisations in this field. The functions performed by the Q.A. Wing are:-

(a) Formulating the procurement specifications suitable for Contracting.

(b) Assessment of vendors against their application for registration with DGS&D or against tender enquiries before placement of contracts.

(c) Maintain directories of suppliers registered as manufacturers, stockists, Indian Agents to foreign manufacturers etc.

(d) Providing advice to DGS&D on all technical issues in the purchase activities.

(e) Technical evaluation of offers wherever requested for.

(f) Evaluation and certification of the quality of supplies.

(g) Quality' Audit/Failure Analysis of supplies at consignee's end.

(h) Providing similar services to other Departments and Central Govts. State Govts., Public Sector Undertakings against their direct procurement.

(i) Inter-action with Indentors and Industry for failure analysis and upgradation of quality of procurement to meet diversified needs and keeping up with changing increasing quality needs of the users.

(j) Inter-action with BIS and other government bodies, contribution / participation in their standardisation and certification activities.

Quality management of stores:
Important stages where quality gets built in the procurement cycle of DGS&D as well as other similar organisations are formulation of procurement specification, selection of vendors, inspection/ evaluation of stores, quality audit through test checks and joint investigation failure analysis for the stores received by consignees.

Formulation of technical specification for tenders
Technical Specifications for any of the items being procured by a Government Department are formulated in such a way that there are broadbased, identify the items unambiguiously and are in line with national / international standards. Wherever the standards are defficient i.e. a particular parameter has not been mentioned, the Q.A.

Wing includes these parameters keeping in view the customer's requirement, status of the technology / practices in the country etc. Other aspects like energy conservation, eco-friendness etc. are also added keeping in view the prevailing practices. Stipulation of the correct and clear specifications in the Tender Enquiries is the foremost stage for building/ensuring the quality in the products being procured.

Selectiono of vendors/registration of firms:
The registration activity of DGS&D provides the basis for development through interaction and preparation of approved list of vendors for supply of the items required by Govt. Departments /Agencies. DGS&D registers the firms in various categories e.g. as manufacturers both indigeneous and foreign, authorised agents/distributor of manufacturers, assemblers and compulsory enlistment of Indian agents of foreign suppliers. The registration of Indian manufacturing firms has been decentralised and is handled from 20 different centres covering almost all the major States.

The process includes assessment of manufacturing capacities and confirmation of financial status of the firms from their Bankers. Where firm is not borne on the approved list for any particular item, the Quality Assurance Wing carries out assessment of manufacturers capacity/capability on specific request from the purchase organisation. All this helps the purchase organisations in identification and proper selection of vendors for placement of contract for ensuring quality and timely delivery of the stores. The work done for registration of firms during 1998-99 (upto Dec.98) is given in the following table:-

1. Status of application made for registration		
a)	Applications brought forward as on 1.4.98	128
b)	Fresh applications received upto 31.12.98	527
c)	Total number of applications disposed of.	516
d)	Balance as on 31.12.98	139

II. Fresh registration granted:

Indian	Firms	Foreign Firms	Indian Agents
SSI	Non SSI		
123	44	5	166

III. Renewals/additional items registration

	Renewals/Addl. items registration granted		:	190
IV.	a)	Applications rejected	:	89
	b)	No. of adverse inspection Reports received	:	152
V.	a)	No. of firms banned	.	–
	b)	No.of firms de-registered	:	11

Inspection /evaluation of stores

This is the major activity performed by the Quality Assurance officers. Quality Assurance Wing perform the function not only against the contracts concluded by DGS&D but also against the contracts received from other organisations as the when requested. In this activity, the Quality Assurance Wing faces stiff competition from other organisations like Rail India Technical and Economic Services (RITES), Central Organisation for Modernisation of Workshops (COFMOW), National Thermal Power Corporation (NTPC) and Engineers India Limited (EIL).

Therefore, in the sphere of activity, Quality Assurance Wing operates in a competitive market. Even though the drawal against RC has gone substantially over the years because of the delinking of the States and PSUs, the workload for third party inspection has remained stationary. If the organisation had limited its activities only to inspection of RC related items, their workload would have been much less as compared to the present level. Approximately, 50% of the workload is generated for inspection of RC related goods and remaining 50% originate because of direct orders placed by organisation to Quality Assurance Wing for inspecting their goods from the suppliers not connected with DGS&D.

During the current year, vigorous efforts were made to sustain the present level of business generation inspite of keen competition in the market. The QA Wing of DGS&D could already secure orders worth Rs. 2377 crores upto December, 1998 as against Rs. 2953 crores during the last financial year.The following table indicates the Quality Assurance work done by the Quality Assurance Wing:

Year	95-96	96-97	97-98	98-99 upto Dec. 98
1. No. of Orders received	38272.00	36749.00	37514.00	29290.00
2. Value of orders received (Rs.in crores)	2663.00	2852.94	3036.96	2302.58
3. Value of orders Inspected (Rs. in Crores)	2666.72	2765.01	2953.11	2377.49
4. No. of Inspection documents issued				
a) Inspection Notes	44731	41689	38762	28768
b) Inspection Certificates	22396	20960	15825	11646
Total	6712 7	62649	40460	40414

The break up of value of orders inspected against DGS&D Contracts and direct orders is as follows:

(value in Rs. Crores)

Year	DGS&D		Direct		Total
1995-96	1378.37	51.69%	1288.35	48.31%	2666.72
1996-97	1338.37	48.40%	1426.73	51.60%	2765.01
1997-98	1452.86	49.20%	1500.25	50.80%	2953.11
1998-99 (Upto Dec.98)	1284.04	54.10%	1093.45	45.90%	2377.49

The region-wise and Directorate-wise value of Inspection work done is furnished below:

(Rs. in Crores)

	95-96	96-97	97-98	98-99 upto Dec. 98
Northern region				
Delhi	363.42	433.50	294.08	251.46
Kanpur	72.31	82.29	75.82	68.96
Chandigarh	–	–	93.16	90.39
	435.73	515.79	463.06	410.81
Eastern region				
Calcutta	844.39	705.52	769.62	817.63
Jamshed	125.91	170.84	183.73	125.65
	970.30	876.36	953.35	943.28
Western region				
Mumbai	262.64	309.90	280.00	112.00
Bhilai	794.97	867.06	876.18	616.47
Ahmedabad	–	–	106.57	69.18

	1057.61	1176.96	1262.75	797.65
Southern region				
Chennai	103.34	94.08	118.13	85.01
Banglore	98.17	101.82	87.16	56.13
Hyderabad	–	–	68.66	84.43
	201.51	195.90	273.95	225.75
Total	2665.15	2765.01	2953.11	2377.49
Inspn. abroad	1.57	–	–	–
Grand total	2666.72	2765.01	2953.11	2377.49

Quality audit through test checks

Quality Assurance Wing has adopted system of checking the quality of stores received by the consignee on a random basis. Basic purpose for this quality audit is to reassure the compliance of the quality of stores received by the consignees. The test check is done on a random basis and is being controlled by the Deputy Director General of Zones. The feed back from this activity is utilised for upgradation of specifications, test procedures followed during the pre-despatch inspection and also the method of stamping /sealing of the stores. The statistics of complaints received on grounds of quality are given in the following table.

Even though all possible measures are taken before accepting the stores and allowing the firm to despatch, there are instances where the stores received by the consignees do not fully meet with the requirements of the specifications. Under the conditions of the contract, consignees have right to reject such stores. Before the stores are finally rejected by the consignees the Q.A. Wing arranges joint investigations at the consignees' premises in respect of such alleged deficient stores where the contractor's representatives are also allowed to be present for analysing the features.

(value in Crores)

Year work	Value - of Inspection over total work done	Value of Received	Complaints justified justified	Percentage of complaints
1	2	3	4	5
1995-96	2667.12	2.34	0.93	0.03
1996-97	2765.01	5.03	1.23	0.04
1997-98	2953.11	4.63	0.92	0.03
1998-99 (upto Dec.98)	2377.43	2.90	0.59	0.02

Recommendations/conclusions drawn by the joint inspection teams help the purchase officer in taking a final decision on the replacement/rectification of such stores, as well as updation of specifications/testing procedures.

World bank aided projects

DGS&D handles procurement of various World Bank aided projects. Q.A. Wing imparts Quality Assurance cover for these purchases too, by way of formulation of equipment specifications, analysis of offers and inspection evaluation of stores received for these projects.

Human resource development

The officers from the Q.A. Wing were deputed for various training programmes, seminars and workshops. Most of the officers at the Director level have already been given training in the area of quality system as per

ISO 9000. The training is being planned for officers at other levels to apprise them with the latest techniques in quality management and other related areas.

The Q.A. Wing has also been participating in the activities of Training Directorate of the DGS&D of imparting trainings to not only purchase and Q.A. officers but also to trade and indentors.

Diversification of activities

After decentralisation of purchase activities of the DGS&D, efforts are now being made to generate additional work by contacting various State Government Departments, Municipal Corporations, State Government Undertakings, Zila Parishads etc. As a result of which additional work could be secured from the following organisations during 1998-99.

1. Haldia Dock Complex, Calcutta
2. State Govt. of Goa
3. Tamilnadu Textbook Corpn.
4. Kerala Water Authority
5. Municipal Commissioner, Pimpri, Pune
6. Metro Water & Sewage Board, Hyderabad
7. Chief Engr., Navy, Mumbai
8. A.P. Textbook Corpn.
9. Tirupati Municipality
10. Baroda Municipal Corpn.
11. U.P. Jal Nigam
12. MTNL Mumbai & Western Railways
13. M.P. Govt.
14. MCD Delhi

15. W.B. Govt.
16. Coal India
17. U.P. Bhoomi Sudhar Nigam
18. J&K Govt.
19. Karnataka Backward Classes Dev. Corpn. Ltd.
20. Sports Dev. Authority, Tamil Nadu
21. Bangalore Mahanagar Palika
22. SIPCOT, Chennai
23. Railway Board

Supporting directorates

In order to ensure that the organisation render efficient services to its clients and at the same time keep pace with the changing economic scenario, a few supporting Directorates are also exist to effect necessary changes in the purchase policies and to advise the organisation inter-alia on the different aspects of purchase management. At present following supporting Directorates are functioning in the DGS&D:

Administration directorate

This Directorate looks after the personnel matters ranging from recruitment to retirement of officers/staff. During the period under report, available promotional vacancies were filled up after following the laid down procedures in order to boost the morale of the employees. The Administration ' Directorate at Headquarters also advises the Regional offices on all administrative matters.The details of staff strength of DGS&D as on 31.12.98 are given below:

	Gazetted	Non-Gazetted	Total
Sanctioned	631	2910	3541
Actual	592	2282	2874

Following decentralisation of ad-hoc procurement in 1992 and delinking of the payment against procurement made by the State Governments and the Public Sector Undertakings against DGS&D contracts from the Chief Controller of Accounts in 1996, the work of the DGS&D/ CCA has been on the decline. Efforts were also made to reduce manpower by imposing cut, transferring staff with the work etc. The reduction however has not been commensurate with the reduction in the workload. The S.I.U. has been engaged to assess the staff requirement. The report of S.I.U. is in its finalisation stage.

Coordination directorate

This Directorate assists in formulation of policies and procedure for procurement of stores. Keeping in view the liberalised economy and the policies announced by the Govt. from time to time this Directorate constantly review the existing instructions as are delineated in Manual of office Procedures for Supplies, Inspection and Disposal,which was last brought out in 1992 and wherever necessary modify the existing purchase policies and procedures to bring them in conformity with the Government policies. A book titled 'CITIZENS' CHARTER' of the DGS&D has been brought out, bringing out the role and functions of the DGS&D and its commitments, obligations of the Consumers, Suppliers etc.

This book has been sent to all the offices under the administrative control of the DGS&D, Indenting Departments and Apex Body Associations/Chambers of Commerce. A copy of the Citizen's Charter is kept in the office of the Public Relations officer both at Headquarters and in the field offices for reference by the visitors. The gist of the book is also displayed prominently in these offices for the guidance of the Industry as well as Users Departments.

Keeping in view the changes in the Government policies announced from time to time following policy/ procedural guidelines have been issued during this period.

(i) With the implementation of Decentralisation of Purchase Policy, adhoc procurement by DGS&D will be on exceptional basis only. Keeping this aspect in view the guidelines for coverage of demand have been modified. Coverage will be made on technically acceptable offers by considering their financial/ technical, production capabilities and their capacity to meet the delivery requirements. In all adhoc contracts, the contracted firm(s) will have to furnish 10 per cent Performance Security.

(ii) The adhoc indents will now be grouped into only two categories,viz. 'Ordinary'/'Urgent' indents depending upon the urgency of the delivery requirements instead of the existing guidelines, categorisations Ordinary/Urgent/Express operational.

(iii) As per amended General Financial Rules, in all adhoc purchases, the firms who are note DGS&D/ NSIC irrespective of the stores for which they are registered, will be asked to furnish Earnest Money Deposit to the extent of 2% of the Estimated Value subject to a ceiling of Rs. 2 lakhs.

(iv) The guidelines to give special treatment to NTC/BIC mills in the procurement of woollen & cotton textiles has been withdrawn in line with the current Government policy.

(v) In line with the instructions issued by the Central Vigilance Commission, Post-Tender Negotiations have been banned in adhoc purchases, with effect from 13.1.1999 except negotation with L.1. (Lowest Tenderer).

(vi) Unsuccessful tenderers will be informed, as far as possible the reasons for non-acceptance of their tender.

(vii) The powers delegated to purchase officers to grant extension in delivery period without consulting the indentor has been reduced to three months from six months,

Management Information Services (MIS DTE.)

The Management Information Services (MIS) Directorate is primarily engaged in•providing required: information tot monitoring the progress in the coverage of indents, right from the stage of their receipt in DGS&D to the completion of supplies both at micro and macro levels, through computerised information system.'

This Directorate also provides data on various aspects of purchase, Inspection and Disposals activities of DGS&D for administrative policy and analytical purposes. Information for monitoring of contracts pending for finalization after the completion of supplies is also provided by MIS Dte. right from indent case sheets, contractual documents (like A/T, SIO, R/Cs drawals etc.) inspection notes, amendment letters and such other documents.

Bulletin on Market prices is brought out every month indicating the price trends of selected commodities for the use of purchase officer, based on data collected from various offices, newspapers etc. A review was undertaken to modify the bulletin by a Committee under the Chairmanship of DDG(A). Bulletin has now been modified.

To acquaint the purchase officers with the latest fiscal policies of Government influencing the purchases of DGS&D, a fortnightly bulletin, "Economic Intelligence" is also brought out by MIS Dte. The MIS Dte. is also responsible for bringing out the Annual Administration Report of DGS&D and providing material for the Performance Budget and Annual Report of Deptt. of Supply All data on R/Cs is computerised. Annual R/C Booklet is issued every year in January. A monthly bulletin is also published every month which contains updated information on rate Contracts concluded afresh, extended and expired, Tender Notices issued and other matters of general interest to the industry as well as indenting departments.

The copies of these bulletins are also available for sale. Free copies are also sent to heads of the indenting departments. Besides this, all Tender Notices issued by DGS&D area fed into the computer and flashed over NICNET to every NIC computter centre in the country.

Market intelligence cell and costs cell

With a view to gather, compile and maintain an upto date data bank in a systematic manner to arrive at reasonable prices of the products to be brought on the Rate Contracts, two Cell viz. Market Inttelligence Cell (MIC) and Costs Cell are functioning in the DGS&D. The tasks assigned to them are:

Market intelligence cell

a) To gather and compile information on the prices of end products and input raw materials;

b) In relation to the existing items on R/C and for new products proposed to be brought on R/C, MIC will collect the names of possible sources with a view to improve participation by the industry in DGS&D purchases;

c) Data on price trends for various items on RC will also be compiled to the extent feasible;

d) To consider suggesting new items for conclusion of the rate contracts;

e) To assist the Purchase Directorates in collecting/ compiling information required to assess prices of particular products;

f) Any other data/information on the aspect of gathering market/raw material prices will be attended on specific suggestions/requests of Purchase Directorates and

g) Any other related functions.

Costs cell

a) To analyse and work out the reasonable cost;

b) To compare the RC prices with the market prices (data to be obtained -from the Market Intelligence Cell and Purchase Directorates) vis-a-vis the reasonable cost worked out. This will be on the request of DDGs for item selection;

c) To make Purchase and available the above data/ information to Directorates on the basis of their needs and

d) Any other related functions.

During 1998 the Cost Cell has completed cost analysis in respect of 9 items associating about 40 suppliers. Apart from this, efforts have been made with Bureau of Industrial Costs & Prices, Ministry of Industry to undertake cost study in respect of 10 selected items for which the annual drawal has been high during the preceding years. The above efforts have helped in procuring items of mass consumption at a reasonable and competitive price.

Litigation branch

Litigation Dte. plays an important role in the working of DGS&D. In all Arbitration cases referred to Arbitration and in court Cases instituted by firms against DGS&D/

UOI or vice versa, the Litigation Dte. helps the Purchase Dtes. in defending the interest of Union of India. Litigation Dte. works under the independent control of OSD (litigation)' and 3 Section Officers to man the work load. Dy. Director/Assistant Directors of Arbitration Groups appear before the Arbitrators to defend the interest of Union of India in cases where value of such cases does not exceed Rs. 3 lacs.

In Regional Offices the Assistant Director (Supplies) look after Court and Arbitration Cases and keep a watch on the progress of each and every case pending various courts or before the Arbitrator.

Training directorate

Training is one of the effective and tested tools for performance enhancement as well as upgradation of' skills and knowledge of the personnel. Everyone has potential for perfection and training helps in its unfolding

Keeping above factors in view Training Directorate is engaged in the HRD activities of officers and staff of DGS&D, and in conducting seminars by Industry and State Governments. The Institute of Supply and Quality Management (ISQM) was set up in December, 1997 within the premises of DGS&D under the Plan Scheme to augment the training facilities in the field of Purchase and Quality Management as also to offer expertise in the area of Consultancy Service in such sectors.

Necessary infrastructures has been created in the Institute of Supply and Quiality Management (ISQM) for conducting the training programme for the officers and staff of DGS&D as well as representatives of Trade and Industry. During this year upto December '98, 603 participants were trained in 48 different courses.

DGS&D and industries/indentors

DGS&D acts as a bridge between the suppliers on side and the buyers on the other. It saves buyers from botheration of tendering themselves for the common user items needed by them and provides a ready market Government Purchases to the suppliers. For constant interaction between the DGS&D, Suppliers and Use periodical meetings are hold.

Working Environment and Records Management

To improve the working environment in DGS&D, a number of steps were taken which inter-alia include clearance of revision pension cases, departmental proceedings, updating of records, etc. A special drive for disposal of unserviceable furniture/obsolete office equipments was undertaken. A special drive for weeding out of the old records and disposal of unusable furniture/obsolete of ice equipments was undertaken.

During this drive, about 59 477 files were reviewed and 22,513 files which have lost their relevance have been destroyed. Records Management, being an important aspect of the overall functioning of the office, continued to get special attention during the ear 1998-99 also. Performance during the year 1998-99 (upto 31.12.98) is given below:-

a)	Files recorded during the year	43,939
b)	Files reviewed during the year	59,477
c)	Files identified for sending to Central record room.	Nil
d)	Files weeded out	22,513

Computeristion

Computerisation of purchase and Quality Assurance activities have been undertaken for better monitoring. The system as well as the software have been provided by National Informatics Centre. Computerisation and inter-connectivity have already been completed at DGS&D Headquarters, DS&D Mumbai, Chennai and QA Wing at New Delhi, Chennai, Mumbai, Calcutta, Bhillai, Bangalore an Hyderabad. Computerisation is likely to be completed during this financial year at DS&D, Calcutta and QA Wing office at Kanpur, Chandigarh, Pune and Guwahati. As a result Of computerisation . and connectivity, the Department is in a position to generate item-wise monthly drawal report.

For quality assurance centres Ernakulam, Jamshedpur and Ludhiana computerisation and inter-connectivity will be taken up in the next financial year. A 'Home Page' in NIC website on the Internet had been established. In order to facilitate timely availability of information on Rate Contract to the DDOs spread over throughout the country. It has been decided to make this information available on the website of DGS&D.

The Department also took an extensive audit of the hardwsare/software to meet the requirement of Y2K compliance. Information Facilitation Centre (IFC), opened on the advice of Administrative Reforms and Public Grievançes is functional at all DGS&D offices since June, 97. This has further strengthened the existing system of attending to the enquiries of large number of visitors coming to this office. The IFC is fully computerised and is closely monitoring the complaint with concerned Purchase Directorates. A register is also being maintained in the IFC, for the visitors for recording their remarks/ suggestions. Any complaints registered are brought to the knowledge of the concerned Directorates/Offices for prompt action thereon.

Financial Performance of DGS&D

The DGS&D is essentially a Service Organisation catering mainly to the procurement needs of various Central

Government Departments, State Governments, Public Sector, Undertakings etc. The activities of the Organisation come under the non-plan Head expect for the training and consultancy activities which is going to be supported by plan provision. The Budget allocation is essentially to meet the cost of staff and other incidental matters. The Budget allocation during the last five year has been as follows:

	1994-95	1995-96	1996-97	1997-98	1998-99
		(Rs. in crores)			
B.E.	19.45	21.19	21.30	24.24	33.74
R.E.	20.21	21.30	23.60	30.60	33.93
ACTUAL	19.55	20.96	21.56	29.98	26.33 (upto Dec.98)

GS&D earns revenue through the fees charged for procurement, Inspection and Disposal. A moderate fee of 0.5% is charged for procurement for stores. A similar fee is charged for inspection of stores also. In addition, some revenue is earned by sale of tender forms and publications of DGS&D. The total revenue earned during the last five years is as follows:

Revenue earned

	1994-95	1995-96	1996-97	1997-98	1998-99 (Upto Dec. 98)
Procurement	11.14	13.62	14.86	10.17	7.29
Inspection	15.78	17.43	19.07	16.30	11.65
Disposal	0.06	–	0.28	0.24	–
Other Receipts	2.68	1.30	1.71	2.53	1.56
Total Receipts	29.66	32.35	35.92	29.24	20.50

3

National Test House

National Test House was established in 1912 on a modest scale for the Railways, primarily for evaluation of certain indigenous products aimed at import substitution. It has grown into a laboratory of national importance in the field of testing, evaluation and analysis.

The main functions of the N.T.H. are:—

(a) Testing and evaluation of materials, products, equipments, apparatus and systems in practically all branches of Science and Technology except food, drugs and pharmaceuticals, arms and ammunitions.

(b) Research and Development in testing technology and related areas, including consultancy for failure analysis and allied problems.

(c) Helping industries in developing indigenous products for import substitution and in their quality assurance programmes.

(d) Calibration at the level of Echelon-II and maintenance of appropriate standards and references in areas of its competence.

(e) Helping N.A.B.L. (National Accreditation Board for Testing and Calibration Laboratories) for accrediting testing laboratories.

(f) Association with B.I.S. for evolving National and International Specifications and Standards.

(g) Training of Scientists, Technologists, Technicians in testing technology.

National Test House also participates in various National as well as International Seminars and Symposia relevance and arranges discussions and demonstrations f creating quality consciousness among small entrepreneurs and the public at large. NTH also arranges in-house training of its staff a encourages interaction with higher institutions of learning and research. Selected staff are sponsored for specialised training courses in the country and abroad ;Ii a view to up-dating their knowledge.

Organisation

NTH has its Headquarters at Calcutta and Regional Laboratories at Calcutta, Mumbai, Chennai, Ghaziabad, Guwahati and Jaipur with testing facilities specific to the regions. The details of staff strength are given below.

	Gazetted	Non-Gazetted	Total
Sanctioned	205	589	794
Actual	177	465	642

Committees constituted for NTH

Two high powered Committees exist to advise NTH policy and various administrative matters. These are Executive Committee and (ii) Technical Advisory Council.

Executive committee

(i) An Executive Committee functions under the Chairmanship of Secretary to take decisions on administrative and financial matters. The Committee has the powers to take decisions on NTH proposals in respect f which the Department of Supply is competent. The decisions taken by the Committee on such proposals would be implemented straight way without further examination where, however the proposals require Consultations/ approval of other Ministries/Departments, the decision of the Executive Committee would be taken up with the concerned Ministry/Department and, processed further on the basis of approval or otherwise by those Ministries/ Departments. The other members of the Executive Committee are DG(NTH), Joint Secretary (Supply), Financial Adviser (Supply), one officer from DGS&D, Two scientists to be recommanded by DG(NTH). The Director, NTH(ER) is the Member Secretary.

Technical advisory council

The Technical Advisory Council for NTH (TAC) as been reconstituted in 1997 under the Chairmanship of DG(NTH) and a representative from the Department of Supply, a number of scientists and engineers from the various institutions are being nominated for the council along with all regional Heads of the NTH as members.

The main function of the Advisory Council is to advise for procurement of sophisticated equipments for NTH in the various disciplines. To fully utilise the budget provision for the NTH for procuring the equipments the help of the members of the TAC representing the BIS, NPL, Quality Assurance Wing of DGS&D are taken depending upon the requirements of the Industry.

Plan activity

To enable the NTH to play its role effectively in the field of quality control, material evaluation, standardisation and assistance in industrial development, it has been brought under the Science and Technology Plan Scheme. The scheme envisages augmentation and modernisation of testing facilities and setting up of regional Test Houses for the benefit of small scale industries in particular. The activities of the NTH are being regularly covered under the Scheme since 5th Five year Plan (1974-78). In the Annual Plan 1998-99 Rs. 4.80 Crores have been provided to NTH. Of which Rs. 3.24 crores have been placed at the disposal of CPWD for implementation of Land and Building works and the balance of Rs. 1.56 crores for meeting the expenditure in Equipment and Machinery and recurring nature of items.

Facilities available

Besides facilities for testing in almost all areas according to national and international specifications, limited facilities for Standards (Echelon-II level) and Calibration are available in Mechanical and Electrical areas in the Eastern Regional Centre. Similar facilities are also available, in a limited way, at other Centres in northern, western and southern regions.The NTH is at present providing testing and evaluation facilities in the following main disciplines:

a) Chemical Engineering;

b) Civil Engineering;

c) Rubber, Plastics and Textiles;

d) Electrical Engineering;

e) Electronics;

f) Mechanical Engg. (Heavy and Light Mechanical);

g) Non-Destructive Testing;

During the year 1998-99 upto December 1998 33 nos of new equipments have been purchased. The NTH is also providing Industrial Quality Consultancy Services (IQCS) in the following specialised, areas.

(a) Techno managerial service for setting up of testing and calibration laboratory.

(b) Material identification consultancy relating to import substitution.

(c) Failure analysis for engineering materials and plan/ system and remedial measures.

(d) Quality improvisation of paints and allied materials, fine chemicals, pesticides etc.

(e) Development of test and calibration methodology.

(f) Strength, Serviceability Durability (SSD) consultancy for civil construction.

(g) Interpretation of radiographs and grading of severity of defects with reference to standards.

A Computerised Management Information System for both administrative and technical functions has been installed in all the Regional branches of the NTH at Calcutta, Mumbai, Chennai and Ghaziabad as well as at the Jaipur Centre of the NTH.

The main areas covered under the system are Sample Monitoring, Equipments Procurement Monitoring, Budget Monitoring, Personnel Information, Library Information and Store Information.

Action has been initiated for networking and Store Information. Action has been initiated for networking of all the computers installed in the NTH.

Action has also been initiated to computerise the technical as well as the administrative activities of the newly established centre of the NTH at Guwahati.

Testing of samples

Region/Centre-wise testing of samples :

The number of samples tested region-wise is as follows:

Name of the region	1996-97	1997-98	1998-99 (upto Nov. 98)
		(In thousands only)	
Calcutta	10.95	8.23	5.50
Mumbai	2.38	2.21	1.30
Chennai	3.11	2.46	1.90
Ghaziabad	3.14	4.44	2.84
Jaipur	2.10	2.25	2.18
Guwahati	0.17	0.33	0.34
Total	21.85	19.92	14.06

Source-wise testing of samples

The source-wise samples origin and reporting thereon is as follows:

(In absolute terms and in percentages)

Year	Receipts				Disposals			
	DGS&D Govt. Deptt. Deptt.	Other for Govt.	Total ate	Priv- Deptt. Deptt.	DGS&D Govt. Govt.	Other for	Total ate	Priv-
	1	2	3	4	5	6	7	8
1996-97								
(a)	1327	7187	8514	12152	2110	7571	9681	12171
(b)	6.40	34.8	41.20	58.80	9.70	34.60	44.30	55.70
1997-98								
(a)	1077	8987	10064	9720	1062	8398	9460	10461
(b)	5.44	45.43	50.87	49.13	5.62	44.44	47.45	52.51
1998-99 (Upto Nov. 98)								
(a)	721	6989	7710	7263	598	6588	7186	6875
(b)	4.82	46.68	51.49	48.51	4.25	46.85	51.11	48.59

(a) represents number of samples in absolute terms.

(b) represents number of samples in percentages.

NTH was established primarily to develop quality products and thereby contribute towards development of the nation. It was, therefore, never envisaged as a profit, earning commercial organisation. NTH is now putting effort to increase revenue earning through its services. IIM, Calcutta has been assigned the job of conducting a study to optimise the resources of NTH and suggest measures for reducing the gap between revenue earning and expenditure. However, this will take some time to materialise.

Calibration

The N.T.H. has undertaken calibration work in a number of cases and issued calibration certificates pertaining to Electrical and Mechanical equipments during the year 1998-99(upto Nov., 1998) as follows:

1.	Electrical	166
2.	Mechanical	355
	Total	521

Special work done and help to industries

(i) The Scientists of NTH (SR) have taken up institute test of Pressure Meters for soil bearing capacity in Bangalore.

(ii) The Scientists of NTH(ER) fabricated necessary, fixture for testing Fibre reinforced plastic materials (FRP) as per Standards.

(iii) The Scientists of NTH (NR) acrylic paint evaluation.

(iv) The Scientists of NTH (ER) have started concrete testing by Ultrasonic concrete Tester.

(v) The Scientists of NTH (JPR) provided consultancy services to M/s. Saboo Minerals at Jodhpur in the field of building construction in Haryana and Punjab where cement has to be used in high salinety areas. Suggestions were given for solving the problem.

(vi) The Scientists of NTH(ER) undertook testing of conduits for electrical ilnstallations.

(vii) The Scientists of NTH(ER) tested Bond Strength of 40 mm TMT bars by designing special arrangement.

(viii) The Scientists of NTH(ER) calibrated a number of gauges by designing a special fixture for calibration.

(ix) The Scientists of NTH(ER) undertook the testing of Thermoplastic paints for road.

(x) The Scientists of NTH (SR) tested sample of compressed Kraft paper used for flooring inner part of vehicle.

(xi) A development work was undertaken by the scientists of Paint Lab. of NTH(ER) for the test "Resistance of Weight Abrasion for oil distemper".

(xii) Scientists of NDT lab. of NTH(ER) have assessed a sample of old Reaction vessel for its suitability for use at Shahzanpur (UP) at firm's premises.

NTH-BIS interaction

The National Test-House (NTH) collaborates with the Bureau of Indian Standards (BIS) in evolving national and international specifications and standards. Currently, the NTH is represented on 150 Councils, Sectional Committees, Panels of BIS and also furnishes data and expertise for drawing up the national .

The NTH has also undertaken various testing Sub-Committees and technical standards jobs for BIS in connection with the Certification Marks Scheme. Eight scientists took part in BIS meetings and offered comments for discussion in the BIS Committee Meetings.

NTH-DST ineraction

Eight samples under NABL Proficiency Programme were evaluated by NTH scientists. 2 scientists of NTH attended Training Courses under NABL Programme. Under the NABL Lab. Accreditation Programme scientists of NTH assessed and accreditated M/s Kidao Lab., Chennai and M/s Garden Reacla Scientists from. BIS and DST interacted with NTH (SR) scientists in connection with accreditation of NTH (SR) laboratories.

R & D Activities

(a) Team of NTH scientists studied the various properties viz. Mechanical, Chemical and metallurgical of Steel ring of 1-450 KVA SKL Make DC Set for Import substitution.

(b) The NTH (ER) scientists have undertaken the development work for composite pigments tests used in synthetic enamels in collaboration with BIS Technologies.

(c) Scientists of NTH(ER) developed and modified the calibration of extensiometer which was obtained from unused machine parts.

(d) Scientists of NTH(ER) carried out 11 Bend Test -of grouting concrete" and "Bend Test of Bitumen bars water proofing compound".

(e) NTH scientists undertook the testing of "Pitch Impregnated Fibre pipes and fittings for drainage purpose" and ageing test on 11 Linoleum sheets and Tiles".

(f) Scientists of NTH(ER) electrical lab. undertook special type of tests viz. Load characteristics Short Circuit tests and temperature wise tests on welding generator.

(g) Scientists of RPT Lab. of NTH(ER) undertook testing for water proofing and colour fastness against washing.

Training

A number of trainees were trained in various fields of technology by the scientists of NTH from all branches by conducting 8 different courses.

(a) 10 persons were trained in Sampling, Testing and quality evaluation of building material excluding cement additives.

(b) 40 persons were trained in Mechanical Testing.

(c) 8 persons were trained for orientation course in Paint and allied products.

(d) 17 Scientific officers were trained in Interpretation of weld radiographs.

(e) Scientist-in Charge, NTH (JPR) delivered lecture and trained trainees on quality control in ceramics.

Seminars/workshops/interaction with Industries

Thirty one Scientists of NTH attended Seminars/ Workshops in various fields of technology at different forums in all parts of the country during April to November, 1998. One Scientist of NTH attended Workshop on "Metrology Why not" organised by NCSL, USA held at Albuquerque, USA. A technical talk on "Benchmarking- A topic to achieve competitive Edge" was-delivered by the Director General, NTH at Deptt.' of Statistics, Calcutta University. National Test House participated in the "12th Industrial India Trade Fair" organised jointly by Bengal Chamber of Commerce and Industry and Govt. of West Bengal at Calcutta Maidan. Various testing Services rendered by NTH have been exhibited there to publicise the activities of NTH.

Awareness programme for the customers of NTH

(a) NTH (NR) and (ER) organised RC Holders meeting to provide NTH services for availability of quality product.

(b) NTH(ER) participated in Industrial Trade fair to project NTH services to the delegates and visitors. NTH (SR) participated in the Exhibition organised on the occasion of National Conference held at Bangalore.

(c) Activities of NTH in various fields focussed through leading newspapers of India.

(d) Brochure on NTH activities prepared and distributed to Trade and Industry.

(e) Citizen's Charter prepared and distributed to Trade and Industry.

(f) NTH organised interaction with industries for making them aware of the services rendered by the NTH.

(g) All the regions of NTH celebrated the 50th Anniversary of India's Independence by arranging open houses in a befitting manner.

Land and building

To meet the emerging demand of industry for testing in the new areas, a new laboratory complex of NTH is being constructed at Salt Lake, Calcutta at a cost of Rs. 34.24 crores. The Revised Cost Estimates of the complex was considered by the Expenditure Finance Committee (EFC). This comprises of four building blocks namely—Main Building, Heavy Material Testing Building, Metrology Laboratory and Acoustics Laboratory.

The HMT Block and Metrology Lab. of the Salt lake Complex is fully completed and have already been taken over by NTH(ER) and shifted a portion of their existing laboratory from Alipore, Calcutta. The main building has been completed upto 7th storey level and the flooring work have been completed upto 5th floor.

The Auditorium roof casting and internal work of the Acoustic lab. is under progress. It is expected that the entire complex would be completed by December, 1999.

Receipts and expenditure

The relevant 'details of receipts and expenditure at the six centres is as follows

(Rupees in lacs)

(Receipt)

Name of the region/centre		1996-97	1997-98	1998-99 (upto Nov.98)
i)	Calcutta	58.49	56.46	40.62
ii)	Mumbai	14.02	14.84	11.91
iii)	Chennai	19.45	20.25	12.26
iv)	Ghaziabad	25.84	37.04	26.80
V)	Jaipur	12.73	15.14	11.87
vi)	Guwahati	1.94	3.75	3.59
	Total	132.47	147.98	107.05

Accredation of NTH Lab

The Central Boiler Board, Ministry of Industry, Govt. of India, recognised NDT lab. of NTH(ER), Calcutta as (i) competent authority for Certification of Welders and (ii) Well known material testing laboratory under the Indian Boiler Regulations. Certification in above respects have also been issued in favour of NTH(ER), Calcutta by Central. Boiler Board.

Study Conducted by Indian Institute of Management, Calcutta

On the recommendations of the Parliamentary Standing Committee on Commerce regarding optimal utilisation of the potential of NTH and its financial viability, a study was entrusted to the Indian Institute of Management, Calcutta. The final report of the study has been received. Actions have been initiated to implement as per the direction of the Parliamentary Committee. Another study to examine the feasibility of bringing various laboratories presently under the control of different Ministries/ Departments, under one umbrella, was also entrusted to Indian Institute of Management (IIM), Calcutta. Draft report of the study has since been received and comments of the concerned Ministries have been sought.

4

Chief Controller of Accounts

The Office of the Chief Controller of Accounts Department of Supply, is the Departmental Accounts organisation attached to the Department of Supply and came into existence with effect from 1.7.1976. The Secretary of the Department is the Chief Accounting Authority for the discharge of the accounting functions. The Secretary is assisted by the Financial Advisor and the Chief Controller of Accounts. The main functions of the Supply Accounts Organisation include:

(i) Payment of the Bills preferred against constracts concluded by the Director General of Supplies and Disposals and its Regional Offices, and raising of claims against the Accounts officer of the consignees concerned.

(ii) Accounting of sale proceeds of surplus and obsolete stores disposed of through the Disposal Wing of the DGS&D and remittance of the receipts of the Accounts Officers of the stock holder after adjustment of Departmental charges and Auctioneers' Commission.

(iii) Payment of clearing charges at Ports for imported stores.

(iv) Payment and accounting functions on behalf of the Department of Supply, DGS&D, NTH and CCA Offices.

(v) Compilation of accounts of the Department and its constituents.

(vi) Internal inspection of payment and accounts records maintained by various offices under the Department.

Organisation

The Chief Controller of Accounts has its Headquarters at New Delhi and its regional Offices are located at Mumbai, Calcutta and Chennai. The CCA is assisted by two Controller of Accounts at New Delhi and one Deputy Controller of Accounts each at Regional offices of Mumbai, Chennai and Calcutta. The sanctioned strength and the actual strength of the Organisation as on 31.12.1998 is as under:

	Gazetted	Non- Gazetted	Total
Sanctioned	104	932	1036
Actual	110	644	754

Following decentralisation of ad-hoc procurement in 1992 and delinking of the payments against procurement made by the State Governments and Public Sector Undertakings against DGS&D rate contracts from the Chief Controller of Accounts Office w.e.f 1.10.96 and 1.4.97 respectively, the work with the DGS&D as well as the CCA has been on the decline. Accordingly, the staff requirement of the CCA's office based on existing work load is under assessment by the Department, pending the final assessment a ban on direct recruitment has been placed in the CCA's office barring some recruitment's, which are being made selectively where considered inescapable.

Allocation of work

Each office responsible for payment of supplier's bills has been allotted a region/state. Accordingly, Suppliers located in a particular region/state can obtain payment only from that Controller/Dy. Controller of Accounts to whom that region/state has been allotted. The details of alloted region/states are as under:

Office	Allocated Region
1	2
1. Controller of Accounts, New Delhi. Haryana & New Delhi.	Punjab, Rajasthan, UP, Himachal Pradesh, MP, J&K,
2. Deputy Controller of Accounts, Calcutta. ura, Nagaland, Meghalaya, & Mizoram	West Bengal, Assam, Bihar, Sikkim, Orissa, Manipur, Trip- Arunachal Pradesh
3. Deputy Controller of Accounts, Mumbai.	Maharashtra, Gujarat & Goa
4. Deputy Controller of Accounts, Chennai. Pondicherry	Andhra Pradesh, Tamil Nadu Karnataka, Kerala &

Some of the Accounting work and payments are, however, centralised at the following stations:-

a) New Delhi

i) Accounting procedure for disposal of surplus stores.

ii) Payments, Accounts etc. of bills relating to Acceptance of Tenders placed by DGS&D for supply of stores to pre-deposit parties.

iii) Payment of bills against rate/running contracts issued by some Directorates of DGS&D for stores like POL Products & Gases.

iv) Contracts relating to payment to foreign suppliers located in UK/Europe/USA/Canada, whose payment is made through Letters of Credit opened on State Bank of India, London/New York.

b) Calcutta — Payments relating to jute supplies including those for supplies to pre-deposit parties.

Volume of payments

During the period from 1.4.98 to 31.12.98, payments amounting to Rs. 1528.30 crores were made against various contracts placed by DGS&D. The regionwise break-up is as follows:

Office	No. of Bills (Rs. in crores)	Payments
New Delhi	87,036	742.61
Calcutta	14,521	496.67
Mumbai	17,530	209.42
Chennai	11,649	79.60
Total	1,30,736	1,528.30

Foreign payments

Payments in respect of contracts placed on foreign suppliers in USA/UK are made through Letters of Credit established directly with the State Bank of India, New York, and London to facilitate prompt payments. After verification of correctness of the payments and Bank charges, outward claims are raised against the Accounts Officers of the consignees to obtain reimbursements.

Payments to the tune of Rs. 11.67 crores were made to foreign suppliers during the year 1998-99. A separate World Bank Payment Cell looks after the payment and accounting work in respect of the centralised procurement made by DGS&D for the World Bank aided projects.

Computerisation of accounts

To reduce the time gap between payment of supplier's bill and raising claim on the Accounts Officer of the consignee and to increase overall efficiency of the office, two modules have been developed with the technical assistance of the National Informatics Centre.

Supply payment modules

The supply payment module has been successfully implemented at New Delhi, Mumbai and Chennai. Drawal Reports are being generated. Supply module has been installed at Calcutta office recently and reports are expected to be generated by the end of March, 1999.

Supply accounts modules

Supply Account Module has been partially implemented in Delhi and in the Regional offices and includes weekly RBI advice, consignees Accounts Officer wise report. The claim portion of the module is under development and include advice modification, accounts preparation and debit clearance under RBD Suspense/PAO suspense.

Electronic connectivity

Electronic connectivity between DOS, DGS&D, Dy. CA Mumbai, Dy. CA Chennai, Dy CA Calcutta and CCA Headquarters office has been established. Efforts are being made towards common compatibility of the system between the DGS&D and CCA's office.

5

Vigilance

The vigilance set up in the Department is functioning under the over all supervision of the Secretary who in turn is assisted by the Joint Secretary as Chief Vigilance officer, an Under Secretary, a Section Officer and other subordinate staff.

The Chief Vigilance Officer is responsible for regulating and coordinating all vigilance activities in the department as well as its attached and subordinate offices. In discharge of his functions, he interacts with the Department of Personnel and Training, Central Vigilance Commission and the Central Bureau of Investigation. During the period under report, sustained efforts were continued to tone up the administration and to maintain discipline among the staff of the department and also in its attached and subordinate offices. With a view to minimising corruption and improving the efficiency, the department has continued to take the following measures:

i) The role of vigilance being contributory to the goal of efficiency in the organisation, system improvement and simplification of procedure have been given more attention to ensure efficacy of the management.

ii) The officers/staff working in sensitive post are rotated periodically.

iii) Enforcement of regular inspection and surprise checks of sensitive spots conducted to impress upon the fact that only a clean administration can give the best performance and productivity.

iv) Effective follow-up action was taken to investigate the complaints containing allegation of verifiable nature such as negligence, excercise of discretion without observing prudence leading to undue favour to a party/loss to the organisation.

v) A close watch maintained over the officer/staff of doubtful integrity.

vi) The vigilance machinery has been made more effective by timely review and monitoring of the results of vigilance functions.

The CVO in the Department initiates and conducts proceedings for banning business dealings of the Government in the non-statutory sphere with firms found guilty of malpractice in relation to their business dealings with the Government.

While conducting such proceedings, he acts in a quasi-judicial capacity. An order passed by the CVO, Department of Supply, banning business dealings with a firm implies that all Department/Ministries/Offices of the Government of India are forbidden from dealing with that firm. The CVO is assisted by one Under Secretary (Vigilance) and one Section Officer (Vigilance).

In the DGS&D, an attached office of the Department of Supply, the vigilance functions are supervised by a Director of Deputy Secretary rank. He is assisted by two Deputy Directors and two Section Officers. In the National Test House, a subordinate office of the Department of Supply, the vigilance functions are attended to by a Scientist (SD) in the scale of Deputy Secretary in addition to his other work.

In the Office of Chief Controller of Accounts, a subordinate office of Department of Supply, the vigilance functions are attended to by a Controller of Accounts of that office in addition to other work.

Statistics

Statistical abstracts in respect of disciplinary/vigilance cases dealt with in the Department of Supply including its attached and subordinate offices as on 31.12.98 is as under:

	Gazetted	Non Gazetted
1. No. of disciplinary/ vigilance cases pending as on 01.04.98	14	06
2. No. of disciplinary/ vigilance cases started during 1.4.98 to 31.12.98	09	01
3. No. of disciplinary/ vigilance cases disposed of during 1.4.97 to 31.12.97	10	03
4. Action taken in respect of disciplinary/vigilance cases disposed of		
(a) Reduction in pay/rank	–	–
(b) withholding of pension	–	–
(c) Reduction in pay	02	01
(d) Withholding of increment	01	–
(e) Censure	–	–
(f) Warning	07	–
(g) Exoneration	–	02
5. No. of disciplinary/vigilance cases pending as on 31.12.98	13	04

6

Public Grievances

The Department of Supply, keeping in view the functions assigned to it under the Govt. of India (Allocation of Business) Rules, does not directly come into interaction with the general public. In view of the nature of functions, the grievances against purchases made through the Dte. General of Supplies and Disposals (DGS&D), payments made by the office of Chief Controller of Accounts and testing of samples done by the National Test House, have been brought into the ambit of public grievances.

An elaborate Public Grievances redressal machinery exists in -he Department of Supply Secretariat as well as its attached and subordinate offices viz. Directorate General of Supplies and Disposals (DGS&D), the office of Chief Controller of Accounts (CCA) and National Test House (NTH) including their regional offices. The Joint Secretary in the Department functions as the Director of Public Grievances and oversees the disposal of grievances in attached and subordinate organisations.

The parties riot satisfied with the redressal of their grievances at respective levels in different offices can directly approach the Joint Secretary in the Department of supply. The Director of Grievances has been vested with powers to call for files/papers connected with the grievances and can take decision thereon with the approval of Secretary.

The offices observe every Wednesday as a meetingless day so that the trade representatives can meet the officers. In addition, one hour every day between 1230 to 1330 hours is set apart for meeting trade representatives, with priority being given to outstation parties. For convenience, the name, designation, room number and telephone number of the concerned grievances officers have been displayed prominently in the respective offices.

The local telephone directory also carries the required information in this regard. The representatives of the firms often approach Secretary and other Senior officers in the Department for redressal of their grievances and the appointments are liberally granted unless there are extreme exigencies.

The officers of the rank of Deputy Secretary and above function as Public Grievances officers in the Department and its attached/subordinate offices. DGS&D, an attached office of the Department has a full fledged Directorate of Complaints and Public Grievances headed by a Director and assisted by a Public Relations Officer. The primary function of this directorate is to guide trade as well as indentors in all procedural and contractual matters pertaining to DGS&D.

The Directorate also redresses complaints and grievances of the trade regarding delay and inaction on part of the Purchase and Quality Assurance Wings. At the same time, it also facilitates settlement of outstanding claims by coordinating between Purchase Directorates of DGS&D and the Accounts office concerned.

The progress of public grievances is monitored by holding periodic meetings with concerned Purchase Officers under the Chairmanship of DG(S&D). The grievances pertain to contractual matters where besides the above grievances machinery, the contract provides for arbitration of, disputes by independent Arbitrator. The existing system of attending to the enquiries of large number of visitors has been further strengthened in DGS&D by opening 'Information Facilitation Counter' (IFC) under instructions of Department of Administrative Reforms and Public Grievances.

The IFC is fully computerised and is closely monitoring the complaints with concerned Purchase Directorates. A register is also being maintained in the IFC for the visitors for recording their remarks/ suggestions. Any complaints so registered are brought to the knowledge of the concerned Directorates/Offices for prompt action thereon.

The DGS&D presents monthly reports to DC(S&D) and Department of Supply besides coordinating and expediting the concerned authorities. The data on grievances received from all P.G. units is being transmitted to D/AR&PG regularly through the software developed by them. Besides, reviews of the Public Grievances are also being undertaken, from time to time, at the level of Secretary.

For users/suppliers' convenience the DGS&D is also publishing the Annual Booklet of Rate Contract items and Monthly Bulletins. The details of all live Rate Contracts as on 1st date of the year on different firms giving details of item-wise rates etc. are published in the Annual Rate Contract Booklet.

The monthly bulletins include information relating to RICs concluded in the previous month. Tender notices for R/Cs as well as adhoc purchases issued by DGS&D Head Qrs. and Regional Offices and any other information relating to policy/procedures of DGS&D are also published in the monthly bulletin. National Test House is a premier Scientific Institution engaged in testing, evaluation, quality assurance and standardisation of materials and finished products. There is direct interaction with the public for getting quotation for test fee, deposition of sample and receipt for sample and test fee etc. These aspects have been computerized and all the above work can be done on a single window "Sample room".

There facilities are available in all the units of the NTH. Grievance Officers for each of the regions have been designated under the control of the DG, NTH. The Directors/Scientists-in-Charges of the different regions of the NTH have been entrusted with the work of hearing and receiving public grievances between 10.00 hours to 13.00 hours on every Wednesday.

Trade representatives are also meeting the Director/ Scientists-in-Charge on all other working days. A locked Complaint Box is kept at a suitable place for receiving complaint, if any, by the public and is opened regularly for necessary action. A complaint Register is also kept in each region where all public complaint indicating action taken to dispose the complaint is available.

Controller of Accounts at HQ of the office of the CCA has been designated as Grievance Officer to hear and redress the grievances. Grievance Officers for each of the regions have also been designated. The office of the CCA has issued a citizen's charter to provide better services to suppliers and has given wider publicity to it. The last Wednesday of each month has been fixed as 'Open Darbar' in which Chief Controller of accounts hears the complaints from 3.00 P.M. to 4.00 P.M. against acts of omission and harassment on the part of officials of the organisation.

Grievances which are not solved at the lower level are heard in the Open Darbar. A suggestion box has been installed at the reception counter of Headquarters as well as at Regional Offices for improvement in the system of grievance redressal process. To provide information regarding payments of bills to suppliers a Public Relation officer has been nominated at Information and Facilitation Counter at Headquarters as well as at regional Offices.

There is planned and constant monitoring of pending cases through monthly/quarterly reports which are put up to Public Grievances Officer. Besides, Public Grievances officer also holds meetings with Senior Officers of Attached/Subordinate offices to review the progress of disposal of grievances.

During year, twice the pendency was reviewed by Director (PG) and appropriate instructions for disposal were issued. Consequently, there has been for disposal were issued. Consequently, there has been substantial reduction in the pending grievances. The results of the review were also brought to the notice of results of the review were also brought to the notice of Secretary.

Implementation of official language policy

Department of Supply, its attached and subordinate offices viz, DGS&D, CCA and NTH continued their efforts to implement various measures to promote and augment the progressive use of Hindi in official work. In compliance with the Constitutional and statutory requirements of section 3(3) of official Languages Act, 1963, all documents required to be issued bilingually were issued bilingually by the Department of Supply, CCA and NTH.

All communications received in Hindi were replied to in Hindi by all the offices. Almost all the officers and employees in the Deptt. of Supply have the knowledge of Hindi language. It has nominated one stenographer and 4 typists for Hindi stenography and Hindi type training.

DGS&D has nominated 5 stenographers , 24 typists and 30 employees, office of the Chief controller of Accounts, New Delhi have nominated 2 typists and NTH, Calcutta has nominated one LDC and 3 employees for Hindi stenography, Hindi type and Hindi Language trainings respectively. Their regional offices have also nominated officials for the above mentioned training. Cash award schemes , such as Incentive Scheme for original noting and drafting in Hindi and Hindi Dictation Scheme, formulated and circulated by the Department of OL for promoting the use of Hindi in Official work, were continued in the Department. This year ten employees and three officers were given cash prizes under these scheme.

Various incentive Schemes for promoting use of Hindi are also in force in its attached and subordinate offices. 8 officials in the Headquarter office of DGS&D were awarded prize and certificates under these schemes. Similar Schemes were implemented in its regional offices in which 32 employees were given prizes. These schemes were also implemented in the Headquarter offices of the CCA and NTH and in their regional offices as well and prizes were given to the successful participants.

Meetings of the Official Language Implementation Committee of the Department were convened regularly in which progress made/achieved by the Department and its other offices was discussed. Its three meetings were convened till 31st December, 1998 and the fourth meeting will be convened before 31st March, 1999. OLICs are functioning in all the attached and subordinate offices of the Department and their meetings are convened regularly in which progress made in the use of Hindi is reviewed.

Hindi workshops were organised in Department of Supply, DGS&D, CCA and NTH offices with a view to motivate and encourage employes as well as officers to do their official work in Hindi.. Department of Supply has imparted training to 9 employees and office of the CCA has imparted training to 14 employees in these workshops. To assess the position regarding progressive use of Hindi in various offices under the Department and with a view to encourage the officers and employees working in those offices to do their official work in Hindi, inspections were carried out.

The Department has inspected 5 offices during the year. The Department has published sixth edition of its own publication *Poorti Bhasha Saraswati*. The articles etc written in Hindi by the officials working in the Department anjd in offices under its administrative control are published in the magazine. Office of the CCA, New Delhi published a house journal in Hindi named "Vartika" and office of the DGS&D published a Hindi magazine named *Poorti Gunata Manjusha*. Besides DGS&D has prepared a glossary also.

In compliance with the Official Language Policy, Hindi fortnight was celebrated from 1st to 15th September, 1998 in the Department. Various activities such as Hindi workshop, Quiz and Hindi Essay Competition ware organised during this period. Cash prizes were given by the Secretary of the Department to the successful participants.

Hindi Day/Fortnight was also organised in the various offices of the Department. Hindi Essay competition, debate, summary writing, Hindi typing competition, Hindi stenography competition, Hindi noting and drafting competition and quiz programmes were organised in these offices and cash prizes as well as certificates were awarded to the employees.

7

Trends in India's Foreign Trade

During the current year, as per provisional estimates exports amounted to Rs. 1,0 1, 850 crores in April to December, 1998 as compared to Rs. 91,192 crores during April to December, 1997 registering a growth of 11 .7% in Rupee terms. Imports have registered an increase of 23.2% in Rupee terms having increased to Rs. 1,32,447 crores in April to December, 1998 from Rs. 1,07,523 crores during April to December, 1997. The trade deficit during April to December, 1998 is estimated at Rs. 30,597 crores. The details of foreign trade in Rupee terms and dollar terms for the period April -December, 1998-99 are given in Table I(a) and I(b) respectively

Trends in India's foreign trade

Commodity trends

During April to November, 1998, the principal commodities which registered significant increase in exports over the corresponding period of the previous year include tea, guargum meal, rice, leather manufactures excluding footwear, castor oil, coal, gems and jewellery readymade garments, natural silk textiles, coir and coir manufactures, floriculture products, mica and handicrafts. Commodities that witnessed the moderate growth up to 15% include spices, coffee, tobacco (manufactured), cashew, fruits and vegetables, processed fruits and juices, miscellaneous processed items, shellac, basic chemicals, pharmaceuticals & cosmetics, man-made textiles, madeups, etc., plastic and linoleum, rubber glass and other products, jute manufactures and sports goods.

Exports of other cereals, pulses, unmanufactured tobacco, sesame and niger seeds, ground nut, oil meal, marine products, sugar and molasses, meat and meat products, spirit and beverage, iron ore, processed minerals, other ores and minerals, leather footwear, residual chemicals and allied products, engineering goods, electronic goods, project goods, cotton yarn, fabrics, made-ups, etc., wool and woollen manufactures, carpets, cotton raw including waste and petroleum products declined during the period.

Export commodities

The export performance of principal commodities/groups during 1997-98 and April to November, 1998 are reviewed in the following paragraphs.

Plantations

Plantation crops primarily comprise tea and coffee. Exports of plantation crops increased during April to November, 1998 by 3 1.8% in Rupee terms. Exports of coffee increased by 15.3% during this period to Rs. 1, 225 crores from 1 062 crores during the same period of last year. Exports of tea increased from Rs. 971 crores during April to November, 1997 to Rs. 1,454 crores during April to November, 1998 registering a positive growth of 49.7%.

Agriculture and allied products

This group comprises a wide variety of agricultural products covering cereals, pulses, tobacco, spices, nuts and seeds, oilmeals, guargum meals, castor oil, shellac, sugar and molasses, processed food, meat and meat products, etc. Share of items under the group

'Agricultural and allied products' was 11.3% in total exports during April to November, 1998. During April to November, 1998, the exports of agricultural and allied products showed an increase of 13.8% from Rs. 8,919 crores during April to November, 1997 to Rs. 10, 151 crores during April to November, 1998.

The items which have indicated significant increase during this period as compared to the correspondence period of the previous year are rice, guargum meal, castor oil, miscellaneous processed items. The items which recorded decline in exports are other cereals, tobacco (unmanufactured), sesame and niger seed, ground nut, oil meals, sugar and molasses, meat and meat products, spirit and beverage & pulses.

Marine products

The exports of marine products are Rs. 2,973 crores during April to November, 1998 as against Rs. 2,990 crores during April to November, 1997 indicating a decrease of 0.6 %.

Ores and minerals

Ores and minerals are traditional items of exports. Their contribution in the total exports is about 2.4% during April to November, 1998. The main item of exports in this category ore iron ore, manganese ore, chrome ore, aluminum, mica and coal. During April to November, 1998, the exports of ores & minerals were valued at Rs. 2,183 crores registering a decline of 10.8% over the same period of last year. Iron ore and processed minerals have shown a sharp decline during this period and mica has registered a positive growth of 20% during April to November, 1998 as compared to the corresponding period of the previous year.

Leather and leather manufactures

The value of exports of leather and leather manufactures

has increased from Rs. 3,694 crores during April to November, 1997 to Rs. 4,269 crores during April to November, 1998, showing a positive growth of 15.6%. Leather goods account for 4. 1 % share in the total exports during April to November, 1998, 'Footwear' exports constitutes 29% of the exports of leather and leather products and exports of leather footwear declined by 19.4% during April to November, 1998 as compared with corresponding period of the previous year. Most of the leather products are exported to developed countries like Germany, France, U.S.A., U.K., Italy, Japan including CIS countries.

Gems and jewellery

Gems and Jewellery is a major export item accounting for about 17.3% of our total exports during April to November, 1998. The exports of gems and jewellery during April to November, 1998 amounted to Rs. 15,583 crores as compared to Rs. 17,672 crores; during the corresponding period of lost year, showing a positive growth rate of 33.5%.

Chemicals and allied products

Chemicals and allied products have a positive growth of 1.8% during April to November, 1998 over the same period of the previous year in Rupee terms. The plastic and linoleum products in the international market are very competitive and stringent environmental and public health controls need to be maintained. Quality Control in terms of packaging standards, delivery schedules require further attention if a continuous increase is to be maintained.

Engineering goods

The share of engineering goods contributes 10.9% to the total exports during April to November, 1998. The main items under the group 'Engineering Goods' are ferro

alloys, nonferrous metals, machine tools, machinery and instruments, transport equipment, residual engineering items, etc. Exports off engineering goods amounted to Rs. 9,834 crores during April cc to November, 1998 as against Rs. 10,139 crores during April to November, 1997 showing a decline of 3%. Other products covered under this group are capital goods and consumer durables.

Electronic and computer software

In the event of technological advancement and breakthrough in industrial infrastructure, electronics and computer software industry has been identified as a thrust sector for export. The non-traditional sector consists broadly of consumer electronics, control instrumentation and industrial electronics, computer systems, communication equipment, components and software.

Electronic goods excluding software has a share of 1.4% of India's exports during the period April to November, 1998. Exports of electronic goods excluding software during April to November, 1998 are valued at Rs. 1,220 crores as compared to Rs. 1,886 crores during April to November, 1997 showing a decline of 35.3%.

Textiles

Textiles including carpets, handicrafts and raw cotton are the major traditional export items accounting for nearly 27.7% share in the total exports during April to November, 1998. Total value of Indian textiles exports during April to November, 1998 increased to Rs. 21,588 crores, from Rs. 20,039 crores during the corresponding period of previous year showing a positive growth rate of 7.7%. Coir & coir manufactures recorded the highest growth in this sector of about 33.3% followed by natural silk textiles (30.1%) and readymade garments (24.9%) and lute manufactures (8.3%) and man-made textile made-ups, etc. (0.7%). Cotton yarn fabrics made-ups, etc. and wool and woollen manufactures recorded negative growths of 10% and 12.3 % respectively. Handicrafts recorded a positive growth of 36.3% during April to November, 1998 compared to the corresponding period of the previous year. Raw cotton including waste and carpets showed a decline of 78.6% and 8.3% respectively during April to November, 1998.

Handicrafts

The main items of exports of handicrafts are various types of handmade carpets and works of art, such as metal artware, textiles (hand printed), woodwares and zari goods. Exports of carpets declined during April to November, 1998 to Rs. 1,278 crores from Rs. 1,394 crores, during April to November, 1997 indicating a negative growth of 8.3%. During April to November, 1998, handicrafts exports increased to Rs. 1 865 crores from Rs. 1 368 crores during the corresponding period of the lost year showing a positive growth of 36.3%.

Trends in India's imports

The trends in India's principal imports during the year 1997-98 as compared to 1996-97, total imports amounted to Rs. 1, 17,948 crores during April to November, 1998 as compared to Rs. 92,989 crores during the same period of the lost year showing a positive growth rate of 26.8% in Rupee terms.

Imports of items under bulk category comprising inter-alia, POL, fertilizers, edible oils, sugar, newsprint, paper board and manufactures, etc. registered an increase to Rs. 37,708 crores during April to November, 1998 from Rs. 36,61 3 crores during April to November, 1997 reflecting a growth of 3%. The imports of sugar increased to Rs. 768 crores during April to November, 1998 showing an increase of 477.4%. The other major items which witnessed an increase are wheat (62%), edible oil (132.8%), fertilizer crude (46.8%), sulphur and unroasted pyrites (12.7%) and paper board and manufactures (9.6%).

Items which recorded negative growth are cereal preparations (68.9%), fertilizer manufactured (12.6%), petroleum crude and products (1 0.9%), newsprint (6.5%), metalliferous ores and scrap (4%), nonferrous metals (9.4%), pulp and waste paper (10%), iron and steel (0.5%) and crude rubber including synthetic (2.3%).

In other items, major growth has been recorded during April to November, 1998 over the same period of the last year in such items as project goods, (99%), nonmetal mineral manufactures (59.4%), other raw minerals (38.3%), pearls, precious, semiprecious stones (24.4%), dyeing and tanning materials (20.8%), raw hides and skins (27.3%), textiles yarn, fabric, etc. (31.5%), professional instruments, etc. (32.8%), electronic goods including computer software (23.6%) and leather (9%).

High decline has been recorded in such items as pulses (62.7%), wool raw (24.8%), transport equipment (17.3%), silk raw (2.9%) and synthetic and regenerated fibres (28.8%) and fruits & nuts (1 6.2%).

Imports of major products are reviewed in the following paragraphs.

Crude oil and petroleum products

The imports of petroleum crude and products during April to November, 1998 were valued at Rs. 18,431 crores as against Rs. 20,686 crores during April to November, 1997 showing a decline of 10.9%.

Fertilizers

The total imports of fertilizers have declined from Rs. 3,281 crores during April to November, 1997 to Rs. 3,163 crores during April to November, 1998 showing a negative growth of (3.6%). This includes crude fertilizers as well as those of manufactured and sulphur and unroasted pyrites.

Pearls, precious and semiprecious stones

The diamond industry in the country draws heavily on imports of rough precious and semiprecious stones. Imports of pearls and precious and semiprecious stones amounted to Rs. 9,813 crores during April to November, 1998 as compared to Rs. 7,890 crores during the corresponding period of the previous year showing a positive growth of 24.4%.

Capital goods

Imports of Capital goods largely represented by machinery, including transport equipments, project goods and professional instruments have shown an increase from Rs. 16,449 crores during April to November, 1997 to Rs. 20,404 crores during April to November, 1998 showing a growth of 24%. In this category, project goods have shown a higher growth of (99%) followed by professional instruments (32.8%), electrical machinery (47.7%) and non-electrical machinery (3.7%) during April to November, 1998 as compared to corresponding period of the previous year. Decline has been registered in transport equipment (1 7.3%).

Chemicals and chemical materials

Organic and inorganic chemical materials and medicinal & pharmaceuticals products constituted the major components of imports under this category. The imports of organic and inorganic chemicals rose to Rs. 7,660 crores during April to November, 1998 from Rs. 6,982 crores during April to November, 1997, showing a positive growth of 9.7%.

The medicinal and pharmaceutical products have registered an increase from Rs. 898 crores during April to November, 1997 to Rs. 986 crores during the period April to November, 1998 showing a positive growth of 9.8%.

Direction of India's foreign trade

The trends of India's export to and import from different regions are given in table-IV & V respectively. The exports figures in respect of regions and sub-regions shown in table IV do not include export of crude oil from Mumbai high and petroleum products to respective countries of consignment, but these are included in the aggregate of exports. During April to November, 1998, Asia and Oceania accounted for 34.8% of India's total exports, West Europe (27.4%), America (25.6%), Africa (6.4%) and East Europe (3.1 %).

During April to November, 1998, Asia and Oceania was the largest supplier of goods and accounted for 45.2% of our imports, followed by West Europe 32.2%, America 11 %, Africa 8.5% and East Europe 2%.

A comparison of respective shares of sources of our imports reveals that regions whose shares have increased during April to November, 1998 compared to the corresponding period of the last year include West Europe from 29.9% to 32.2%, Africa from 7% to 8.5%. Imports have declined from Asia and Oceania i.e. from 48. 1 % to 45.2%, America 11.9% to 11% and East Europe from 3. 1 % to 2%.

8

Export Processing Zones

The Export Processing Zones (EPZs) set up as enclaves, separated from the Domestic Tariff Area by fiscal barriers, are intended to provide an internationally competitive duty free environment for export production at low cost. This enables the products of EPZs to be competitive, both quality-wise and price-wise, in the international market. India has seven EPZs at Kandla (Gujarat), Santacruz (Mumbai), Falta (West Bengal), NOIDA (U.P.), Cochin (Kerala), Chennai (Tamil Nodu) and Visakhapatnam (Andhra Pradesh).

The Santacruz Electronics Export Processing Zone (SEEPZ) is meant exclusively for export of electronics and gem and jewellery items whereas the other zones are multi-product Zones.

Export oriented zones

The Export Oriented Units (EOUs) Scheme introduced in early 1981, is complementary to the EPZ Scheme. It adopts the some production regime but offers a wide option in locations with reference to factors like source of raw materials, ports of export, hinterland facilities, avail ability of technological skills, existence of an industrial base and the need for a larger area of land for the project. 1,186 units are in operation under the scheme at present

Infrastructure

Each of the Zones provides basic infrastructure such as developed land for construction of factory sheds, standard design factory buildings providing ready-built sheds, roads, power, water supply and drainage. In addition, Customs clearance is arranged within the Zones at no extra charge. Provision is made for locating banking/post office facilities and offices of clearing agents in the Service Centre located in each of the Zones. EOUs on the other hand have to put up their own infrastructure. At present 527 units are in operation in Export Processing Zones as on 31.10.1998.

Product coverage

While the EPZ operating units broadly fall under the product groups of electronics, engineering items, chemicals and allied products, gem and jewellery; textiles, garments, plastics and rubber products. EOUs are mainly concentrated in textiles and yarn, food processing, electronics, chemicals, plastics, granites and minerals/ores. Majority of the units are located in Tamil Nadu Andhra Pradesh, Karnataka, Maharashtra and Gujarat.

Export performance

Exports from EOU/EPZ units which stood at Rs. 13,067.64 crores in 1996-97 rose to Rs. 14,514.30 crores in 1997-98 representing a growth of over 11%. Details of exports from EPZs/EOUs during the last three years are indicated below:

(Rs. in crores)

Year	EPZs	EOUs	Total
1995-96	3235.63	7009.00	10244.63
1996-97	4338.92	8728.72	13067.64
1997-98	4817.30	9697.00	14514.30
1998-99	3350.50	9000.00	12350.00

Export promotion measures

The policy and procedures applicable to EPZ units are under constant review and improvements are brought about from time to time. The special package for revival of exports announced by Commerce Minister in the Parliament on 5.8.1998, include the following specific measures for boosting exports from EOU/EPZ units:

1. Enhancement of corporate tax holiday from 5 years to 10 years;
2. Subcontracting facility in the domestic tariff area; and
3. Exports through courier.

Private/joint sector EPzs

Government has permitted development of EPZs by private, state or joint sector. The Inter-Ministerial Committee on private EPZs has already cleared three proposals for setting up of private EPZs in Bombay, Surat and Kancheepuram. In addition, establishment of an EPZ at Greater NOIDA by Government of U.P. has also been cleared.

Export Promotion Industrial Park (EPIP) scheme

A centrally sponsored 'Export Promotion Industrial Park' (EPIP) Scheme has been introduced in 1993-94 with a view to involving the State Governments in the creation of infrastructural facilities for export oriented production.

The scheme provides that 75% of the capital expenditure incurred towards creation of such facilities, ordinarily limited to Rs. 10 crores in each case, will be met from a central grant to the State Governments. In addition, a maintenance grant equivalent to 2% of export turnover of each unit·established therein will also be made available to State Governments for a period of 5 years from the date of commercial production of that unit.

The Central Government has so far approved 19 proposals for establishment of EPIPs in the States of Punjab, Haryana, Himachal Pradesh, Rajasthan, Karnataka, Kerala, Maharashtra, Tamil Nadu, Andhra Pradesh, Uttar Pradesh, Gujarat, Bihar, Jammu & Kashmir, Assam, Madhya Pradesh, West Bengal, Orissa, Meghalaya and Manipur. While the EPIP in Rajasthan at Sitapura (District Jaipur) has since been completed, the Park at Suraipur, District Gautambudh Nagar (Uttar Pradesh), Hoodi, District Bangalore (Karnataka) and Ambarnath District Thane (Maharashtra) are nearing completion. Other Parks are at various stages of implementation.

Export houses, trading houses & super star trading houses

The objective of the scheme of Export Houses, Trading Houses, Star Trading Houses and Super Star Trading Houses is to give recognition to the established exporters and large Export Houses to build up the marketing infrastructure and expertise required for export promotion.

The Registered Exporters having a record of Export performance over a number of years are granted the status of Export Houses/Trading Houses/Star Trading Houses/Super Star Trading Houses subject to the fulfilment of minimum annual average export performance in terms of FOB value or net foreign exchange earnings on physical exports prescribed in the EXIM Policy.

The Export Houses, Trading Houses, Star Trading Houses and Super Star Trading Houses' Scheme allows the Registered Exporters certain additional benefits available to them under the policy.

9

Economic Development

The year 1991 marks a watershed in the economic history of India, as the country went through a paradigm shift-from one of the most highly regulated economies of the world which was essentially inward-looking to a market-oriented system, reducing the role of Government in making economic decisions, as the means to achieve higher growth of the economy and its rapid integration with the rest of the world.

An economic stabilisation programme and structural reforms covering trade, industry, taxation, financial sector and capital market were put through turning the worst economic crisis that confronted India since Independence into an opportunity to usher in a quiet revolution which would enable the country to attain a trajectory of higher growth and, along with it, social equity.

Developments in the Gulf region in 1990 exerted pressures on India's balance of payments and with outflow of capital, mainly NRI deposits, the foreign exchange reserves declined to about one billion dollars (barely two weeks of imports) in June 1991. The country was for the first time on the verge of defaulting on its external debt. There was no choice but to have recourse to a structural adjustment programme with the International Monetary Fund providing a standby credit for a stabilisation programme coupled with wide-ranging reforms.

The first steps were in the area of Trade Policy by devaluing the rupee by 22 per cent in dollar terms, eliminating export subsidy and reducing import licensing restrictions. A dual exchange rate system was ushered in but by March 1993, it was unified and a fully floating exchange rate regime in which the exchange rate is determined by market forces of demand and supply came into being. The foreign exchange market was widened and deepened, and in August 1994, the rupee was made fully convertible on current account, trade and non-trade. The downward adjustment of the rupee was designed to improve the country's international competitiveness and correct the imbalances in trade and current accounts.

Beginning with the 1991-92 Budget, Government also launched a phased reduction of import tariff bringing down the maximum from 300 per cent in 1990 to 50 per cent by march 1995. The changes resulted in lowering the import-weighted average tariff from 87 per cent in 1991 to 27 per cent in March 1995. The dispersion of tariffs was also significantly reduced and quantitiative restrictions were substantially eased. The trade reforms undertaken from 1991 helped to reduce the anti-export bias of Indian industry which was being exposed to both domestic and international competition.

The thrust of the Export-Import Policy (1992-97), made coterminus with the Eighth Five year Plan, is export promotion which is crucial for balance of payment and at the same time the Policy facilitates the import of production inputs required for sustaining increased industrial growth and exports.

Exports have responded impressively to the policy reforms and after the slowdown in the first two years under the impact of macrostabilisation measures, grew by an average of 18-19 per cent in the subsequent three years (1993-94 to 1995-96) in dollar terms. Exports have now diversified both commoditywise and countrywise with an increasing share going to the rest of Asia, particularly East and South East Asia with which India is trying to evolve increased trade and investment cooperation, given the rapid growth and the dynamism of these economies.

India's exports have undoubtedly gained from the expansion in world trade-as will be seen from the fact that a slowdown in global exports in 1996 has also effected India's exports to some extent in the current year-but the Government is confident that the export target of 38 billion dollars in 1996-97 would be achieved as against the 31.8 billion in 1995-96. A target of 75 billion dollars of exports by 2,000 A.D. has been set and this would mean maintaining an annual export growth of around 20 per cent in dollar terms over the next four years. This would facilitate a steady rise in the ratio of exports and imports in GDP and take India closer to one per cent as its share of world trade by the year 2001. Changes in the direction of India's trade from 1960-61 are brought out in Table IV.

In recent years, a largest percentage of imports are covered by exports—88 per cent in 1995-96. Imports have also increased with industry stagin a strong recovery from 1993-94 onwards to record double digitrates of growth. The higher import bill also reflects the demand for mass consumption items like pulses and edible oils apart from the growing dependence on imports of petroleum crude and products to keep pace with the rapid growth in energy use in the country.

The Economic Survey–1996—97 is a balanced appraisal of the past performance of the economy, attributing the gains to the policy of economic reform and liberalisaton, pursued during the last five years and presents a picture of cautious optimism for the future.

While attributing the past gains to the policy of liberalisation, the Survey asserts that the policy would need to be pursued with greater vigour in future to carry the economy to higher growth path. It attributes "the loss of momentum" in the economy to "the marked slow down in the pace of reforms preceding and during the election period", but adds "this has been revived with a series of measures in recent months."

The Survey says "the initial spurt of reforms from 1991—92 t 1993—94 was very successful on all accounts, resulting in a jump in economic growth in 1994—95 to 7.2 per cent." It says GDP grew by 7.1 per cent in 1995—96 despite the slowdown in the momentum of reform and adds, econmic growth in 1996—97 is estimated by the CSO to be around 6.8 per cent (GDP at factor cost). The Eight Plan, it says is thus likely to end with an average growth of 6.5 per cent per annum, 0.9 per cent higher than the target rate of 5.6 per cent and 0.5 per cent point higher than the actual achievement of the Seventh Plan. More important for the future is the fact that the average growth during the latest three years is 7 per cent, probably placing India among the top ten performers in the world during the period."

However, when it comes to a review of sectoral performance that he Survey is compelled to be more realistic. It says "the economy in 1996–97 so far presents a mixed picture." Although, it says "overall economic growth remains high at 6.8 per cent, and agriculture has rebounded, the growth of manufacturing value added has slowed and the performance of key infrastructure sectors, especially power and crude oil, is weak. The annual rate of inflation (point to point) has risen t actual long—term levels and export growth has decelerated markedly in recent months."

On agriculture, the Survey says "production in

1996—97 is expected to show good recovery from the slower growth in 1995—96. The growth is projected at 3 per cent after a fall of 0.4 per cent in 1995–96. The sharp decline in foodgrains production by 3.4 per cent, which was responsible for the slow growth in 1995–96, is expected to be reversed by; an increase of 3.3 per cent in 1996—97. Foodgrains production is expected to recover to 191.2 million tonnes, only marginally lower than the level of production in 1994—95. The recovery is primarily due to coarse cereals, as well as anticipated rise in wheat production, which suffered a sharp setback in 1995—96." Commercial crop production has done extremely well in 1996—97 with oilseeds and cotton expected to reach record levels of 24.1 and 14.1 million tonnes respectively.

The momentum of growth witnessed in 1995—96 with a GDP growth of over 7 per cent, has been maintained in 1996—97, thus providing increasing evidence that the growth potential has improved as a result of the reforms initiated in 1991. With the growing participation of virtually the entire spectrum of political opinion inthe reform process, there is a good prospect that a higher growth rate would become a permanent feature of the economy.

The initial spurt of reforms from 1991—92 to 1993—94 was very successful by all accounts, resulting in a jump in economic growth to 7.2 per cent in 1994—95 (in terms of GDP at factor cost). Since 1994—95, however, there was a marked slow down in the pace of reforms. Nevertheless, GDP grew by 7.1 per cent in 1995—96. The slackening of reforms preceding and during the election period may have been responsible for some loss of momentum, but this has been revived with a series of measures in recent months.

Economic growth in 1996—97 is estimated by CSO to be around 6.8 per cent (GDP at factor cost). Thus, the

Eighth Plan is likely to end with an average growth of 6.5 per cent per annum, 0.9 per cent point higher than the target rate of 5.6 per cent, and 0.5 per cent point higher than the actual achievement of the Seventh Plan. More important for the future is the fact that the average growth during the latest three years is 7 per cent, probably placing India among the top ten performers in the world during this period.

As the final year of the Eighth Plan draws to a close, a comparison of some salient dimensions of some salilent dimensions of economic performance between the Eighth Plan period and its predecessor reveals the following:

— Overall economic growth has been faster;

— The manufacturing sector has grown almost 2 per cent points faster per year in the Eighth Plan period;

— Agriculture and allied sectors have grown at about 3.5 per cent per annum in both periods;

— Both exports and imports have grown significantly faster in the Eighth Plan period;

— The balance of payments has strengthened considerably, with trade and current account deficits declining as ratios of GDP, while exports and imports have grown rapidly both in value terms as well as in proportion to GDP.

— The Central Government's fiscal deficit as a proportion of GDP has declined significantly;

— The average rate of gross domestic savings has risen substantially from 20.6 per cent of GDP in the Seventh Plan period to 23.9 per cent in the first four years of the Eighth Plan;

— With the exception of telecommunications, the rate of

growth of net output (value added) of infrastructure sectors has slowed;

— The average rate of inflation has risen somewhat, though remaining below double digits.

Total gross domestic saving reached a new peak of 25.6 per cent of GDP in 1995—96, exceeding its previous peak of 24.9 per cent of GDP in 1994–95. This seems to vindicate the reform strategy of encouraging savings by expanding saving and investment opportunities, rather than giving special incentives.

Gross domestic investment (adjusted), as a proportion of GDP at current prices, rose even faster than gross domestic saving in 1995—96 to a high of 27.4 per cent from 26 per cent in the previous year. Gross domestic investment in real terms, as a proportion of GDP at constant prices, reached a new peak of 27.1 per cent, exceeding the previous peak of 25.9 per cent in 1990—91. Gross fixed capital formation which is even more important for productivity and growth, reached a new peak of 24.1 per cent of GDP in 1995—96. Private sector investment appears to have responded vigorously to the policy of promoting competition, removing policy distortions and hurdles, and improving access to factors of production (e.g. technology, capital).

Estimates of savings and investment in 1996—97 are not yet available. Indicators are mixed. On the one hand, domestic capital goods production is buoyent and disbursement of financial institutions are significantly higher, on the other hand, capital goods imports have declined, non—oil imports are lower in the first nine months of the year, corporate demand for credit appears slack, and sanctions of financial institutions are substantially lower.

The economy in 1996—97 so far presents a mixed

picture in other dimensions as well. Although overall economic growth remains high at 6.8 per cent, and agriculture has rebounded, the growth of manufacturing value added has slowed and the performance of key infrastructure sectors, especially power and crude oil, is weak. The annual rate of inflation (point to point) has risen back to average long—term levels and export growth has decelerated markedly in recent months. Despite the slowdown in exports, a combination of sluggish imports and reasonably buoyant inflows of invisibles and capital flows have led to a build—up of foreign exchange reserves by over $ 2.5 billion.

In the previous chapter, we described the situation as it prevailed in 1960-61. We shall now proceed to take a brief review of the progress made during the past decade. The last year for which some data are available is 1968-69. Therefore, in the following review, we shall cover the period from 1960-61 to 1968-69.

National Income again offers a useful summary measure to judge the performance of the economy in a given period. The particular measure of national income we shall use is specifically termed Net National Product at Factor Cost. We shall briefly refer to it as NNP. We have earlier mentioned that the NNP was Rs. 13,308 crores in 1960-61. It increased to Rs. 28,800 crores in 1968-69 was 216.4. The NNP increased annually by about 6 percentage points during 1961-62 and 1962-63; by almost 17 percentage points in 1963-64; by 26 percentage points in the next two years; by 23 percentage points in 1966-67; by 32 percentage points in 1967-68; and finally, by 6 percentage points in 1968-69. Over the eight years from 1960-61 to 1968-69, the NNP more than doubled.

This is a spectacular performance if it were all real. Unfortunately it is not all real. During the eight years from 1960-61 to 1968-69, the prices of commodities have almost doubled. This means that a rupee in 1968-69 does not mean the same thing as it did in 1960-61. Hence, to judge the real increase in NNP, we should ask what would the NNP be if the prices had remained unchanged. In other words, we should value the NNP in subsequent years at prices as they prevailed in 1960-61. We shall refer to this as Net National Product at Constant (1960-61) Prices. From such a series, it becomes clear that the NNP increased by only 26.5 per cent in eight years and not by 116.4 per cnet as appeared earlier. Thus the real increase in the NNP is only 26.5 per cent in eight years; the balance of apparent increase is a reflection of the increase in prices.

The growth in the NNP has not been steady. This is because agricultural production, which constitutes almost half of the total, is still liable to wide fluctuations from year to year. The real increase in the NNP by 6 percentage points in 1963-64 and again by 8 percentage points in 1964-65 was because of the good agricultural season in those two years. This was followed by two very bad years and the NNP actually declined in 1965-66 and remained at the same low level in 1966-67. Fortunately, the year 1967-68 turned out to be a very good year and the NNP jumped by 10 percentage points. The year 1968-69 was also a good year and the NNP is estimated to have advanced by another 2 percentage points.

Thus the anunal fluctuations in agricultural production explain the unsteady growth of the NNP. But in a period as long as 8 to 10 years, one must take good years along with bad years and reckon the fact that the real increase in NNP in eight years was only 26.5 per cent which is a compound growth rate of less than 3 per cent per annum.

The growth in the NNP must be placed alongside the growth in population. The population of the Indian

Union in 1961 was 434 million. We shall know what it is when the census is taken this year. However, in the meanwhile, the population is estimated to have been growing at the annual rate of 2.5 per cent. Clearly, therefore, a growth of NNP at an annual rate of no more than 3 per cent is barely sufficient to keep pace with the growth in population; it leaves little margin to make a net improvement in the economic condition of the people. This becomes clear if we divide the NNP by the estimated population each year to get the NNP per capita. If this is done, it becomes clear that the per capita NNP increased from Rs. 306.7 in 1960-61 to just Rs. 321.3 in 1967-68 and Rs. 319.4 in 1968-69. This is an increase at best of only 4.5 per cent in eight years which is about half a per cent per annum. This summarises the performance of the economy during the past decade.

As mentioned earlier, per capita private consumer expenditure gives a more direct measure of the well-being or standard of living of a people. We have seen that the per capita private consumer expenditure was Rs. 276.3 in 1960-61. In are given the relevant data for the subsequent years. In order to assess the real changes in the per capita consumer expenditure in subsequent years at constant (1960-61) prices for the years from 1960-61 to 1968-69.

It will be seen that the per capita consumer expenditure increased from Rs. 276.3 in 1960-61 to Rs. 285.5 (at 1960-61 prices) in 1968-69. The per capita consumer expenditure shows a sudden increase (Rs. 296.0) in 1964-65 and then a sudden fall (Rs. 269.8 and Rs. 271.8) in the following two years. This is a reflection of the bumper agricultural production in 1964-65 and poor production in the following two years. The average per capita consumption during the three years 1964-65, 1965-66 and 1966-67 was Rs. 279.2 per annum. It seems more likely that the real consumption was maintained more or less at this level by carrying some of the large stocks of 1964-65 into the next two years rather than allowing it to fluctuate along with fluctuations in agricultural production. For the same reason, we should smoothen out the fluctuations in the first three years as also in the last two years. When this is done, the estimates of per capita consumer expenditure in the nine years appear as shown in. They seem more reasonable and plausible.

The upshot of the whole exercise is that the per capita consumer expenditure rose from Rs. 276.3 in 1960-61 to Rs. 289.6 in 1968-69, that is by 4.8 per cent in eight years or by about half a per cent per annum. It is obvious that it could not have risen by any more because, we have seen as the per capita income rose at best by 4.5 per cent in the eight years. Incidentally, we may note that the per capita consumer expenditure seems to have increased a little more than has the per capita national income. The reasons seem to be firstly that the large increase in national income registered in the last two years has been mainly on account of the large increase in the production of foodgrains in these years and secondly that the net domestic capital formation as a proportion of the net domestic expenditure has gone down sharply in these two years.

This brings us to the next point namely how are these small gains of development distributed between different sections of the population–between the rural and urban populations and between the richer and poorer sections of these populations? More specifically, we ask: The average consumer expenditure in the country rose by 4.8 per cent in real terms (that is at constant prices) in the eight years from 1960-61 and 1968-69. Did this happen equally in the case of the rural and urban populations and equally in the case of the richer and poorer sections of these populations? These questions are crucial while assessing whether anything is happening to the poor of this country; whether their lot has improved materially as a result of the economic development of the past decade. If the per capita consumption in the country has risen by no more than 4.8 per cent in eight years, it is obvious that little noticeable could have happened in the nature of alleviation of poverty unless the poorer sections have profited proportionately more than the average and much more so than the rich. Did this happen during the past decade? We shall examine the facts.

Rural-urban differential

As mentioned earlier, the National Sample Survey (NSS) offers estimates of private consumer expenditure in rural and urban areas separately. In we give the NSS estimates of per capita consumer expenditure for the rural and urban populations for the years 1960-61 and 1967-68. In order to make the estimates for 1967-68 comparable with those for 1960-61, the estimates for 1967-68 must be expressed at prices prevailing in 1960-61. This is done in the second line of the Table.

As earlier mentioned, the NSS estimate of per capita private consumer expenditure for 1960-61 (Rs. 278.8) is in close agreement with the corresponding official estimate (Rs. 276.3); the NSS estimate is higher than the official estimate by less than one per cent (0.9 per cent). However, the NSS estimate of per capita private consumer expenditure for 1967-68 at 1960-61 prices (Rs. 256.2) is much below the corresponding official estimate (Rs. 287.0). Indeed the NSS estimate is short of the official estimate by as much as 10.7 per cent.

It seems that the NSS estimate of per capita private consumer expenditure for 1967-68 is an underestimate. This becomes clear if we compare it with the NSS estimate for 1960-61. It will be seen that, compared at constant 1960-61 prices, the NSS estimate for 1967-68 (Rs. 256.2) is below the NSS estimate for 1960-61 (Rs. 278.8) by as much as 8.1 per cent. Hence, if we rely on the NSS estimates, it would appear that the per capita consumption declined by as much as 8.1 per cent during the seven years from 1960-61 to 1967-68. This appears unlikely. Hence, we must conclude that the NSS estimate of per capita consumer expenditure in 1967-68 is in fact an underestimate.

We shall later examine the reasons for and the nature of this underestimation. For the present, we propose to revise the NSS estimates of rural and urban per capita consumer expenditure, both in 1960-61 and 1967-68, in order to bring them in accord with the official estimates of per capita national consumption in those years. * It will be noticed that the revision is only slight for 1960-61 but is very considerable for 1967-68.

From the estimates of per capita rural and urban consumer expenditure thus revised, it will be seen that the per capita national consumer expenditure increased from Rs.276.3 in 1960-61 to Rs. 287.0 in 1967-68 that is by 3.9 per cent. In the same period, the per capita rural consumer expenditure increased from Rs. 258.8 to Rs. 268.6 that is by 3.8 per cent, while the per capita urban consumer expenditure increased from Rs. 356.4 to Rs. 364.9 that is by 2.4 per cent. Thus it seems that the average consumption in the rural area has improved a little more, though only slightly, than the average consumptions in urban area. Consequently, the rural-urban difference has been reduced a little. For instance, in 1960-61, the per capita urban consumption (Rs. 356.4) was 37.7 per cent higher than the per capita rural consumptions (Rs. 258.8). In 1967-68, the per capita urban consumption (Rs. 364.9) was only 35.9 per cent higher than the per capita rural consumption. We shall later examine the process through which the rural-urban difference has been thus reduced, even if only slightly.

Overall economic growth in terms of Gross Domestic Product (GDP) at constant factor cost improved from 0.8% in 1991-92 to 6.3% in 1994-95 and 7% in 1995-96 aided by a growth rate of 2.4% by agriculture and allied sectors, 11.7% by industry and construction sector and 7% by services. Overall economic growth during the first four year of the 8th Plan (1992-97) averaged 5.9% per annum compared with the planned target of 5.6%.

The domestic savings rate measured in terms of gross domestic savings as a proportion of GDP at current market prices increased from an average rate of 21.3% in 1992-93 and 1993-94 to 24.4% in 1994-95. The rate of domestic investment measured in terms of gross domestic capital formation as a proportion of GDP at current market prices increased from 21.6% in 1993-94 to 25.2% in 1994-95.

Industrial production which was virtually stagnant in 1991-92 increased by 9.4% and 12.1% in 1995-96 supported by a growth rate of 6.9% in mining, 13.6% in manufacturing and 8.1% in electricity generation. As per the latest information available, industrial growth deceleration to 8.5% in April-June 1996 due to deceleration of growth rates in all the sub-sectors (3.6% in mining, 10.4% manufacturing and 2.2% in electricity generation). As per growth rates by use-based classification, capital goods sector recorded a growth rate of 14.2%, intermediate goods 11.9%, consumer durables 11.1% and consumer non-durables 8.6% in April-June 1996. However, the growth rate of basic goods sub-sector having a weight of 39.4% in the overall industrial production was only 4% in April-June 1996.

Seven infrastructural sectors, namely, electricity,

coal, steel, cement, crude oil and petroleum product & fertilizer with a combined weight of 31% in the Index of Industrial Production (IIP) recorded a growth rate of 7.8% in 1995-96. But their growth rate decelerated to 3.2% in April-August 1996 due to poor performance of electricity generation (growth rate of only 2.4%) and crude oil production (decline of production by 10.4%).

The outlook of agricultural production in 1996-97 is excellent with foodgrains output likely to reach 197 million tonnes compared with 185 million tonnes in 1995-96. This is primarily due to this year's rainfall distribution being the best in the past five years. The late withdrawal of monsoon has further ensured bright prospects for rabi production this year.

The estimate of foodgrains production in 1995-96 has been scaled down to 185 million tonnes representing a sharp decline of nearly 6 million tonnes over the prec * eeding year. The shortfall was substantial (about 3 million tonnes) in wheat output, besides short-fall of production of rice and coarse cereals. Consequently wheat procurement dropped steeply to 8.2 million tonnes compared to 12.3 million tonnes in the preceding year. Public stock (Central Pool) of foodgrains was about 22.1 million tonnes as on September 1, 1996.

Economic census and surveys

The Central Statistical Organisation (CSO) conducted the first economic census in 1977 to bridge the data gaps in the unorganised sectors of non-agricultural economy. The economic census was aimed at providing basic information on distribution of non-agricultural enterprises and to provide a frame for follow-up surveys for collection of detailed information about the structure of enterprises, investments, input, output, emploument, etc. The first economic census was followed by two sample surveys-one in 1978-79 relating to unorganised manufacturing and the second in 979-80 devoted to trade, transport, hotels and restaurants, storage and warehousing and services.

The second Economic Census was conducted in 1980 during the houselisting operations of 1981 Population Census with increased scope and coverage. It covered all enterprises (establishments and own-account enterprises) in the non-agricultural sector excluding crop production and plantation. Based on the information thrown up by this Census, three follow-up surveys were carried out, one in 1983-84 on hotels and restaurants, transport, storage and warehousing and services; second in 1984-85 on unorganised manufacturing and third in 1985-86 on wholesale and retail trade. The frame of 1980 Census was updated during 1987-88 in 64 towns. On the basis of Economic Census 1980 and updated frame, four sample surveys were conducted.

The third Economic Census 1990 was conducted along with the houselisting operations of 1991 Population Census in all states/union territories except Jammu and Kashmir. The data processing of Economic Census 1990 was undertaken in a decentralised manner by state/ union territories. Some of the states/union territories utilised the services of Regional Computer Centres at Calcutta and Chandigarh. The all India results of Economic Census 1990 brought out shortly by the CSO for which processing and tabulation has been done by the Computer Centre, Department of SAtatistics. On the basis of the frame thrown up by Economic Census 1990, a follow-up survey covering sectors of mining and quarrying and storage and warehousing was conducted during 1992-93 and another survey on hotels and restaurants and transport was conducted during January to September, 1994.

According to 1980 Economic Census, there were 18.4 million enterprises in the country (excluding Assam) employing 53.6 million persons. Among these, these were 16.9 million enterprises (58.4 per cent in rural areas) engaged in non-agricultural activitties employing 50.7 million persons (43.3 per cent in rural areas). As per of the results of Economic Census 1990, there were 25 million enterprises out-of which 22.7 million were in the non-agricultural sector. The total number of persons usually working were of the order of 72.1 million out of which 40.2 million were hired workers. A total of 17.7 million enterprises operated without any hired labour on a regular basis and were mainly run by the households themselves.

Ministry of Finance is responsible for administration of finances of the Government. It is concerned with all economic and financial matters affecting the country as a whole including mobilisation of resources for development and other purposes. It regulates expenditure of Government including transfer of resources to the states. This Ministry comprises three departments, namely, (i) Economic Affairs, (ii) Expenditure and (iii) Revenue.

The Department of Economic Affairs consists of seven main divisions namely, (i) Economic, (ii) Banking, (iii) Insurance, (iv) Budget, (v) Investment, (vi) External Finance and (vii) Currency and Coinage. This Department inter alia monitors current economic trends and advises Government on all matters of internal and external economic management including working of commercial banks, term-lending institutions, investments regulations, external assistance, etc. Preparation of the Budget of the Union of India as well as the state governments and union territory administrations with legislature when under President's rule and their presentation to Parliament is also the responsibility of this Department.

The Department of Expenditure comprises eight main divisions, namely, (i) Plan finance Division, (ii) Establishment Division, (iii) Cost Accounts Branch, (iv) Controller General of Accounts, (v) Finance Commission Division, (vi) Implementation Cell, (vii) Integrated Finance Division and (viii) Staff Inspection Unit.

Department of Revenue exercises control in respect of revenue matters relating to direct and indirect Union taxes through two statutory boards namely, Central Board of Direct Taxes and the Central Board of Excise and Customs. This Department is also entrusted with the administration and enforcement of controls and regulatory measures provided in the enactments concerning Central sales tax, stamp duties, gold control, foreign exchange and other relevant fiscal statutes. Control over production and disposal of opium and its products is also vested with this Department.

The Finance Minister Mr. P. Chidambaram presented an innovative, well—balanced and virtually a tax—free budget for 1997—98, which should boost savings and investment and help the economy to bounce back with vigour. Many of Mr. Chidambaram's proposals were on expected lines, but his comprehensive package would be received with aplomb all round because of his demonstrated commitment to contain fiscal deficit and advance the reform process.

Undoubtedly, the Finance Minister must have been greatly concerned over the industrial slowdown and the prolonged sluggishness of the capital market, which will now get a shot—in—the—arm by the range of his tax and non—tax measures.

The Corporate sector must be more than satisfied

with the Finance Minister's response to their oftrepeated suggestions while tax—payers in general would get substantial relief from across—the—board lowering of rates. Mr. Chidambaram hopes to restore buoyancy to direct tax revenues so as to raise the tax—GDP ratio and the share of direct taxes in the total tax revenues of Government. He has sought to widen the base of taxation by making it obligatory on residents of large metropolitan areas owning vehicle, telephone or immovable property to file tax returns. A new simplified scheme is being introduced for retail traders to evoke better compliance replacing the presumptive tax scheme which did not yield the desired results.

To harness black money for productive purposes, especially infrastructure, and for financing the Basic Minimum Services Programme he has announced a voluntary disclosure of income and wealth scheme with certain immunity for those coming forward to disclose their cash holdings or assets. The scheme will be in force till the end of 1997.

As expected, Mr. Chidambaram not only abolished the remaining 7.5 per cent surcharge but also reduced the corporate tax rate to 35 per cent while foreign companies would bear 48 per cent. The rate reduction for foreign companies coupled with the decision to raise the aggregate limit of investment in a company by institutional investors from 24 to 30 per cent should attract larger flows of both direct and portfolio investments. For non—resident Indians, the capital gains tax arising on transfer of securities has been reduced to 10 per cent bringing them on par with foreign institutional investors.

Apart from fulfilling his promise to limit fiscal deficit to 5 per cent of GDP in the current year, Mr. Chidambaram has kept the deficit in 1997—98 at 4.5 per cent with a hope of further lowering it to under 4 per cent in the next budget. This would have a salutary impact on the international investor community.

Adhering to his undertaking last year, Mr. Chidambaram has announced the phasing out of the system of ad hoc treasury bills, which have been used to monestise the budget deficits, from April 1st this year. Instead, a scheme of ways and means advances by the Reserve Bank of India to the Central Government is being introduced to take care of mismatches in government's receipts and payments. Mr. Chidambaram has assured that this would not become a permanent source of financing budgetary deficits. Details of the scheme are being announced by the Reserve Bank. The RBI will, however, continue to support government's borrowing programme and the budget for 1997–98 assumes a limit of Rs. 16000 crore for such support. Mr. Chidambaram described the new arrangement as a bold and radical change, intended to strengthen fiscal discipline and also provide greater autonomy to the Reserve Bank in the conduct of monetary policy. The conventional budget deficit has now lost its relevance and the Gross Fiscal Deficit will become the key indicator of total deficit. The Finance Minister has announced that he would introduce a new instrument of capital indexed bonds to provide investors an effective hedge against inflation.

In the spirit of cooperative fedetalism embodied in the Common Minimum Programme of the United Front Government, the Finance Minister has accepted the Tenth Finance Commission's recommendation for a single, divisible pool of taxes to be shared between the Centre and the States. He said Government would adopt the proportion of 29 per cent recommended by the Commission. However, this matter would have to be the subject matter of a constitutional amendment and many

States are pleading for a much higher percentage of devolution than the 29 per cent the Fnance Commission has recommended.

Along with fiscal adjustment, Mr. Chidambaram has given a definite push to the reform process, which had slowed down before process, which had slowed down before and after last year's elections to the Lok Sabha. On the much awaited stand of Government on private sector entering the insurance business, Mr. Chidambaram has come up with a limited opening in the areas of pension business and health insurance. The Life Insurance and General Insurance Corporations will continue to enjoy their monopoly over life and non—life and non—health insurance business.

But companies with majority Indian ownership and control will be permitted to enter health insurance, GIC and LIC can also have joint ventures in pension and health insurance business.

Though Mr. Chidambaram did not refer to any restructuring of public sector enterprises, he said, Government would delegate more managerial and commercial autonomy to all public undertakings. Nine well performing enterprises would be helped to become global giants. Though disinvestment in public undertakings did not take off in 1996—97, the Finance Minister has endorsed the Disinvestment Commission's scheme of disinvestment on the basis of their periodical reports. The budget for the coming year expects to realise Rs. 4800 crore from disinvestment.

In his budget speech, the Finance Minister also announced a new oil exploration licensing policy, under which companies like Oil and Natural Gas Corporation and oil India Limited, will be paid international price of oil for new discoveries. Royalty payments will be fixed on an ad—valorem basis.

The companies will have freedom for marketing crude oil and gas in the domestic market. tax holidays, duty concessions and abolition of cess for the new exploration blocks are provided for in the new policy. Mr. Chidambaram hoped that Indian and foreign companies would respond positively to the new policy which will include a separate tax code to facilitate new investments. Oil exploration and industrial parks will qualify for five year tax holiday in addition to telecommunications.

It is rarely that a Finance Minister gets encomiums from various sectoins of the society for his budget proposals. But Mr. P. Chidambaram has managed to achieve such kudos with his budget proposals for 1997–98. The capital market, the corporate sector as well as the ordinary salaried class have al welcomed his proposals, as Mr. Chidambaram has tried to give something to all of them in the hope that they will all be enthused to help him raise more resources to be ploughed back into the economy.

Of course, the former Finance Minister, Dr. Manmohan Singh, who was the architect of initiating the current economic reforms policy in 1991, has said that the euphoria over the budget proposals may not last if the present government was unable to muster a consensus for resolving certain contentious macro—economic issues. But even he is forced to admit that the most significant element of Mr. Chidambaram's budget is that India has not given up on reforms. Dr. Singh has also appreciated the direction of reform in indirect taxes and restructuring of customs duty proposed in the budget.

Mr. Chidambaram's task was not an easy one. He happens to be the Finance Minister in a coalition government formed by 13 parties and supported by a major party from outside. Even in the best of times, no

Finance Minister can be have his way entirely while farming the budget proposals, as he has to take the entire Cabinet along. So Mr. Chidambaram's situation can be better appreciated.

Moreover he was presenting the budget at a time when the picture on the industrial fronts as well as on exports was not rosy. The capital market has been down for months (the sensitive index of the Mumbai stock exchange touched a three—year low last december). Industry in general had its misgiving on many crucial issues. The morale was rather low all round.

In a situation like this, Mr. Chidambaram had to do something which will psychologically lift the morale of various groups. This boosting up of the psychological morale is what he has done successfully through some bold proposals in the 1997–98 budget.

Now to analyse some of the major proposals contained in the budget. Mr. Chidambaram outlines his approach and says that "a good tax policy should aim at moderate rates, a widex tax base, simpler procedural rules and securing greater compliance. Households and the corporate sector are our best savers; we must reward them."

With this objective in mind, he has rationalised the personal income–tax structure, keeping the rate at the lowest slab at 10 per cent and the highest at 30 per cent (as against 15 per cent and 40 per cent respectively so far). He has also increased the standard deduction to Rs. 20,000 and has proposed that senior citizens having income upto Rs. 1,00,000 would not have to pay any tax. Thus with one stroke he has earned the gratitude of 12 million people who are assessed to income tax now.

To broaden the net wider, he has proposed that in future those who satisfy any of the two following economic criteria—ownership of a four-wheeler vehicle, a telephone, a house or have undertaken foreign travel in the previous year—should voluntarily file their tax returns. No one can seriously object to this proposals; but in attempting to widen the tax base, one hopes the government will ensure that unnecessary harassment is avoided.

Of course, the Finance Minister has introduced a voluntary disclosure scheme to harness black money. The measure has naturally created some controversy and entical questions have been raised. It remains to be seen how far the present scheme—which is different from similar schemes introduced earlier—is successful.

After trying to win the confidence of the individual tax payer, Mr. Chidambaram turns his attention next to the corporate sector. By abolishing the 7.5 per cent surcharge on corporate tax and reducing the rate of taxation for domestic companies to 35 per cent and for foreign companies to 48 per cent, he has conceded one of the long-term demands of industry.

His proposal in the 1996–97 budget for a Minimum Alternate tax (MAT) had some sections of industry u in arms. By now exempting export profits from MAT and bringing about modifications in the application of MAT, he has assuaged the feelings created by his last year's proposal.

Another major concession Mr. Chidambaram has given is the abolition of tax on corporate dividends in the hands of the shareholders. This single proposal, along with abolition o fthe surcharge on corporate tax and MAT modifications, has been such a morale booster for the capital market that the Mumbai stock sensitive index gained over 400 points in two trading days after the presentation of the budget.

Other proposals specifically aimed at improving the sentiment of the stock markets include acceptance in principle of buy–back of share by companies subject to certain conditions and the one–time permission to stockbrokers to corporatise their businesses without attracting tax on capital gains. Companies raising funds from the capital market will be required to give an annual statement disclosing the end—use of such funds. This is intended to restore the faith of small investors in stocks. With regard to indirect taxes also, Mr. Chidambaram has taken some bold measures which have all been welcomed by industry in general. He has outlined that the goal was to achieve the average level of tariffs prevalent in ASEAN countries by the turn of the century. This will give time to Indian industry adjust to these changes. With that objective in mind, he has reduced the peak rate of customs duty from 50 per cent to 40 per cent.

He has reduced the duty on capital goods from 25 to 20 per cent and added that over the next two to three years, these rates would need to be further adjusted to conform to levels prevalent in other developing Asian countries.

Duties have been reduced on raw materials used by steel, chemical and textile industries. Stating that "if there is one science that will dominate the 21st century, it is the information technology and if there is one industry in which India can emerge as a world leader, it is the information technology," Mr. Chidambaram has given a number of concessions to encourage this industry.

Tourism is a major foreign exchange earner and there are specific proposals to boost investment in this sector. Coupled with the abolition of surcharge on corporate tax, one should see some surge in investment in this industry.

Like in customs duty, the Fnance Minister has given across the board concessions in central excise also. Last July, he said, he had promised that within three years "we shall have a four—rate tax structure." With this objective in view, he has introduced three rates—8 per cent, 13 per cent and 18 per cent. Jute industry has been given a special treatment, as he has exempted all jute and jute products from excise duty, Excise duty has been cut in respect of several items of mass consumption.

The 1997—98 Union Budget has broken new grounds in terms of carrying forward the liberalisation process and tax reforms by attempting to impart growth impulses to the economy. The Budget initiatives are important for more reasons than one presumably because the macro economic parameters of the economy were onthe downswing throughout most of the last year of the Eighth Plan (1997—98) with inflation rearing its head, trends in industrial production and foreign trade remaining none too ecouraging and capital markets coasting on thin trading for even blue chip companies. The 1997—98 Budget, as such, was expected to address these serious maladies so as to ensure that the economic activity gathered momentum and also to herals hope for realising the seven per cent growth target set for the Ninth Plan for which 1997–98 Budget is the inaugural year.

The Finance Minister Mr. P. Chidambaram did not dash hopes on all these things as the Budget he presented was a deft exercise in attempting to satisfy every constituency—be it salaried class, trade and industry, investors, both domestic and foreign and instiitutionals. In a master stroke, the Finance Minister attempted to rope in only one segment under the tax net and that is the services sector which is now contributing 40 per cent to the GDP. The logic is that "services" are products as much as "manufactured goods" and it was historic underestimation of this segment that had led to the neglect of any attempt to bring this into the tax net. But the credit for bringing services under the tax net must redound to the glory of the reform architect Dr. Manmohan Singh who initiated a modest but momentous beginning by introducing services tax on telephones and stock brokerage. Later, it was extended t advertising, courier and radio paging. From nowhere, the services tax fetched Rs. 970 crore for the exchequer in the fiscal year 1996—97.

It is but natural that the 1997—98 Union Budget should extend the services tax to some more aeas. The Finance Minister did not hesitate to do so and in his second budget after assuming office in July 1996, Mr. P. Chidambaram has confined his tax mobilisation effort to mop up Rs. 1205 crore only by bringing a few more services under the tax net and revising postal rates. The Budget for 1997—98 extends the service tax to cover a host of well–known services embracing transportation of goods by road, consulting engineers, custom house, steamer and clearing and forwarding agents, air travel agents, tour operators and car rental agencies, out—door caterers, pandal contractors and mandap keepers and man—power recruitment agencies. While the proposals on service tax are estimated to yield a revenue of Rs. 1200 crore in a full year, in the next fiscal year, a credit of Rs. 900 crore alone is being taken into account. The remaineder Rs. 305 crore for next year is being realised by revision of tariffs for some postal services, the proceeds of which would be for the development of postal services and in partially bridging the deficit on the numerous services being provided by the Postal Department.

A particularly noteworthy feature of the 1997—98 Budget is that it has given away massive customs tax relief amounting to Rs. 2625 crore and the reason for that as provided by the Finance Minister was that "our goal must be to achieve rapid and broad–based growth." While Mr. P. Chidambaram reduced the peak rate of customs duty from 50 to 40 per cent in a bid to align the country's tariff structure with international standards, he also reduced customs duty on capital goods from 20 to 15 per cent. Some of the intermediate inputs which witnessed cuts include steel industry inputs, cold rolled coils of iron andsteel, duty on ships brought for breaking, organic and inorganic chemicals, dyes, pigments, paints and varnishes, glues, enzymes and modified starches.

In tune with the tenet of emerging cooperative federalism, which is the hall—mark of the 13—party coalition government at the Centre, the Budget has accepted the alternative devolution formula seeking to bring in all taxes collected bythe Centre into a single divisible pool and apportion 29 per cent to the States as recommended by the Tenth Finance Commission.

The Budget of 1997—98 is a veritable bag of sops for Indian corporates and tax—payers as duty was cut across—the—board. In personal income tax, the existing rates of 15, 30 and 40 per cent is proposed to be replaced by 10, 20 and 30 per cent. The rate would be 10 per cent in the slab of Rs. 40,000 to Rs. 60,000, 20 per cent in the slab of Rs. 60,000 to Rs. 15,000 and 30 per cent for all income above Rs. 150,000. The limit on standard deductions has been raised to Rs. 20,000 which would apply uniformly to all salaried tax payers. In widening the tax net, the Budget proposed an amendment of Section 139 of the I.T. Act by which residents of large metropolises who satisfy economic criteria such as ownership of a four–wheel vehicle, telephone, flats and undertaking foreign travel in the previous year should voluntarily file their tax returns. Failure to do so would entail a simple notice from the I.T. Department. Yet another related scheme announced in the Budget pertains to the Voluntary Disclosure Scheme (VDS). Following the mandate of the National Development Council (NDC), the Minister announced the VDS to tap black money for productive purposes by which any disclosed income would be taxed at the revised highest rate of 30 per cent, the states would receive 77.5 of the proceeds on this score while the balance would be spent on bolstering the Basic Minimum Services. The scheme would start on a date to be notified by the Finance Minister and end on December 31, 1997. Some category of people would not be liable to secure immunity under this scheme and they include those held for offences under the Drugs and Psychotropic Substances, Arms Act, ordinarily punishable under the IPC and the Anti—Corruption Act.

A reappraisal of the country's Science and Technology (S&T) policy is called for in the wake of economic liberalization and the emerging globalization research and development (R&D) The basic object of the reappraisal would be to provide better assistance to the country's industrial growth and exports, industrial growth and exports, besides enhancing the quality of life of the people.

Several eminent scientists and technocrats have highlighted the inadequacies of the current approach to S & T. The government's S & T policy has been termed "short sighted" at the recent 84th session of the Indian Science Congress. In the words of a well-known scientist, if the government went on "underplaying S & T at it has been doing since the economic reforms started", there would be hardly any science left in this country in another 5-10 years.

Main issues

Though S & T is to be given high priority in the Ninth Plan, it should address several fundamental problems hindering its effective application. A brief overview of the main issues that need to be addressed would reveal several soft options but few hard choices for the planners.

The country' R&D expenditure declined from a little over one per cent to 0.86 per cent of the gross national product (GNP) during 1990-95 and the trend has not been reversed. Though this is relatively high among developing countries, it is very small compared with 2.5 per cent of GNP spent by developed countries in general. India's R&D expenditure is around $ 1 billion. The United States spends 200 times more than India on R&D, while Japan and South Korea allot 140 times more. Though we have the third largest manpower with some science and technology qualification, we do not have any advantage in terms of specialized skills and training.

No doubt the Plan allocation for S&T has considerably increased from Rs. 15 crore in the I Plan to Rs. 9,180 crore in the VIII Plan. However, a major share has gone to Defence, Space and Atomic Energy. For example, the 1995-96 budget estimates of the Departments of Atomic Energy and Space were Rs. 1,001 crore and Rs. 911 crore, respectively.

More than money, young people today shy away from science. In 1950-51, there were 1,27,000 students enrolled in the science stream and in 1993, we have 10 million of them. But, the percentage of students opting for science at the undergraduate level was 32 in 1950-51, which declined to 19 in 1993. Again, the top 32 per cent opted for science in 1950, but today only the middle and the lower 19 go for it. Management, accountancy and financial disciplines attract more. Computer software is the lone exception in terms of popularity but the numbers for employment will soon become limited, especially at the specialization level. Over the past one decade., the number of students enrolling for degrees in science has stagnated at the same level.

Indian S&T is at a crossroads. Globalization and the need for self-reliance, apparently contradictory in terms of their objectives, call for a realistic mix of policies. The myth of import of technology has been blasted loud and clear by unequivocal and frank warning by no less a person than Dr. A.P.J. Abdul Kalam and a few other scientists. Dr. Kalam pointed out that there is no such thing as a free lunch in the import of technology. It we are not careful, we would often end up with less relevant, obsolete, eco—unfriendly technologies from developed countries, except in a few cases. We should accept the reluctance of developed countries to transfer technology in frontier areas and take up the challenge of developing our own technology in critical fields.

Unfortunately, liberalization has misled some people into believing that self-reliance has no relevance! Nothing could be more harmful to the interests of the country. In fact, at one time, the Confederation of the Indian Industry suggested the elimination of all restrictions on technology imports and foreign collaboration. While the removal cannot be 100 per cent, considerable liberalization has indeed taken place. Since the new Industrial Policy (1991), automatic approvals by the Reserve Bank for technology imports are allowed in cases pertaining to specific industries, where the total lump sum payment does not exceed Rs. 1 crore and the royalties on domestic sales and exports do not exceed five per cent and eight per cent, respectively. In 1994, for instance, 340 out of 915 cases got automatic approval. Hidden behind the plea for a 100 per cent automatic approval is a reluctance on the part of the industry to undertake any R&D so long as foreign products and processes are available and can be sold at high profit. In other words, this is described as "black box" approach, where one deals with technology as if it is a black box meant for trade only! It is an easy option but it cannot be adopted in the long-term interests of the country.

The truth is globalization is not a one-way street. Where there is expertise and resources, it becomes a two-way street, as for example, in India. Today, a wave of collaborative R&D is sweeping the world. Networking with premier R&D organizations around the world is becoming profitable. The evolution of a worldwide information network has made real time-management of production and marketing possible anywhere in the world. Leading companies from the US are coming to India since the country offers research facilities at low cost, a good science base, a fair legal framework and freedom and flexibility of operations. There is new breed of entrepreneurs in India who value quality and prompt delivery. With adequate intellectual property safeguards, more and more R&D firms are tying up with Indian counterparts, known for their world class research. For example, the National Chemical Laboratory(NCL),Pune, has licensed some of its patents to a Us firm. The Indian Institute of Chemical Technology, Hyderabad, has collaboration with DuPunt in agrochemical research. NCL is offering its services to China.

The Council of Scientific and Industrial Research (CSIR) has responded to this trend effectively. CSIR will soon have a "virtual" laboratory to monitor the data on what is being perfected or experimented in its laboratories. CSIR is no longer dependent entirely on government funds. It is supposed to earn up to 50 per cent of its experditure through commercial use of its products and processes. CSIR's external cash flow is expected to reach Rs. 145 crore during 1995-96. There is a suggestion from the private sector that the CSIR laboratories be converted into corporations and made the to compete in the market and sell their products and processes. However, many of the laboratories do not have effective competitors in the private sector.

About 75 per cent of the R&D expenditure is ment by the government on laboratories under its control. Only 25 per cent is met by the industry. However, the R&D expenditure by companies accounts for less than 0.1 per cent of their turnover. But the industry is slowly realizing the value of collaboration with research instiutions. For instance, three Indian Pharmaceutical companies have recently signed long-term agreements with government research laboratories for R&D in new drugs.

Industry is accused of not interacting closely with universities. It is a pity that the interaction between government laboratories and academic institutions has remained minimal. The Mashelkar Cpmmittee (1993) had made several specific recommendations for providing incentives to researchers and for exposing them to the international scientific community.

The Ninth Plan approach paper has indicated that emphasis would be made on networking between the research institutions/nationl laboratories both for development and marketing of technology. In order to achieve these objectives, the existing S&T infrastructure will be modernised through major investment by industry. Efforts would alsobe made to dispense with hierarchical bureucracy in the R&D institutions adequate delegation of powers, according to the approach paper.

Initiatives from Academic Bodies: Some initiatives from academic institutions are noteworthy. The Indian Institute of Science, Bangalore, is setting up special research cells for dealing with wpecific industrial problems in areas such as telecommunication, food processing, software engineering and drug design. The

IIT, Chennai has set up a Center for Industrial Consultancy and Sponsored Research.

And Miles to Go: One test of technological excellence is the number of patents sealed in critical areas. A survey (1994) of the National Council for Applied Econmic Research of scientists working in Central government laboratories showec that the average number of patents applid for a scientist wa 0.13 and the patents obtained was 0.09. In terms of technology, the perceived gaps between the status quo and the state-of-the-art technology is 15-20 years in the paper industry, 10-15 years in cement, 10 years in polymers and 5-10 years in the paint industry. In specific cases, the gap would have since narrowed but the figures indicate the long road ahead in catching up with the state-of-the-art technology.

Addressing the Problem: Several initiatives have been taken to address the problem of enhancing the level of technology. The Technology Development Fund (TDF), created in 1994-95 to be financed from the five per cent cess on imported technologies through collaboration is expected to procure around Rs. 100 crore for the Department of Science and Technology. The TDF is expected to promote indigenous technology, especially in the small-scale sector. A Technology Development Board has been set up to assist in the use of the TDF. The approach paper says that besides continuing the initiatives taken during 1996-97, a Corpus Fund for financing research projects in frontier areas of scinece by distinguished scientists of any age, will be created. Efforts would also be made during the Ninth Plan to generate maximum resources for R&D from the production and service sectors.

Another initiative is the setting up of mission mode projects such as the one on fly-ash disposal and utilization. Yet another idea being tried is the location of clusters of industries (e.g. leather and jute) and supporting them with better facilities such as housing and health care.

However, the scheme offering tax deduction for sponsored research has not taken off in a big way. Only a few industries have responded to the broadcasting of 125 per cent weighted tax deduction for sponsored research in a national laboratory. This shows that the industry cannot be motivated by limited tax cuts alone. Market-driven demand seems to be a better incentive.

— The financial sector has a vital role in promoting efficiency and growth. It intermediates the flow of funds from those who want to save a part of their income to those who want to invest in productive assets. The efficiency of intermediation depends on the width, depth and diversity of the financial system. Till about two decades ago, a large part of household savings was either invested directly in physical assets, or put in bank deposits and Government small saving schemes. It is only since the late eighties that the equity market has started to play a role in this intermediation process. Other markets and short-term money markets, remain relatively segmented and underdeveloped. In recent decades, the Government and its subsidiary institutions and agencies, have had an overwhelming and all encompassing role. This has played a part in slowing the evolution and development of thse markets. The extensive system of controls, rules, regulations and procedures, directly or indirectly affects the development of these markets. We need to clear this web in the interest of both savers and those who invest in productive assets. Tax deductions and exemptions cannot be a substitute for reforms of policy and procedures. they can, however, create further distortions.

— The two most serious problems in the financial system are the lack of flexibility in intermediary behaviour and the segmentation of various markets and sets of financial intermediaries. Well developed markets are interconnected; demand-supply imabalances in one market overflow into related markets thereby dampening shocks and disturbances. This inter-connection also ensures that interest rates and returns in any market, reflect the broad demand-supply conditions in the overall market for savings. A rise in the demand for funds for investment, above the existing flow of funds from savings, leads to a rise in the interest rate or rate of return in all markets. The time lag may differ from market to market depending on economic factors. Conversely, a decline in demand for funds for investment below saving, leads to a fall in interest rates across the board. This does not happen in segmented markets. Adjustment in interest rates is also delayed by the slow speed of response of intermediaries and their lack of flexibility. Because of the historical role of the government and its subsidiary organisations in controlling and directing all financial activity, the autonomy and flexibility if intermediaries was greatly circumscribed. Consequently, adjustment to demand-supply imbalance in each segment was also very slow. Over the last five years a series of reforms. The widening and acceleration of reforms will increase the flexibility and responsiveness of the intermediaries and promote integration.

— The anuual (point-to-point) inflation rate in the first half of the currint financial year (April-September) ranged between a low of 4.2 per cent to a high of 6.6 per cent. The price rise of this magnitude could be regarded as modest given the hefty increase of 18 per cent in the administered prices of petrolium products in early July, 1996. Even in the next two months October-November 1996, the annual price rise was still below 7 per cent. However, there was a clear indication of inflationary pressures resurfacing due to the persistant rise in the prices of many of the agricultural commodities—mainly foodgrains—right from the middle of current financial year. By the end of December 1996, the annual inflation rate had crossed 7 per cent. The normal seasonal decline in the post-harvest period generally seen during November-December did not happen this year and hence the uptrend in prices was unabated in the third quarter of 1996-97. The containment of inflationary pressures in 1996-97. The containment of inflationary pressures in 1997-98 will require prudent fiscal and monetary policies and appropriate supply side policy measures to control price increases in primary articles.

— During the last financila year 1995-96, sanctions of financial assistance by development finance institutions recorded a growth rate of 18.5 per cent, while disbursements grew by 17.4 per cent. For investment institutions, the financial assistance sanctioned and disbursed declined by 31.4 per cent and 6.0 per cent, respectively, because of sluggish capital market conditions. During the first nine months of the current fiancial year (April-December 1996), The all India financial institutions disbursed Rs. 26813 crore as against Rs. 23187 crore disbursed in April-December 1995, implying an annual growth rate of 15.6 per cent. However, financial assistance sanctioned by them recorded a decline of 26.6 per cent. It appears that these institutions are mostly disbursing the pending sanctions of 1995-96. Development finance institutions disbursed Rs. 22256.9 crore as against Rs. 19088.1 crore in April-

December 1995, the annual growth rate being 16.6 per cent. Assistance sanctioned by them, however, declined by 30 per cent. As UTI has become part of SEBI mutual fund discipline its loan sanctions and disbursements are being eliminated, as per SEBI guidelines relating to mutual funds.

— Most of the development finance institutions raised resources during the year through issue of bonds. Their interest rates have also become more or less market-based, in consonance with the ongoing liberalisation in the financial sector. Their interest rates increased in 1995-96 and in the first half of 1996-97, reflecting higher demand for funds on account of revival in real sector activities. Since October 1996, the minimum lending rate of DFIs, (excluding interest tax) has been reduced to 16.5 per cent from 17 per cent earlier.

— All India financial Institutions and the SEBI, led by IDBI, set up the North Eastern Development Finance corporation Ltd. (NEDFI) in the last financial year to cater exclusively to the financial needs of the industries in the North Eastern Region. The National Securities Depository Ltd. (NSDL), promoted by IDBI, UTI and National Stock Exchange of India (NSE) in December 1995, to maintain an electronic record of securities ownership details, started operations on November 8, 1996. IDBI got linked to the Society for Worldwide Interbank Fiancial Telecommunication (SWIFT) network tht processes and exchanges messages relating to overseas banking and foreign exchange business.

— In 1995.96, Small Industries Development Bank of India (SIDBI) set up a Technology Development and Modernisation Fund. This has an initial corpus of Rs. 200 crore. It will directly assist the SSIs in enhancing their export capabilities. SIDBI has also relaxed the norms under special schemes, to facilitate a greater flow of funds to industrially backward areas. It has widened the scope of the National Equity Fund and extended it to cover the whole country except for metropolitan cities. ICICI expanded its fee-based corporate advisory services to facilitate the creation of better projects and improvement in business environment. It initiated efforts in areas such as public sector restructuring and infrastructure projects. Industrial Reconstruction Bank India (IRB) has moved into business oriented activities from simple revival of sick units and also expanded its merchant banking activities. The Industrial Reconstruction Bank (Transfer of Under takings and Repeal) Ordinance, 1997 with a view to converting IRBI into a company under Companies Act, 1956, and transforming it into a full fledged financial institution.

Establishment Division is the nerve centre for the entire gamut of the service conditions of the Central Government employees having financial content. These activities are, therefore, spread over a vast spectrum of their service conditions right from the date of appointment to the date of retirement. Basically, these include revision/prescription of pay scales, fixation of pay and various allowances. The proposals received from various ministers/departments of the Government of India seeking calrification in regard to revision of pay scales, prescription of pay scales, increments, deputation allowance and cadre review of various categories of posts are examined in this Ministry keeping in view the equity and comparable relativities and duties. During 1994-95, 5th Central Pay Commission has been set up to review and make recommendation on the emoluments structure and service conditions, having financial bearing, of the Central Government employees.

Plan finance

Plan Finance-I Division handles matters relating to finances and plan outlays of states. It releases Central assistance to states for their Annual Plans (including for externally aided projects), Hill Areas Development Programme, Border Area Development Programme, Plan and Non-Plan revenue deficit grants and Centre's share to the Calamity Relief Fund (CRF) of the States. For 1994-95, the revised estimates of Central assistance to states for their Annual Plans amounted to Rs. 16,543.37 crore consisting of normal Central assistance-Rs. 10,914.97 crore, Special Central Assistance Rs. 973.00 crore, Special Plan Loan-Rs. 630.00 crore, Additional Central assistance for externally aided and other projects-Rs. 3,540.40 crore and Special Central Assistance for Hill Areas-Rs. 320.00 crore and Special Central Assistance for Border and Other Special Areas-Rs. 165.00 crore.

Against this, Rs. 16,599.71 crore was actually released to the states during 1994-95 on the basis of the provisional expenditure details furnished by them. Further, Plan and Non-Plan revenue deficit grants of Rs. 2,679.97 crore and Rs. 1,088.63 crore respectively and Centre's share of Rs. 462.64 crore to the Calamity Relief Fund of the states were also released to them. In addition, a grant of Rs. 17.95 crore was also released to Madhya Pradesh during 1994-95 for Bhopal Gas Tragedy Action Plan.

Plan Finance II Division deals with maters relating to the Central Plan. These cover the estimates of resources for Central Plan including internal and extra budgetary resources, Plan outlays of different ministries/departments of the Central Government, appraisal of Plan projects/schemes before they are submitted to Public Investment Board (PIB)/Expenditure Finance Committee (EFC) etc. Plan Finance II is also the Secretariat of the PIB.

The PIB considers investment proposals of the Central Government ministries in regard to their public sector undertakings. Under the existing guidelines, central sector projects costing Rs. 50 crore and above are considered by PIB. Secretary (Expenditure) is the Chairman of the PIB and Joint Secretary (Plan Finance II) acts as the Secretary to the Board. During the period between 1 January and 31 December 1994, 11 meetings of PIB were held and 30 projects with a total capital cost of Rs. 11,404.51 crore were recommended for approval.

Estimation of internal and extra budgetary resource for financing the Annual Plan of the central public sector undertakings is an important activity of this Division. Recently, GOM was constituted under the Chairmanship of Finance Minister to review the proposals of sick PSUs for capital restructuring. Plan Finance II Division is mainly responsible to examine these proposals.

Under the Constitution, a Finance Commission is to be constituted every fifth year or at such earlier time as the President considers necessary to make recommendations to the President as to (i) the distribution between the Union and the states of the net proceeds of taxes which are to be, or may be, divided between them and the allocation between the states of the respective share of such proceeds; (ii) the principles which should govern the grants-in-aid of the revenues of the states in need of such assistance out of the Commission by the President in the interest of sound finance. The recommendations of the * Commission together with an explanatory memorandum as to the action taken thereon are laid before each House of Parliament. Ten Finance Commissions have been consituted since the commencement of the Constitution.

The Tenth Finance Commission constituted in pursuance of Article 280 of the Constitution by the

Presidential Order dated 15 June 1992 submitted its report for the period 1995-2000 on 26 November 1994. Government accepted the recommendations of the Commission regarding devolution of Income-tax, Union excise duties, additional duties of excise in lieu of sales tax, grants in lieu of tax on railway passenger fares, grants-in-aid to cover non-plan gap on revenue account, financing of relief expenditure, grants for upgradation and special problems, grants for local bodies and debt relief. The report along with an explanatory menorandum on the action taken on the recommendations contained therein was placed on the table of each of the House of Parliament on 14 March 1995.

Finance Commission division implements the recommendations of the Finance Commission and also takes follow-up action on various observations of the Commission as contained in its report. Finance Commission Division also take advance action for setting up of the next Finance Commission.

Cost Accounts Branch of Ministry of Finance, Department of Expenditure renders professional assstance to different ministries and other agencies of Central Government in studies relating to cost aspects. This organisation was set up by the Government of India during World War II when defence contracts had to be placed on cost plus basis and the cost and price had to be vertified by an independent agency.

After Independence and with the growth of industrialisation, the role of the organisation changed and it became a body to render professional assistance to different ministries, committees and other agencies of the Government in cost, price fixation, reasonableness of prices charged investment appraisal, cost accounting system and other aspects. This Branch is manned by officers who are professionally qualified cost accounts and chartered accountants and they are members of the Indian Cost Accounts Service (ICAS), a Group-'A' Service constituted by Government of India in 1978. The needs of other ministries-Industry, Commerce, Petroleum and Natural Gas, Central Excise, etc., are also met by this Branch by posting ICAS officers to these ministries on participation basis.

This Branch is headed by Chief Adviser (Cost). He advises Department of Expenditure in the matters relating to the cadre administration of the Indian Cost Accounts Service. The office of the Chief Adviser (Cost) also looks after the training requirements of the Service officers.

The Controller General of Accounts (CGA) is the apex accounting authority of the Central Government and exercises the powers of the President under Article 150 of the Constitution for prescribing the form of Accounts of the Union and state governments on the * Comptroller and Auditor General of India. The functions of the Controller General of Accounts (CGA) include, inter alia, the framing of rules, regulations etc., in the field of accounts and internal audit, the publication of accounts codes and manuals, issue of periodical instructions, cadre management of Civil Accounts personnel. The Junior Accounts Officers' Examination for Central ministries/departments, Cabinet Secretariat and union territories administrations e.g., Delhi, Andaman and Nicobar Islands, etc., is also conducted by the office of the Controller General of Accounts. It is also responsible for Government disbursements and banking arrangements of the various ministries/departments/ offices of the Government of India. The Controller General of Accounts has been closely studying and monitoring the extant system; significant improvements have been brought about in the reconciliation of cash balances of the Government with the RBI so far as civil ministries are concerned. These improvements are also being extended to other self-accounting Ministries of Railways, Defence and Posts and Telecommunications. A publication entitled "Accounts At A Glance" 1993-94 was brought out which gives broad and significant features of Government receipts and expenditure.

The office of the Controller General of Accounts is responsible for consolidation of accounts of Union Government which has been computerised. All the Principal Accounts Offices in Delhi have started transmitting floppies through the software IMPROVE. To speed up the work of consolidation of monthly accounts all the Principal Accounts Offices are being provided with a 386 DX machine along with dial up modern which would enable connectivity of these machines with the 486 machines housed in CGA office.

The Institute of Government Accounts and Finance was set up in February 1992 under the Controller General of Accounts as a Plan Project to impart in-service training on Government accounting, financial management, administrative and establishement matters to officials of the accounting organisation working in Central Government ministries/departments.

A Regional Training Centre has been set up at Calcutta and is fully functional, two more are also to be set up at Bombay and Madras. The Institute also conducted Induction Level training courses for newly recruited accountants. Orientation Training Programmes for the Drawing and Disbursing Officers and officers dealing with Finance and Budget in ministries were conducted by the Institute for some ofthe ministries.

The Management Training Programme on Preparation of Budget and Budgetary Exercises, Personnel Management, and Litigation and Vigilance

Procedure for Controllers of Accounts and other officers were conducted in April and December 1994. The Institute also conducted training for a group of 25 officers of Government of Sri Lanka in May 1994 and five officials of Malawi in August 1994. Induction level orientation training on Government Accounts and Financial Management for Indian Civil Accounts Service Probationers after they complete professional training at National Institute of Financial Management has also been started and will continue to be a regular activity of the Institute.

The Central pension Accounting Office (CPAO), established as a unit of Ministry of Finance, commenced functioning w.e.f. 1 January 1990 for the purpose of administering primarily the scheme of payment of pension to Central Government civil pensioners by public sector banks. The Central Pension Accounting office is fully automated where the entire job right from the stage of receipt of correspondences to their final disposal is done on computer using roacle software having instant information retrieval facilities.

The Staff Inspection Unit (SIU) was set up in 1964 with the objective of securing economy in staff consistent with administrative efficiency and evolving performance standards and work norms. Where the SIU in the course of its work-measurement studies comes across procedures and methods whose revision or modification seems patently necessary and is likely to lead to economy in staff, it incorporates suitable recommendations in its reports. However, items requiring detailed methods study are brought to the notice of Department of Administrative Reforms and Public Grievances for further necessary action. SIU's reports are mandatory and have to be implemented in toto within a specified time frame.

The development so far in 1996—97 in the balance of payments, the Survey says, point to an easing of pressure on the current account and to buoyancy in capital inflows. The deficit on trade account in 1996—97 is expected to be lower than in the previous year, largely due to a sharp deceleration in the growth of non—petroleum imports. The improvement in trade deficit would be partly offset by anticipated decline in invisible receipts, reflecting an increase in payment for factor services and some decline in private transfers. The current account deficit is expected to decline from 1.7 per cent of GDP in 1995—96 to less than 1.4 per cent of GDP in 1996—97. Net capital inflows in 1996—97 are likely to be nearly three–fold over the previous year, largely because of buoyant inflows under non—resident deposits and foreign investment flows, including Euro—equities, and a sizable build—up of foreign exchange reserves. The foreign currency assets of the RBI rose by over US $ 2.8 billion from about US $ 17 billion at the end of March 1996, providing cover of about 5.5 months of imports.

The Survey says, exports during April—December period of 1996–97 grew only by 6.4 per cent as against 19.7 per cent during the previous three years. Among the significant reasons for the decline are slow down in world trade growth in 1996 (by about three percentage points). The latest trend in the growth rate of exports suggests that the initial impact of trade liberalisation is petering out and the trade flows are reverting to their normal trend determined by world demand and domestic activity. Despite the export slow down, self reliance as measured b;y the coverage of imports by exports, has risen by 88.2 per cent in April–December 1996 from 86.7 during 1995—96.

On the capital account, foreign investment continued to dominate capital fows. Total foreign investment (direct plus portfolio) during April–December 1996 surged to over US $ 4 billion, which is more than 50 per cent higher than in the corresponding period of 1995–96. This revival followed a modest decline in such investment flows from US $ 4.9 billion in 1994–95 to US $ 4.3 billion in 1995—96, mainly due to a sharp fall in the issue of Euro—equities. Foreign direct investment flows were US $ 2.1 billion in 1995—96. During April—December 1996. FDI flows were US $ 1.5 billion in the corresponding period of the previous year. Portfolio investment, comprising investment by FIIs and Euro—equities, doubled to over US $ 1.1 billion in the corresponding months of 1995—96.

India's external debt declined from US $ 99.0 billion at end—March 1995 to 92.2 billion at the end of March 1996. The downsizing of external debt resulted in a decline in debt–to–GDP ratio. The share of concessional debt in total debt remains stable at about 45.5 per cent. The share of short–term debt was 5.5 per cent at end–March 1996 and is low by international standards.

The survey does not provide current estimates of either poverty or employment generation, saying that the methodology of estimation is currently under the review of the Planning Commission. However, it says the government has accorded high priority to poverty alleviation programmes through an increase in the Central Plan allocations for social sectors and poverty alleviaton theweaker sections, specially scheduled castes and scheduled tribes and women have been given importance in special programmes of poverty alleviation and employment as well as in several other programmes. The Public Distribution System has also been streamlined recently in order to target the poorer sections of the population.

As outlined in the Update of the Economic Survey,

fiscal deficit, reliable economic infrastructure services and broad–based employment—generating growth remain the key challenges for ecomomic policy. About fiscal deficit, as the Survey itself puts it "the normally difficult task of expenditure management will be accentuated in the coming years by the challenge of accommodating the recommendations of the Fifth Central Pay Commission." Further, as it says "the responsibility for fiscal consolidation and prudence does not rest with the Central Government alone."

About the infrastructure sector, as the Survey rightly puts it, the crux of the problem is of heavy investment. Both for infrastructure and other investment requirements of the economy, the country would need an inflow of foreign direct investment of US $ 10 billion per year as against US $ 2 to 3 billion currently. The Survey rightly exhorts al concerned to "learn from the pragmatic nationalism of China which received around US $ 40 billion of investment in 1996. We must also learn from the flexibility and speed of Indonesia, which modified its policies rapidly in response to perceived competition from China and India, to double foreign investment inflows between 1994 and 1996."

About poverty alleviaton, as the Survey puts it for the vast majority of the people it would have to be through job opportunities stemming through labour intensive Growth. For those at the margins of a market driven economy "the effective provision of minimum social services and special programmes for employment and poverty alleviation, fulfil an essential need." The basic goal, as the Survey puts it "should be to enhance sustainable benefits to the poorest segments of the society, while reducing administrative duplication and wastage and minimising well—known leakages."

Investment in infrastructure is'to be stepped up from the present 3.5%-4% of the GDP to around $ 200 billion (Rs.7,00,000 crore) over the next five years. The Government is taking steps to boost both domestic and foreign investment so as to achieve the target of 12% annual industrial growth and 7% annual GDP growth. The Foreign Investment Promoton Board has been recast to make it a more effective and credible instrument to promote foreign investment in India, through adoption of greater transparency in rules and regulations as well as in the process of award of contracts. Complementary financial sector reforms are being made to ensure that enhanced domestic and foreign funds flow into this and other critical sectors. The response of the entrepreneurs to the policy initiatives has been very encouraging.

The data on foreign collaborations also indicates a strong and positive response to the structural reform measures. The Foreign Investment Promotion Council (FIPC) has been constituted to attract more foreign investment and to achieve the targeted FDI of US $ 10 billion by preparing project reports in selected thrust areas. The FIPC will also determine the exact snags in project implementation so that commencement of production is not unduly delayed.

The indicates that the overall investment in the corporate sector (the summation of Internal Savings, Assistance Disbursed, Capital Raised, and Capital Transfers from Abroad) is much higher than what has been indicated. There might be some double counting because the share premium which has been included in the amount raised from the primary market may also get included as the internal accruals of the corporate sector. Even after the suitable adjustments are made to avoid this double counting, it is likely that overall investment levels from 1992-93 onwards are much higher.

Overall employment in the SSI sector has been steadily increasing. In the ASI factory sector, employment after remaining virtually stagnant for over 10 years since 1980, recorded a growth of 6.2 per cent in 1992-93, the first year after the initiation of the reforms process. This suggests possible reorientation of the structure of production.

Though firm estimates of additional employment generated due to implementation of the IEMs filed or LOIs issued in the post policy period are not availabile, it is understood that nearly 20% of these intentions have actually been implemented and another 20% in different stages of implementation. Additional direct employment likely to be generated by these units would be over 1.7 to 2.0 million persons. Since IEMs/LOIs relate to units which employ more than 50 persons, net additional direct employment that would be generated with their implementation indicate an increase of over 20% to the total employment in respect of this sector.

The grosss profits of public sector enterprises have shown an increase of 21.3% compared to last year. Considering the fact that input costs and salaries and wages have increased by 2033 crore over the previous years, this growth in gross profits is impressive. The profit before tax and net profits have increased by 47.3% and 58.8% respectively over the last year.

The development of world class infrastructure insectors like power, transport and communication is critical for sustained industrial recovery. The Government is already considering extensive application of the market mechanism in these sectors through deregulation of production and distribution.

Foreign investment in these sectors is also being encouraged. In the power sector the policy package for private participation includes reduction of import duties, a five year tax holiday for new power projects and a 16% return on equity. New initiatives have also been considered in the mining sector to promote modernisation and investment.

For infrastructural development, Infrastructure Development Finance Corporation with an authorised capital of Rs. 5000 crore is being set up to act as a direct lender, refinancing agency and provider of financial guarantees. Income of any fund dedicated to infrastructure has been freed from tax. Plan outlay to infrastructure sectors has been increased. To step up investment in infrastructure, a levy of 2% as special customs duty on all imports except those that carry a nil rate of duty or are imported at nil rates of customs duty for export production has also been proposed. Tax concessions have also been extended to infrastructure sector.

While it may be difficult to indicate the industry specific reasons, three factors which have significantly affected the growth rates are:

— The power sector has been behaving erratically and overall growth in April-August was only 2.1 per cent. In fact deceleration in the electricity growth rates is being witnessed since October, 1995.

— In 1995-96 industry was facing a liquidity crunch. To improve the liquidity situation, Reserve Bank revised the CRR twice from 14% to 12%. However, due to the continued pre-emption of funds advances by the Government, easing of liquidity does not seem to have positively favoured the non Government sector.

— Along with the availability of funds there has also been increase in their cost. The overall lending rate of the institutions and commercial banks are in the range of 18 to 20%. With the inflation rate currently running at around 6%, the nominal interest rate for industry at 18 to 20% makes effective real interest rate of 12% to 14% which are perceived very high. The current interest rates are higher than the average return on capital employed which is reported to be around 18% for the corporate sector. This is infact resulting in withholding of investment by entrepreneurs. The sanction of term loans by the financial institutions has declined for the first time during April-July, 1996 by 21.8% compared to the same period in the previous year validating the fact that the investment intentions are being kept pending. IFCI data show further slide in sanctions in August, 1996.

The Government has gradually moved to borrow funds at market related rate of interest. The rate of interest on Gilt Securities, therefore, tend to become the bench-mark interest rate. While lending to the corporate sector and deciding the prime lending rates for such lending, the financial intermediary would require to add additional transaction and monitoring cost and the perceived risk in such transactoins. There are no precise estimates of these costs which financial intermidiaries will have to incorporate. However, the ceiling of non performance assets indicated by Reserve Bank of India provide us the likely bad debts in lending to the corporate sector. The transaction and monitoring cost of the corporate loan could roughly be taken as additional 10% markup. This makes the calculation of PLR which might subconsciously being followed by the financial intermediaries. According to this assessment, the minimum PLR for the financial intermediaries 15.8% to 16% for commercial banks and financial institutions. Since the bench mark rate is determined by Gilt Securities rates, there is little possibility of PLR coming down in the medium term given the risk averse nature of the financial intermidiaries in India.

The other possibility of interest rates coming down basically rests on excess supply of loanable funds. The information on the monetary variable upto 13th September, 1996 indicate that the Government's pre-emption from the market continues to exceed 100%. Government is withdrawing more than the total credit created by the commercial bank system. With shortfall in excise the custom collection and government's expenditure liabilities remaining fixed, the possibility of this pre-emption getting reduced is remote. In view of this the excess fund available with the commercial bank would continue to find an out-let in Government securities. This is evident from continuous increase in the holdings of Government securijties in excess of SLR stipulations. Even if Government reduces CRR and releases additional liquidity in the system, additional demand of funds by the Government being so high, almost insatiable, flow of funds to the corporate sector may not increase. Further any decrease in the interest rate of Gilt Securities if it is marginal, will not induce commercial banks and institutions to off load their surplus fund in the corporate sector because the perceived risk may be higher than the ratio of non performance assets being prescribed would indicate. An alternative risk perception scenario could be based on the ratio of outstanding commercial banks credit in sick/ weak industrial units which have been around 14% in 1990s. Given the risk averse nature of the financial intermediaries in India the risk perception is bound to be higher than that indicated by the non-performance asset ratio. In view of this and continued government's pre—emption of resources from market, in the medium term the possibility of interest rates coming down appears to be remote.

An estimate of all anticipated receipts and expenditure of the Union for the ensuing financial year is laid before the Parliament. This is known as 'Annual Financial Statements' or 'Budget' and covers Central Government's transactions of all Kinds, in and outside India, occuring during the preceding year, the year in which the statement is prepared as well as the ensuring year or the 'Budget Year' as it is known.

The presentation of Budget is followed by a general discussion on it in both Houses of Parliament. Estimates of expenditure from the Consolidated Fund of India are placed before the Lok Sabha in the form of 'Demands of Grants'. All withdrawals of money from the Consolidated Fund are thereafter authorised by an Appropriation Act passed by Parliament every year. Tax proposals of Budget are embodied in a Bill which is passed as the 'Finance Act' of the year. Estimates of receipts and expenditure are similarly presented by state government's in their legislatures before the beginning of the financial year and legislative sanction for expenditure is secured through similar procedure.

Tax concession

However, municipalities looking to municipal bonds as a feasible option should not forget that their popularity abroad is due to their tax exemption status. For the most part, the bond holder in the US do not have to pay federal taxes on the interest and usually do not have to paystate or local taxes if the bond is issued in the state of his or her residence. A California resident would not have to pay state taxes on Califormia bonds, for instance, New York City obligations are TRIPLE TAXEXEMPT to gcity residents whose income is taxed at federal, state and local levels. However, in India it is debatable whether there is tax exemption from interest income for municipal bonds as there is no Constitutional backing for the tax exemption. There are strong opinions to make kthese bonds tax free initially to entice the investors.

Government too in t;he recent budget has given positive signal for same tax benefit to the infrastructure sector.

From the investors' point of view the primary issue is redemption. For this there has to be an active secondary market for debt instruments. During the past few years debenture financing has been on rising trend inspite of poor secondary markeft conditions. Investors were more enthusiastic towards the dept issue as compared to equity offerings. Keeping in view this trend BSE and NSE had to start separate trading wing in, the debt instruments. Among all the stock exchanges in India, NSE seems to be the best bet as it is more popular for the debt instruments. OTCEI can be the other alternative for listing of municipal bonds due to its market facilities. However, OTCEI now a days is no body's baby. How far it will succeed in giving tje adequate return to investors of municipal bonds only the time will tell.

The availability of market intermediaries and faster listing arrangements hold the key to future success of municipal bondss. Even if all the above problems are set right the legal risk in the event of default remains to be clearly defined. Given the instability of octroi as a future revenue source debt servicing ability of the issue becomes a crucial issue considering the rates they would have to offer. Authorities seem to be silent about the investors who face default risk on account of non receipt of redemption amount from municipalities. Bankruptcy laws need amendment to cover such institutions. SEBI can think of Municipal Bond Insurance policies underwritten by private investors guaranteeing municipal bonds in the event of default. The insurance can be purchased either by the issuing government entity or the investor, it provides that bonds will be purchased from investors at par should default occur. Such insurance is available in the US from a number of large insurance companies, but a major portion is written by two organisations: American Municipal Bond Assurance Corporation (AM-BAC), a private corporation, and Municipal Bond Insurance Association (MBIA), a pool of private insurance.

Insured municipal bonds will enjoy the highest rating resulting in greater marketability and lower cost to the issuers. In such a situation, at least initially, undue emphasis of market to accept only top quality issues will have no importance. From the investor's stand point, however, their yield would be typically lower than similarly rated uninsured bonds as the cost of insurance will be passed on by the issuer to the investor. Setting up Municipal Investment Trust (MIT) can be yet another alternative to minimize risk exposure of investor. These unit popular in the US. They buy municipal bonds and pass the tax-free income on to shareholders. Bonds in the trust's portfolio are normally held until maturity, unlike the constant trading of bonds in an open-ended municipal bond fund's portfolio. The trust offers diversification, professional management of the portfolio, and monthly interest, compared with the semi annual payments made by individual municipal bonds.

The issue of rating is yet another crucial issue to be addressed. Given the reputaion that municipalities enjoy coupled with the lack of commercial glamour of municipal projects, rating may be the only macharism to make such bonds attractive to investors. Rating agencies however will be making a fool of investors if they give higher rating to municipalities on account of highly depedent single revenue source, i.e. octroi. Let us see the present trend. 65% of ABC revenue comes from octroi. Bombay Municipal Corporation's annual income from octroi is Rs. 650 cr. with 20% increase every year. This means in the event of octroi being withdrawn corporation will not be credit worthy any more and debt service ratio would mount. Crisil however, was cautions to keep the ratings of ABC to investment grade despite the impressive financial structure. Further, keeping in view the accounting principles being followed by some of the municipal corporations there seems to be a problem in getting a rating. For example, according to one report the accounting principles followed the Municipal Corporation or Greater Bombay do not confirm to any prudent accounting standards. Barring the financially healthy civic bodies, most of them are currently meeting even depreciation expenditure out of capital receipt. Unprovided sums run into hundreds of crore of rupees and some do not even provide for the gratuity payments due to its own attached employees. It becomes difficult to make any financial assessment or debt service ratios on account or unreliable accounting systems being followed by municipalities. Hence for bringing the qualitative issue in the market it is desirable that the entire working of municipalities are overhauled. This should be both in terms of revenue earning capabilities as well as expenditure and price of service. It may also be prudent for municipalities to start experimenting with alternative mechanisms of increasing revenues for servicing debt okbligations and decreasing the credit risk. Some of the alternatives may be charging substantial property taxes (e.g. Kerala Mu;n;icipal Corporation), increasing user fees (e.g., Bombay Municipal Corporation) and using ad hoc appraisal methods especially where bonds are subscribed by institutional investors. Thus the success of municipal bonds has a long way to go. But if the impetus is given in the right direction the municipal bonds have a very big role to play in municipal financing.

Policies of the government

The Common Minimum Programme (CMP) provides a clear indication of the Government's commitment to accelerate the process of economic reforms and to address some areas of weakness that have emerged.

Among the major themes of the CMP are:

— An overarching commitment to growth with social justice.

— A growth target of 7 per cent year in the next 10 years.

— A commitment to fiscal prudence with the goal of reducing the fiscal deficit to below 4% of GDP.

— A commitment to strengthen anti-poverty programmes and target subsidies in favour of the poor.

— A commitment to increase investment in the social sectors.

— A commitment to continue the process of tax reform and bring about a phased reduction in customs duties.

— A commitment to decontroal and reform in the agricultural sector.

— A target of maintaining 12 per cent annual growth of industry.

— A target of $ 10 billion a year of foreign direct investment.

— A commitment to reform and restructuring public sector enterprises, including through disinvestment.

— A commitment to developing the infrastructure sectors through all modes of investment, public and private domestic and foreign.

The Government has moved swiftly to implement the agenda outlined in the CMP.

The programme of tax reform has been carried forward along the lines articulated by the Tax Reforms Commitee, import duties have been reduced for a wide range of products. The intension is to eventually move to duty rates comparable to those prevailing in other developing South-East Asian economies, the Modvat system of rebates of excise tax on imputs to the singly most important industrial sector in India, namely, textiles, has been extended, the surcharge on corporate taxation reduced by half and introduced Minimum Alternate Tax as a measure of broadening the base of taxation.

The Government is committed to fiscal prudence by reducing the fiscal deficit to 5 per cent of GDP for 1996-97 as compared to 5.9 per cent in 1995-96 (Revised Estimates). A number of initiatives to deal with three critical areas of weakness in the economy are: agriculture, infrastructure and social sectors. In agriculture, the budget has made allocations for strengthening the capital base of the National Bank for Agricultural and Rural Development, the principal refinance institution in agricultural credit. It has also provided funds for re-capitalising Regional Rural Banks and has launched an important new initiative for private local area banks. Agricultural infrastructure will be strengthened through a large special allocation to finance completion of a number of irrigation schemes.

For infrastructure, a number of fiscal incentives are being provided in the budget. The tax holiday earlier provided for power, telecommunications and road transport has been extended to other infrastructure sectors such as water supply, sewerage and irrigation. It also exempts from income-tax the income of dedicated infrastructure funds which invest in equity and debt instruments of infrastructure companies. The existing income tax incentive available for long-term savings under Section 88 of the Income Tax Act has beden extened to include bonds issued by infrastructure companies or by financial institutions leading to infrastructure projects. The budget has also announced the formation of a new Infrastructure Development Finance Company (IDFC) which will fill some critical gaps in financing of commercially viable infrastructure projects. This institution could act as a direct lender, as a refinance institution, as a channel for multilateral funds and as a provider of various types of financial guarantees for infrastructure projects. The intention is that the IDFC will induce investors in India and abroad to make available long-term funds at the lowest market rates. The budget has alo provided resources for the National Highway Authority of India to help fund its operations.

In the social sectors, a number of schemes have been launched to strengthen the provision of basic minimum services and has generally expanded allocations for social services and anti-poverty programmes.

The Government welcomes foreign investment and has taken a number of concrete steps to achieve this objective. The Foreign Investment Promotion Board has been restructured to make the process of foreign investment approval speedier and more transparent. 350 foreign investment projects have been cleared involving a total foreign equity of US $ 4 billion. A new Foreign investment Promotion Council has been established aimed at reaching out to foreign investors and represent their concerns to the Government. The Government has announced that the list of 35 industries which are eligible for automatic approval of foreign investment upto 51 per cent of equity will be expanded in order to accelerate the approval process. The regulations governing foreign institutional investor have been amended to allow these investors to make equity investments in unlisted companies. Hitherto, they were limited to investing in listed companies only. The limit of investment of 5 per cent of total equity in a single company by an individual FII has been rasied to 10 per cent. The Securities and Exchange Board of India (SEBI) regulations are being amended to allow FIIs to set up 100 per cent debt funds to facilitate FII investment in corporate debt instruments. The guidelines for Euro issues have been liberalised to ease access of Indian companies to international capital markets.

In the area of capital markets, landmark legislation enabling the establishment of depositories for share trading has been passed during the Budget session of Parliament. The first depository is expected to become operational in November this year. Stronger guidelines have been issued for disclosure in the offer documents of primary issues and a number of other steps have been taken to strengthen investor protection. New guidelines have been brought out for mutual funds in general and for money market mutual funds in particular.

The process of financial sector reform has been continued on several fronts. Reserve requirements of banks have been reduced; many more public sector banks have reached capital adequacy norms set out several years ago; regulation of interest rates on bank deposits has been reduced so that they remain only on maturities upto one year; and more private sector banks have become operational. Interest rates charged on loans have been comletely deregulated for Regional Rural Banks to improve their financial viability. It has been decided to allow private sector local area banks to be set up which will operate in two or three districts. These banks will be subject to RBI regulations but will have lower initial capital requirements and will benefit from the interest rate deregulation extended to Regional Rural banks. The process of reforms in the banking sector has borne fruit in the form of significant reduction in non-performing asset of public sector banks and higher profits.

Non-Bank Financial Companies (NBFCs) which comply with the dual requirement of credit rating and prudential norms have been allowed freedom to fixed interest rates on deposits. At the same time, the reserve bank of India has imposed a ceiling on interest rates which can be offered by the mutual benefit financial companies (MBFCs) which do not meet the prudential standards set by RBI.

A number of steps have been taken to strengthen the market for Government securities including the issue of guidelines for primary dealers in Government securities. The first set of such dealers have begun operation. Following the announcement in the budget, legislation is being proposed to provide statutory backing to new, Insurance Regulatory Authority. Similarly, quick action has been taken to establish the Disinvestment Commission announced in the budget.

Traditionally in India municipalities used to operate within the frame work of laws enacted by the state legislature. Sources of raising money by municipal bodies used to be approved by the state legislature which in turn rested on the latter's degree of commitment to the principle of devolution. Article 243x of the Constitution specifically authorise the state legislation to entrust local bodies with powers and functions. Though 73rd and 74th Amendments to the Constitution no doubt stressed the importance of devolution of powers to municipal bodies. State legislature continued to be the resource base for municipalities. However, with the growing pace of urbanization, soaring cost of funds due to intermediaries, sluggish collecton on account of octroi and property taxes and decreased Central and State level capital receipt there had been a mismatch of supply of funds and demand for infrastructural facilities. Faced with a slow down in the economy and declline ingovernment grants there has been a sea change in borrowing mechanism of municipalities. Municipalities had no other opton except to break their shell and access the capital market for raising resources. Much of the inspiration for such rapid development in municipal financing in India comes from the US municipal bond markets where the volume of municipal debt outstanding at the end of 1995 stood at a staggering $ 1015 billion. This marks yet another attempt to reduce government's monopoly and a step towards private sector participation in the development of nfrastructural facilities. The trend setter in this area was Ahmedabad Municipal Corporation (AMC) planning to tap the market with an Rs. 100 crore bond issue. The issue has been rated by Crisil. Bombay Municipal Corporation has been the second entrant in this field by submitting its proposal to crisil. Other municipalities that are planning to tap the market are Coimbatore in Tamil Nadu, surat and Rajkot in Gujarat municipalities of Madras, bangalore, Vijayawada, Nagpur and New bharatpur. However, each of them is playing safe and plans to enter the market oncethe response to AMC is kknown. This move has largely been facolitated by changes made to Article 243 of the Constitution empowering local bodies to function as autonomous institutions. Another factor has been the growing confidence of investors towards to bond market that prompted municipalities to make a grand entry into the bond market.

Municipal bonds are dept obligations issued by a State or local municipal entityl. The funds raised may support a government's general financial needs or may be spent by financing core urban infrastructural facilities like drinking water, sanitary system, road development, hospitals, etc. In general, municipal bonds are issued in form of general obligation bonds (GOBs) and revenue bonds (RBs).

If the Plan objectives and programmes are to be translated into reality, the close co-operation and co-ordination from the States is essential. The economic reform programmes which form a guide-post of the Central direction could succeed only if the States are sincere and committed to the cause. Much of the benefits of direct investment depends on the policy and initiative of the State governments. Reforms can receive greater acceptability only if poverty alleviation measures are implemented vigorously, which has to be done by the States. The development of infrastructure and social sector has ultimately to be implemented by the States.

We have already noted that a vital constraint of growth and development is unchecked population. The family welfare programmes and population control mechanism are in the hands of State governments. Statistics show that some States have advanced in the direction while others are lagging behind. The story of success or failure in this direction has been caused by the extent to which the States are sincere and devoted to the cause. The newly revamped public distribution system of the deva Gowda government has decided to supply 10 kg of food grains at half the PDS price to 60 million families below the poverty line "in order that nobody could complain about the step as the aim was to benefit the poor." It may be recalled that during the Food Ministers' conference at New Delhi in August 1996, the State Food Ministers refused to withdraw the PDS benefits from affluent classes and also to raise the price of ration items. Again, the identification of families below the poverty line lies with the State government. Though the Centre has asked the States to set up vigilance committees at the Panchayat level to supervise identification, the success of the scheme will largely depend on how sincere are the agencies entrusted with the responsibility, other things remaining the same.

In order to achieve the seven minimum basic services in particular and the rural development schemes in general, the Centre has instructed the States to constitute vigilance and monitoring committees at the block, district and State levels for the effective implementation of rural development programmes across the country. The government has taken action to strengthen the District Rural Development Agencies (DRDAs) with adequate technical staff at various levels. These are important agencies for poverty alleviation programmes. Thus, at every level of plan efforts, success will depend chiefly on the States' implementation level.

Estimates committees recommendations

It is pertinent here to recall certain observations made by the Lok Sabha Estimates Committee of Parliament in 1992-93. The 19th Report may well be described as a monumental monogram on Defence management and Policy, besides force levels and manpower.

The Committee have felt that the existing statement on defence policy which is, to defend territorial integrity of the country, is a needless over simplification. They have also expressed dismay over the fact that suddenly emerging situations like Gulf War of 1990 should have thrown country's defence planning into dissarray or that country should have fought four wars and launched armed operations in and at the request of neighbouring countries without a clearly articulated and integrated defence policy. The Committee has therefore stressed upon the need for a clear and comprehensive defence policy based on a viably national security doctrine. In the same context the Committee have recommended review and rationalisation of the Officials Secret Act to facilitate a more meaningful debate on national security affairs.

The Committee have suggested revival of dormant national security council for holistic direction of national security affairs at the highest level. From this perspective the Committee have desired that the defence policy makers should take a greater note of emerging threat to the country from air and sea.

With a view to stabilising defence plan expenditure the Committee have called for studying the feasibility of making the defence sector allocation for the entire plan unalterable. This the Committee feel will make defence planning exercise more realistic by co-relating allocation of resources to the task entrusted to the defence services. Commenting on the efficiency of decision making process in the Ministry of Defence, the Committee have observed that often proposals floated for fulfilling the task entrusted to defence services are subjected to such prolonged process of scrutiny and series of clearance that it assumes the form of a hurdle race and in the bargain the services end up with a relatively larger share of anxiety. To mitigate ths situation the Committee have highlighted the need to reform the decision making process in the Ministry of Defence. To this end, they have called for greater powers to be delegated to the three Chief of Staff.

Despite the Estimates Committee's emphatic recommemdations, the Government has been implementing them in a piecemeal manner with the result that many essential items are still to be cleared for procurement by the defence services. This has its cascading effect on defence preparedness due to a lack of appreciation of perspective planning by the nodal

Ministr. Infact, the three services have a Director General for Defence Planning but their recommendations of a long term nature have had little effect on decision makers.

Therefore, the need is to change track in the same manner as government did in the sectors of the economy. Another major imperative is to take out the Defence Budget from the non-plan category and bring it within the overall planning process. This is immensely desirable in order to make the Defence Sector Undertakings enter into diversified manufacture or civilian sector also. The Current year's Defence Budget is of the order of Rs. 27,798 crore as against Rs. 26,879 crore last year. The allocaton for present year include a capital outlay of Rs. 8979 crore on all the three services. Often there is a debate on this capital segment. But in the absence of detailed expenditure Budget documents such discussion becomes an exercise in futility.

A major part of this outlay is committed expenditure on ongoing projects including procurement and construction but does not provide for any new acquisitions sought by any of the services. This is a lacuna and has to be covered up by a projected allocation offunds as and when required for additions to the defence services arsenal. Otherwise there is general demoralisation in the armed services which feel that they are not getting their deserved priority, although the case may be otherwise.

India has a large Army, the fifth biggest in the world. The Navy and Air Force too have their unique position figuring among the top five or six. But strange to say there is a very big communication gap between the Armed Forces and the public and what hits the eye most is the denial of access to the media to the state of defence preparedness

The Press Council of India has admirably defined the role of the press in coverage of defence related matters in its Report (1994) calling for more openness in defence coverage. The Council said the media has an "adversarial role" to the extent that it questions authority, all authority, to look at the otherside. This must be understood and a relationship of creative tension accepted as a democratic necessity. For the rest, they are partners in trying to build a better society".

One must however congratulate the Army Chief General Shankar Roy Choudhary for his frank and forthright advise to his troops and officers to develop media interaction modes and use it as a "force multiplier and not as a force degrader". Infact, this is among the Ten Commandments prepared by the Army Headquarters as advice to troops engaged in low intensity conflict situations. This thus shows the appreciation of the role of the media in giving a boost to defence preparedness in all its magnitude but sadly it remains to be implemented in letter and spirit.

No doubt a good beginning has been made recently by the Army Training Command (ARTRAC) which has organised a number of inter-media Seminars at a number of locations but the feedback has not been as fruitful as it should be. At least the consolation is that after a long time the three services are coming to realise that the print and electronic media are weighty partners in the process of defence preparedness and policy making.

To conclude, it must be understood that the nature of modern warfare is such that it involves the whole nation. Of course Defence Forces play a key role but since war or any external threat requires total mobilisation in a democracy, maximum transparency alone can assure co-operation on the part of the people in every respect

The balance of payments adjustment in the

aftermath of the 1991 crisis has been remarkably smmoth. The adjustment was made possible mainly because of the dynamic growth in exports and large foreign investment flows. International prices of petroleum were also favourable for most part of the period. The balance of payments outlook in the medium term will depend critically on several factors. First of all, as reiterated in earlier Economic Surveys, it is absolutely imperative of sustain rapid export growth to assure external sector viability. Tremendous efforts would be required to ensure this on an increasing base of exports and in the context of a difficult international trading environment. Second, taking into account the importance of POL in the total import bill and the uncertainty surrounding the future movement of oil prices, concerted efforts on the demand and the supply sides are required to contain the POL import bill at manageable levels. The rapid rise in POL consumption in recent years is a matter of concern. The growth of consumption of petroleum products will have to be contained through an appropriate pricing policy, and by effecting energy efficiency in the use of petroleum products in the transport and other sectors of the economy which are major users of petroleum. On the supply side, concerted efforts are required to increase domestic production of crude oil and augment refining capacity. The saving on POL imports will allow sufficient room for imports of raw materials, components and capital goods consistent with the requirements of a growing economy without undue pressure on the balance of payments.

Earnings from tourism have been a mojor component of invisibles. Tourism industry, apart from being a major foreign exchange earner, contributes substantially to sustainable human development, including poverty alleviation, employment generation, environmental regeneration and advancement of women. The sector also helps to pressure and promote handicrafts, arts and the cultural heritage of the country. Inadequate infrastructure has become the main impediment to the accelarated growth of tourism in India. In fact, there is an acute shortage of approved accommodation, transport and other tourism facilities in all the metro cities and other major tourist centers. The Department of Tourism has initiated several measures for attracting large scale private investment in the tourism sector, including declaration of tourism as a priority sector for foreign investment provision of incentives and setting up of an investment facilities cell to provide information about investment opportunities and to facilitate investment. The State/Union Territory Governments are also offering a number of financial and fiscal incentives to tourism industries. These efforts are to be sustained an intensified to make India na all-season attractive tourist destination in the world.

The importance of foreign investment, as a major source of capital flows for sustaining a high current account deficit without imposing an excessive burden on the external debt management ability, has been described amply in the earlier sections. In order to strengthen the balance of payments and garner more foreign savings to meet the investment needs of the economy, India needs to maintain a welcoming stance towards direct foreign investment and continue to clarify policies in areas where there may be ambiguities.

Borrowings under external assistance constitute the most desirable form of debt creating capital flows, because of their favourable terms in regard to period of maturity and interest rates, conferring significant benefit in the form of concessionality. Given the international aid environment, though India may have reached a stage of graduating from being eligible for large flows as in the past, the substantial build-up of aid in the pipeline offers enormous scope for increasing the level of disbursements from the commitments secured so far. India should also take advantage of the offer of currency choice for existing IBRD currency pool loans and the offer of a broad range of terms for new IBRD loan commitments. This provides the borrowers flexibility to select terms that are consistent with their debt management strategy and suited for their debt servicing capability.

Even with the optimistic outlook for foreign investment and sustaining the normal trends in other traditional sources of capital flows, there will still be a large uncovered gap between domestic savings and investment requirements, if the economy were to grow at a sustained rate of about 7 per cent per annum. This will imply that borrowings on commercial terms will be inescapable. However, such borrowings should be consistent with the achievement of a sustainable balance of payments position over the medium and long term.

Capital account convertibility entails some risk of capital flight and possible macroeconomic instability arising from movements of short-term, cross-border capital flows. Such risks and vulnerability remain contained as long as prudent macroeconomic policies are followed and the financial system is sound and flexible to rapidly adapt to changing situations. Thus, a reduction in fiscal deficit, moderation in inflation, a sustained dynamic export performance, strengthening of domestic financial institutions, and a further build-up of foreign exchange reserves are some of the preconditions for a move towards capital account convertibility. It should also be recognized that capital account convertibility indirectly imposes discipline on the conduct of policies by increasing the cost associated with policy failures.

However, strengthening the prudential supervision of financial institutions, and putting in place appropriate institutional arrangements for speedy foreign exchange and payments clearing systems constitute major elements in ensuring a smooth transition to full convertibility.

The investment in Research and Development. (R & D) has increased from a paltry Rs. 20 crore in the First Five Year Plan. Presently there are 214 universities, 400 national laboratories and 1300 in-house R & D centres in the industrial sector. Several Science & Technology departments have been set up in the areas of environment, non-conventional energy resources, bio-technology, ocean development, industrial research, space, atomic energy, defence, health, agriculture and electronics.

Identification and promotion of priority areas in R & D is done by Science an Engineering Research Council (SERC) set up under the Department of Science & Technology (DST). DST supports 12 autonomous research insitutions as well, for furthering research work in several discipline. Technology Information, Forecasting and Assessment Council (TIFAC) has been set up for generating technology forecasting and technology assessment documents and enabling a technology information system that is interactive and nationally accessible.

Industrial research in several diverse fields of scientific activity is being undertaken through a network of 40 laboratories and 81 field stations set up by the Council for Scientific and Industrial Research (CSIR). In the field of bio-technology, more than 24 specialised R & D centres have been developed for pursuing state-of-the-art research. Identical efforts for promoting new avenues of research are being undertaken' in the field of ocean development as well.

The Union Budget for 1996-97 has taken various measures to promote R & D facilities. A matching one time grant has been awarded to CSIR and the Indian Council of Agricultural Research (ICAR) for modernisation of laboratories and institutes. The Technology Development and Application Fund created in 1995-96 has been proposed to be strengthened by Rs. 30 crore. A Five Year Tax Holiday under Section 80-IA of the Income Tax Act has been allowed to companies exclusively create for participation in R & D activities. The existing procedure for awarding weighted deduction under Section 35(2AA) of the Income Tax Act on sums paid for scientific research to a National Laboratory or a University or an IIT has been amended, by deleting the condition of approval by an outside body. In order to encourage R & D efforts, goods developed and patented in India and concurrently in specified countries have been exempted from levy of excise duty for a period of 3 years. The exemption procedure for customs duty on import of equipment and consumables for R & D institutions has been rationalised as well.

The following five committees of the National Development Council were constituted to go into some of the critical areas of development: (i) Committee on Austerity, (ii) Committee on Population, (iii) Committee on Employment, (iv) Committee on Micro-Level Planning; and (v) Committee on Literacy.

The meeting of the National Development Council held on 5 April 1993 considered the report of the NDC Committee on Austerity. The Council generally endorsed the recommendations of the report of the Committee. It was also decided to set up a NDC Committee on Power. Accordingly, NDC Committee on Power under the Chairmanship of Chief Minister, Maharashtra, was constituted to examine measures to make state electricity boards economically viable by recasting tariffs, improving efficiency and considering delinking of distribution from generation.

A Committee headed by Deputy Chairman, Planning Commission was constituted to evolve a suitable formula for distribution of Central assistance to Non-special Category States. The suggestions made by the Committee were discussed by the NDC in its meeting on 23-24 December 1991, wherein a consensus emerged and a revised formula evolved which was made the basis for allocation of Central Plan assistance to the states for the Eighth Plan. Under the criterion of the progress in respect of national objectives, the approved formula highlights four objectives, viz., (a) population control and maternal and child health; (b) universalisation of primary education; (c) on-time completion of externally aided projects; and (d) land reforms.

Achievements

During the 43 year period (1950-51 to 1993-94), Net National Product (NNP) at factor cost at 1980-81 prices increased from 40,454 crore to Rs. 2,02,670 crore implying compound growth rate of 3.8 per cent per annum. Advance estimates of GDP for 1994-95 project a growth rate of 5.3 per cent over 1993-94. During the First Five year Plan (1951-56), national income increased by 3.6 per annum. In the Second Five Year Plan (1956-61), however, the growth rate actually achieved was four per cent annum against the target of 4.5 per cent per annum.

In the Third Plan (1961-66), there was a sharp decline in the growth rate at 2.3 per cent per annum and fell well short of the target at 5.6 per cent per annum. This was primarily due to the steep fall in agricultural production and consequent decline in NNP at factor cost of 4.65 per cent in the last year of the Third Plan. However, during the subsequent three Annual Plans, the economy picked up and the growth rate during 1965-69 was 3.7 per cent per annum. Fourth Five year Plan (1969-74), the growth rate target was fixed at 5.7 per cent in terms of NDP at factor cost. However, the actual growth rate achieved was only 3.3 per cent per annum.

The economy took an up-turn during the Fifth Five Year Plan (1974-79). The growth rate fixed in terms of GDP at factor cost of 4.4 per cent per annum was over-achieved at 4.8 per cent annum for the Fifth Five Year Plan. In 1979-80, however, the economy faced a severe drought resulting in the decline of GDP at factor cost by 5.2 per cent over the previous year. The economy bounced back on the track during the Sixth Plan (1980-85) period when the rate of growth in GDP at factor cost at 5.6 per cent per annum surpassed the target of 5.2 per cent per annum. Despite successive drought condistions during the first three years of the Seventh Plan (1985-90), the economy has fared exceptionally well. The growth rate achieved during Deventh Plan period was six per cent per annum and this surpassed the target of five per cent per annum in GDP at factor cost for the Seventh Plan.

During 1991-92, the country faced a severe fiscal crisis and the balance of payment situation became so critical that exceptional measures had to be restored to. While the growth momentum enabled an increase in GDP by 5.4 per cent in 1990-91, the growth in 1991-92 was only 0.9 per cent. In 1992-93 the economy registered the growth of 4.3 per cent and this had been mainly due to high growth in agriculture and improvement in sectors of trade, hotel and restaurants, transport by other means, storage, communication and the public administration and defence, despite railways and banking and insurance sectors registering a decelerated growth. The GDP from agriculture and allied sectors recorded a growth of 5.1 per cent in 1992-93 as compared to 2.3 per cent in 1991-92.

Important policy reforms had been made during June 1991 towards liberalisation and structural adjustment of the economy. These measures have started showing results. The annual rate of inflation as measured by the wholesale price index declined from 13.6 per cent at the end of 1991-92 to seven per cent in 1992-93. The inflation rate stood at 10.8 per cent in 1993-94. The Eighth Plan has targeted for a GDP growth of 5.6 per cent per year, a substantial reduction in the average annual inflation rate, about five per cent and the average current account deficit of about 1.6 per cent of GDP.

Index of agricultural production with the triennium ending 1969-70 as base, rose from 71.9 at the end of First Plan to 86.7 at the end of Second Plan. During Third Plan performance of agriculture was not quite satisfactory. Widespread drought during 1965-67 slowed down the rate of growth in agricultural production and led to increased import of foodgrains and other items. Index of agricultural production reached the level of 80.8 in 1965-66 and 80.7 in 1966-67. These drought years also witnessed introduction of the best available agricultural technology for the first time in India in the form of high yield variety programme and multiple cropping programme. The folloeing years recorded substantial improvement in agricultural production. As a result, the index, after recovering to 98.9 points in 1967-68 increased steadily to 112.4 in 1973-74. The next year 1974-75 again a bad year for agriculture when the index declined to 103.6. This was followed by considerable improvement in 1975-76 when it touched 125.1. In 1976-77, the index registered a decline of 8.8 points and stood at 116.3 but again shot up to 132.9 in 1977-78 and 138 in 1978-79. The year 1979-80 witnessed a fall by 21 points when index number of agricultural production slipped to 117. It recovered to 135.3 in 1980-81.

The index number of agriculture production steadily rose to 158.4 in 1985-86. There was decline during 1986-87 to 152.5 and 151.3 in 1987-88. Thereafter it picked up steadily to 192 in 1990-91 and came down to 188.5 in 1991-92 and recovered to 195.8 in 1992-93. According to the revised triennium ending 1981-82 as base, the index numbers of agriculture production which stood at 85.9 in 1970-71 rose to 154.8 in 1993-94. During 1982-83 Kharif production was adversely affected due to wayward monsoon which was inadequate, uneven and untimely. Even so, fall in foodgrains production was only marginal, indicated by a drop of 5.4 points in the production index. Agricultural production registered significant improvement in 1983-84 which was near normal year from the point of view of weather conditions. Index of agricultural production increased from 137.5 in 1982-83 to 156.4 in 1983-84 and production of foodgrains touched a record level of 15,237 crore tonnes. Weather conditions during 1984-85 were not very satisfactory. As a result, production of foodgrains declined to 14,554 crore tonnes and index number of agricultural production also declined marginally to 154.6. During Kharif 1985, onset of the south-west monsoon was delayed over central and northern states and its behaviour during the season was erratic over many states. However, weather conditions during the rabi season were on the whole rather favourable to crop production. Consequently, foodgrains output during 1985-86 stood at 15.044 crore tonnes. Weather conditions during 1986-87 continued to be unsatisfactory. Monsoon was delayed over eastern states, while southern states experienced dry spells leading to moisture stress conditions. As a result only 14.342 crore tonnes of foodgrains production could be achieved during 1986-87. The year 1987-88 witnessed severe drought conditions in most parts of the country and the incidence of heavy floods in the eastern states. The foodgrains production consequently further fell down to 14.035 crore tonnes. During 1988-89 production of foodgrains recorded a new peak of 16,982 crore tonnes indicating a substaintial increase of 1.775 crore tonnes over the previous peak of 15.237 crore tonnes achieved in 1983-84. With the rainfall and weather situation being favourable during south-west monsoon 1989, the total foodgrains production reached another record level of 17.065 crore tonnes.

On account of erratic behaviour of south-west monsoon, foodgrains production in 1991-92 fell by 4.6 per cent to 16.337 crore tonnes from a record level of 17.64 crore tonnes in 1990-91. Production of rice and wheat was 7.467 crore tonnes and 5.676 crore tonnes respectively. There was a substantial decline in the production of coarse cereals and pulses. Production of oilseeds in 1991-92 was less than previous year's production of 18.60 crore tonnes. Production of foodgrains during 1992-93 was 17.948 crore tonnes and the production was recorded at 18.212 crore tonnes in 1993-94. Production of foodgrains during 1994-95 is expected to be of the order of 18.636 crore tonnes.

Production of oilseeds is expected to be around 2.251 crore tonnes. The thrust has been given for the growth and diversification of agriculture to achieve self-sufficiency in food and generate surpluses for exports during the Eighth Five year Plan Period (1992-97).

On the irrigation side the potential created on major, medium and minor schemes increased from 22.6 million ha in 1950-51 to 26.25 million ha at the end of the First Plan, 29.08 million ha by Second Plan, 33.57 million ha at the end of Third Plan 37.1 million ha by 1966-69. At the end of 1969-74 the potential created was 44.10 ha. By 1979-80, it touched 56.61 million ha and by 1984-85, it reached 65.22 million ha. Potential created by 1989-90 was 76.52 million ha by 1991-92, 81.09 million ha and by 1992-93 achievement was 83.01 million ha. The anticipated achievement by 1993-94 is 85.05 million ha. The target for 1994-95 isto create additional irrigation potential of 2.62 million hectare.

Under power sector, total installed capacity (including non-utility), which was only 2301 mw in 1950, increased to 78,367 mw by the end of March 1992. Against the capacity addition of 30,538.7 mw in public utilities envisaged during the Eighth Plan period (1992-97), the actual addition during the first three years (1992-95) were 12,674 mw.

Under the rural electrification programme, 4.70 lakh villages had been electrified out of 5.79 lakh villages (as per 1981 Census) by the end of the Seventh Plan, achieving 81.3 per cent level of electrification. Upto December 1994, 4.94 lakh villages were electrified.

Universal elementary education, eradication of illiteracy in the age group of 15-35 and development of vocational education to act as viable alternate stream have been the focal points of all programmes in the education sector during the Eighth Plan. Major initiatives in the form of Operation Black-board, non-formal education programme, Teacher Education, and District Primary Education Programme have been undertaken to achieve the goal of 'Education for All'. As on September 1993, 108.20 million children have been enrolled in primary schools and 39.91 million in upper primary schools. The Eighth Plan during its first three years could achieve an additional enrolment of 11.69 million in the primary schools and 7.06 million in upper primary sections making a total enrolment of 18.7 million during the Eighth Plan.

The emphasis of adult literacy programme has been on sustainability of literacy skills and the achievement of goals of rmediation, continuation and application of skills of actual living conditions. Total Literacy Campaign (TLC) and Post Literacy and continuing education programmes are designed to cater to the above objectives. The Eighth Plan target was to cover 100 million adult illiterates by 1991. About 41 million people have been made literate so far under various programmes.

Under Vocational Education, the Eighth Plan target is to divert about 11.63 lakh higher secondary students to the vocational stream. Upto the end of 1993-94, 9.12 lakh students were enrolled in 16,450 vocational sections approved in 570 schools. In order to boost the programme and activities in Vocational Education, Pt. Sunder Lal Sharma Central Institute of Vocational Education (PSSCIVE) has been established under NCERT at Bhopal on 1 July 1993.

In the higher education sector as on 1994, there are 153 universities, 34 demand universities, 7,958 colleges and total enrolment in the higher education system is about 48 lakh. In addition, there ia a vast network for technical education, including colleges and institutions offering courses in engineering, medical science, management, etc. In the technical education sector new initiatives like Technology Development Missions, establishemnt off corpus fund in the case of IITs, IIMs and IISc, Banglaore have been taken up recently.

Large investments in the industrial and mineral sector particularly from the beginning of the Second Plan have brought about a significant transformation in the industrial scene. This rate of industrial growth has not been uniform during this period. After a steady growth of about eight per cent during the initial period of 14 years, there was fluctuating trend in the industrial growth rate approaching near stagnancy in 1960-68, going upto a level of 9.6 per cent in 1976-77 and dropping to -1.6 per cent in 1979-80. During the last decade (1970-71 to 1979-80) the average growth rate has been about four per cent per annum. The average growth rate of industry in the Sixth Plan period (1980-85) amounts to nearly six per cent which is a small improvement over the average of about 5.3 per cent in the preceding five years.

Seventh Plan envisaged an average annual growth rate of 8.7 per cent in the output of industry sector. In the first year of the Seventh Plan i.e. 1985-86, the actual growth rate achieved was 8.7 per cent as per revised Index of Industrial Production (IIP) (Base 1980-81=100). In 1986-87, second year of the Seventh Plan, growth rate achieved was 9.2 per cent. However in 1987-88, the growth rate declined to 7.3 per cent due to decline in production towards the end of the year following unprecedented drought. In 1988-89, there was agian a recovery in the growth rate and the IIP recorded an increase to 8.7 per cent. In the last year of the Seventh Plan, there was slight deceleration in the growth rate, which was only 8.6 per cent due to sharp decline in growth rates of mining and electricity sectors. During 1990-91, the growth rate was 8.3 per cent and during 1991-92, the growth rate was 0.6 for industrial production. The industrial production registered an increase of 2.3 per cent in 1992-93 and 4.1 per cent in 1993-94.

Government initiated a number of measures late in Sixth Plan and in early years of Seventh Plan with the objective of removing constraints on industrial growth and providing a more liberal and congenial environment for development of industries. A number of steps were taken to liberalise industrial procedures relating to creation of capacity, imports of technology, etc., to encourage competition in Indian industry so as to ensure reasonable prices and improvement in quality. These include re-endorsement of capacities, delicensing of industries including specified MRTP and FERA industries and broad-banding of a large number of industries especially in areas of high technology industries linked with energy production and utilisation, as well as mass consumer goods industries. Provisions of the MRTP Act and FERA regulations were rationalised to facilitate entry into industrial areas of high priority. Expansion of existing units has been liberalised and investment in moderanisation/renovation/replacement as well as export production, has been exempted from industrial licensing. Licensing of new capacity has been liberalised and concept of minimum economic scale introduced to promote production efficiency, taking advantage of economics of scale.

A number of policy measures have been initiated for development of specific industries like textiles, sugar, steel, electronics, etc. Steps have also been taken to tackle the problem of industrial sickness. These include (i) system for early detection of industrial sickness introduced by Reserve Bank of India' (ii) various steps for checking industrial sickness and promoting industrial revival evolved by Industrial Reconstruction Bank of India; (iii) setting up of Board for Industrial and Financial rreconstruction, and (iv) setting up of Small Industries Development Fund in IDBI to provide refinancing assistance not only for development, expansion and modernisation but also for rehabilitation of sick industrial units in small scale sector. The statement on industrial policy announced in July 1991 is being implemented. The new industrial policy emphasises delicensing and technological dynamism. Government has also set up modernisation funds for textiles and jute industries to cater to problems of those industries which account for major share of industrial sickness.

The Government is to establish 70 growth centres to act as a nucleus for industrial growth and promote accelerated development especially in backward areas. Sixty nine centres have already been identified. The process of setting up of the growth centres has been started. There has been an important milestone in the public sector steel capactiy with most of the main units of the Stage-I of the Visakhapatnam Steel Plant having come on stream in 1990-91. The 4 MT expansion programmes of Bhillai Steel Plant and Bokaro Steel Plant have also fully materialised during the year.

In order to have more national generalisation, the past performance can be reviewed separately for two categories, i.e., (i) those efforts related to income generation and self-employment and (ii) others related to self-employment-cum-entrepreneurship category.

The first category covers the programmes/schemes under KVIC, TRYSEM, SEEUY and some other institutions exclusively devoted for self-employment. During 1985-86, KVIC, provided employment opportunities to 39.8 lakh persons whose earning amounted to Rs. 349.53 crores. In the total employment under KVIC Programme the share of SC/ST was about 29% and women's participation about 46%. Under TRYSEM Scheme 200,650 youths were to be trained during 1985-86. Out of this, 56,500 youth were trained and 41.845 were reported taking up self-employment.

The second category by and large, refers to SSI entrepreneurs. Under Indian context the two strategies, i.e., developing entrepreneurship and small industries are interwoven. Between 1973-74 and 1986-87, the number SSIs increased by over three folds generation by about two and half times. It is difficult to assess as to how much oif it is the outcome of planned efforts. But programme wise SIDO conducted more than 1638 EDPs and trained 50,130 potential entrepreneurs during 1978-88. During 1970-86 they conducted 287 programme specially for 6,757 engineer entrepreneurs. IDBI sponsored 550 EDPs benefiting 15,369 entrepreneurs. 6 Since its inception NSTEDB sponsored 147 EDPs benefitting 3,090 potential science & technology entrepreneurs. 7 SBI conducted 125 EDPs during 1978-87 and trained 2,939 persons with success rate of 33 percent. NIESBUD masseurs sponsored 42 EDPs benefitting 1125 potential entrepreneurs. Besides such national bodies large number of programmes were conducted locally by other governmental and non-governmental organisations which have not been recorded systematically. As per one estimate about 1,250 full EDPs of 6 weeks duration are conducted every year benefitting more than 40,000 potential entrepreneurs.

Since entrepreneurship development presently pursued by variety of organisations/agencies with different types of approaches/strategies and also with varying degrees of resources for varied target groups, their rate of success (in terms of the ration of number of entrepreneurs who actually set up their enterprises to the number of persons trained/promoted) naturally show a very wide range of variation (8% of 80%). Recently nationwide study by NIESBUD, however, reported 27.8% success rate as national average since there are experiences of higher rates of success there seems to be enough scope for further improvement in all aspects of EDPs starting from Identification & Selection of Potential Entrepreneurs; and Quality & Content of Training; Support Services; and Availability/accessibility to infrastructural facility.

There are very few, if any, published documents presenting quantitative and qualitative evaluation of EDPs. In the absence of uniform data for all reported programmes, it may be useful to consider cost of emploment generation from the typical programmes separately.

The cost of conducting full entrepreneurship development programmes include cost of initial campaign, identification & selection, 4-6 weeks training, and follow-up for about 4-6 months after the completion of training. These can be estimated from the existing pattern of expenditure. SISIs are conducting integrated EDP with an expenditure of Rs. 56,000/- for TCOs and other voluntary organisations who conduct EDPs sponsored by IDBI and other financial institutions; NSTEDB & NIESBUD, the cost comes in between Rs. 70-80 thousand. Under difficult areas and for special schemes such as women entrepreneurship the coast goes upto Rs. 100,000/-. Considerig 30% as success rate and on an average 30 participants per programme the cost for promoting entrepreneurship comes in between Rs. 6000/- and Rs. 11,000/- (without establishment cost) per entrepreneurs who sets up an enterprise with an investment between few thousand to 35 lakhs. SBI Evaluation Study (1986) 10 further help us understand the pattern and size of investment and return by entrepreneurs promoted through such EDPs. The overall average investment by them was reported as Rs. 3.55 lakhs. To be more precise maximum, i.e., 57.4% invested between 2-5 lakhs; and followed by those 27.9% who invested between 1-2 lakhs; and 8% invested upto Rs. 25,000/- and only 6% invested over Rs. 10 lakhs. In terms of benefits, out of such promoted entrepreneurs 83% sampled units reported making on an average a net profit of Rs. 48,200/- (about 4000/- per month) during 1985.

Another study that provided detailed information about cost/benefit refers to Assam Experiment-Self-Employment through entrepreneurship Motivation Training Centres during 1973-76. With the total expenditure of Rs. 17.96 lack that included the cost of training of officers, all recurring and non-recurring expenditrue of 6 EMTCs in Assam 534 units started functioning (another 593 received financial sanction but not considered for calculating benefits here) and accordingly the cost for promoting each succeessful entrepreneur was reported having net profit between Rs. 300/- to Rs. 1500/- per month (during mid seventies). Further the total amount raised and invested by these entrepreneurs in the area amount raised and invested by these entrepreneurs in the area amounted to Rs. 1.2 crores to which Govt. contributed only 12.25 lakhs as seed money. The evauation study further revealed that more than 90% units thus established provided employment to 1-2 persons besides the self-employed owner.

Another valuable and more recent information related to cost-benefit of a typical entrepreneurship development programme for self-employment (in SBI sector) is available with Rural Development Self-emploment Training Institute (RUDSETI), Gurgaon which has been set up jointly by a Trust and two nationalised banks since 1984. RUDSETI trained 1,832 candidates and 1127 of them have already set up their enterprises, the total of cost on selection, two weeks training counselling and support activities comes to Rs. 795/- per successful self-employed entrepreneurs (this does not include the establishment cost). In addition, the bank financing to these entrepreneurs on an average was reported as Rs. 18,214/- per self-employed person, enterprises set up by these entrepreneurs represented 'business' enterprises 28.7% followed by 'industries' 19.6% and 11.6% 'service units'. It was further revealed that 68% of thus promoted entrepreneurs have started earning net profit between Rs. 500/- to Rs. 1500/- per month.

A number of new measures have been suggested to improve the operational efficiency of planned programmes. Some of these can be cited below:

Planning by its very nature is a participative process in which both the Union government and State governments will collaborate with each other both in formulation and implementation of plans. It has also been suggested in the approach paper to provide additional funds to the poorer States si as to improve their basic minimum services and inter-State allocations would be determined on the basis of identified gaps which deprive people of the benefit of development.

Another irritant of development inbthe planning process is the Centrally-sponsored schemes (CSS). In 1996-96, there were 182 CSS with a total outlay of Rs. 16,000 crore. Many of these schemes relate to subjects falling squarely within the competence of the State governments. It is now proposed that inter-State schemes will remain under the control of the Central government. All other schemes where state management will have operational efficiency would be transferred to the States along with caresponding funds. This will go a long way in improving the operational efficiency of such schemes and establishng better relationship between the Centre and the States. Approximately, half of the total planned public investment is expected to go into agricultural and rural development.

The process of decentralization and grant of autonomy does not stop at the state level, it has to be carried further to the Panchayats. Democratic decentralization through Panchayati raj though established in the fifties in some of the States, did not make any impact in the process of planning. The 73rd constitutional amendment has now changed the contours of decentralized planning. The State governments are now required to endow the Panchayats with the power and authority necessary to enable them to function as institutions of self-government with the responsibility of preparing plans for economic developmint and social justice and implementing them. In the IX Plan, 29 subjects identified in the Eleventh Schedule would be transferred to the Panchayati Raj institutions along with resources and personnel engaged in such works. This will usher in a new era of people-oriented planning in which not only the governments at the Centre and the States, but the people at large, particularly the poor, can fully participate. Participatory planning is essential both for accelerated growth and ensuring social justice.

As we have already said, the growth of population may create tremandous difficulty in increasing employment or improving the economic well-being of the poor. The current high growth of population is mainly due to (a) the large size of the population in the reproductive age-group (estimated contribution 60%), (b) higher fertility due to unmet need for contraception (estimated contribution 20%), and (c) high wanted fertility due to the prevailing high IMR (estimated contribution about 20%). In the IX Plan, special efforts are proposed to be taken to meet all the feltneeds of contraception and reduce the infant and maternal morbidity and mortallity so that there is a reduction in the desired level of fertility. Attempts would be made also to enhance the quality and coverage of family welfare programme by involving medical practioners of all types; Panchayati Raj institutions, industry, agriculture and labour representatives. Along with this, greater emphasis would be given on education and health programmes which would go a long ways in reduting the rate of growth of population.

There has been a considerable sloppage in the growth of capacity in the infrastructure sector during the

VIII Plan. Several measures are suggested to improve the efficiency and capacity utilization of the exiting infrastructural assets. First, greater emphasis will be given to complete ongoing projects so that they start yielding returns as early as possible. Secondly, since this in itself may not meet the requirements of the demand, additional facilities would be ensured for increase in the resource availability for further investment and proper maintenance of existing infrastructural facilities. There is a tendency now to get too many projects cleared without the requisite financial resources in sight which not only causes delay in completion of projects but unnecessarily escalates costs many more times than the original estimate. Project planning would be screened and only those projects would be sanctioned for which funds are in sight and which could be completed early without cost overruns.

In addition, a number of other specific measures are proposed to improve the economic well-being and quality of life. The empowerment of social groups like SCs, STs, OBCs, women and minorities is of crucial importance. A high priority is accorded to empowering these soecial groups both economically and socially to enable them to join the mainstream of national development at the earlist.

Environmental degradation has creaated great damage to the economy. It has also adversely affected the gealth of people. There is a proposal to ensure environmental sustainability of the development process through social mobilization and participation of people at all levels.

In spite of increased production of agricultural commodities, a large number of people are still on the verge of destitution. It is, therefore, proposed to ensure food and nutritional security for all, particualarly the vulnerable sections of the community.

There is a great deal of regional imbalance operating at both inter-State and the intra-State levels. with greater freedom and choice of location that is now available to industry, it is more than likely that some States and some regions would be able to attract more private investment than others. In such a case, more public resourcces should be invested invested in such backward regions.

Self-reliance has been one of the main features of planning in India. In spite of the poening of the economy to international agencies, self-reliance would remain n important component of development policy and strategy. The Ninth Plan would address the issues of external vulnerability and develop suitable strategies for making India a strong and confident player in the international economy.

Planning for sustainable regional development

Ecologically sustainable economic development has become a policy issue of major significance. conceptualizing and analysing sustainable development is very important at the regional level. This paper investigates sustainable in a practical planning context and seeks to highlight the notions of sustainable resource use. Economics provides some guidelines for planning responsibilities, although ecological considerations should also be taken into account. A region is a geographical area consisting of a coherent entity from the standpoint of description, analysis, administration, planning, or policy. Among the various types of regions are homogenous and functional regions. Functional environmental regions are often based on the interactions between environmental resources like ground-water, river, and meteorological systems within a particular region. Homogenous environmental regions are based on the existence of common resources in the area concerned. Regions can also be distinguished as natural regions, economic regions, administrative regions, etc.

Regional development is often critically dependent on the regional availability of resources. A region's economic development may be directly dependent on the resources in the region. Usually, in such cases the dependence is on resources that may serve as essential and cheap productive inputs for economic activities. Concomitantly, the environmental capacity to absorb waste materials and pollution can restrict economic activity. Some regions may depend on export of resources as the main source of income. A regional resource sector may have several effects on the activities in a region such as increased demand for public services, utilities, and infrastructure; demand for labour; capital, space and spin-offs to other private sectors. Thus, the development of a resource sector might lead to shifts in sector allocation, income levels, distribution, and exchange rates.

From the standpoint of welfare, regional sustainable development ensures that the regional population attains an acceptable level of welfare both at present and in the future and that this regional development is not only compatible with ecological circumstances in the long run but also tries to accomplish a globally sustainable development. Consequently, regional sustainable development has to fulfil the following goals:

— It should ensure the regional population a sustained acceptable level of welfare;

— It should not have conflict with sustainable development at a supraregional level;

— It should ensure economic progress and/or developoment of potential of the region concerned;

— It should maintain ecological values and/or relieve constraints of the area concerned; and

— It should ensure the economic and environmental interest of the parties involved.

The economic-ecological interactions arise in general, because concerted socio-economic development requires a compromise between material growth and environmental parameters, including environmental quality and vital natural resources. Although in the short run, the conflict between material growth and environmental quality may be severe, in the long run, a mitigating effect may emerge, because continued economic growth needs a sound resource base and structural protection and upgrading of environmental quality.

Such a coevolutionary development, in both the developed and the developing countries takes for granted that the economy and the ecology ultimately do not conflict with each other. Such coevolution is also based on equitable development options for the present and future generations. It does not necessarily require mutual positive spill-over effects between the economy and the ecology. This idea is echoed in the notion of ecologically sustainable economic development.

This paper, investigates sustainable development in a practical planning context and seeks to highlight the notion of sustainable resource use. An attempt has also been made to provide a practical framework, as renewable stocks of natural resources are key factors of sustainable development.

Indeed at the local level, resources like land, labour and human and physical resources—physical capital to a limited extent are available. Techno—economic surveys can identify the potential resources. But will all the labour force be mobilized for gainful and productive employment? This is a more important task and accompllishing ths depends on the integration of the techno—economic approach with other aspect of the social system and development process. This is the concern of many mono—disciplines like economics, engineering, sociology, psychology, etc. All such studies have pointed out that only at the local level, the basic needs, particularly of vulnerable sections can be identified and they justify larger investment in primary education for promoting health, nutrition, rural development, family size, fertility, literacy and awareness of national culture.

It is true that rural development is in the main equivalent to the development of food and cash croops and their needed inputs—irrigation, fertilizer, seeds and other resource inputs—animal husbandry, dairying and poultry farming, fisheries, forestry and agro—industries. (Dr. Malcolm S. Adisheshiah in Bulletin of Madras Institute of Development Studies, January 1991 P.41). But such investments in agricultural developmentare bound to be more effective when there is adequate investment in human resource development, particularly in literacy and primary education. Between the I and VII Five Year Plans, there has been à decline in agriculture, forestry, animal husbandry, fisheries irrigation, rural development and village and cottage industry from Rs. 45,924.70 crore to Rs. 45,523.02 crore (ie from 54.92% to 23.62% of the total public sector outlay). But in spite of the decline in agricultural outaly, rural development culd have been quickened if only there had been more investment in human resources and human developmen. Local resource mobilization with local planning seems to be a promising vehicle for promoting rural development and alleviating poverty.

Local resource mobilization and substitution of human capital as well as physical capital is in conformity with the experience of some of the

Scandinaviancountriesand Japan in this context. Theyhave been able to substitute the scarce resources with resource mobilizaton at the local level in rural and agricultural sectorsin particular. Such local resources cannot flow to higher levels but can improve productivity at the local level. This resource augmenting effect has the advatage of accelerating agricultural growth.

In such an effort, equity will have to be given special consideration. The disadvantaged population has to be seen not in therole ofobjects of participation but they are to be integrated as the subjects ofoperation. There should be also anb organizational structure which promotes the effective participation of the disadvantagedpopulation. The emergence of local bodies with elected representatives, one hopes, will make it possible to privide thisinfrastructure.

There should be sound planning at the three levels of District Panchayats, Panchayat Samithis and Village Panchayats.

Underutilization may be in the intensity of land use and agricultural productivity or the levels of utilisation of labour force. Measures ofunderutilization can be: (a) a straightforward measure of idle resources, of production capacity at a given level of technology and organization, eg fallow land, unemployment and underemployment according to atime measure; (b) misallocation of resources due to lack of knowledge of superior alternatives or distortion in the structure okf incentives; and (c) underutilization in terms of productivity. According to Prof. Brahmananda, even though aggregate capital may be adequate potentially at the macrolevel, capital in the form of wage goods capacity may be deficient. It is in the process of production of wage goods at the local level through local planning that local resource mobilization can take place and productivity can be improved and social change brought about. At the grass roots level in the rural areas, there is urgent need for improving productivity and promoting social change with better education.

Rural development refers to a number of development programmes. Earlier it was linked only with agricultural development but on the basis of the experience during the last few decades we can speak of holistic rural development which includes agriculture, rural development, rural indutries, and hollistic self—supporting development.

In order to accelerate such a holistic rural development there are three major potential areas for integration which are: (a) stepping up the existing wage employment programme in rural areas ofor capital construction in agriculture and for ecodeveloment; (b) stimulating the growth of households by intergrating them with the existing self—employment programmes like IRDP; and (c) accelerating the pace of social development.

In sum, we will emphasize that poverty alleviation programmes should be properly integratd with over—all development. No rural development is possible without wipping out p[overty or reducing it in stages. The integration of poverty alleviation objective with the over–all development strategy has to be distinguished from the issue of integrating poverty alleviation programmes with the over–all development strategy. The over—all development strategy is concerned with questions like investment priorities, choice of technique and location of projects through trickle down effects. It tries to reduce poverty. A greater and more specific role has to be given to investment in agiven resources, eg bringing down the capital output ratio to a certain level sector by sector). But integration of poverty alleviation programmes with over–all development strategy tries to ensure that poverty alleviation programmes subserve the goals of over—all development. At present, the schemes for increasing incomes and employment do not adequately take care of it. In this also there should be a greater role both for human resource development and human development.

Sustainable regional planning

Sustainable development has become a key catch-phrase in eonomic planning and resource management. However, the interpretation of this concept is still obscure, and definitions of it are abundant ranging from continued economic growth to steady economics where economic growth to steady state economies where economic growth mainly serves to compensate for environmental degradation.

Sustainability, as defined by the Brundtland Commission, is essentially a holistic notion, and as such all aspects of the system need to be included in it. Now, the same may also be defined as the preservation of the production possibilities of an economy to produce useful goods and services. Such a definition could provide some guidance on the rate at which one can exploit exhaustible resources or the level of degradation of renewable resources that may be permitted. However, this raises another issue that in the production of such goods and services, man-made capital and natural resources (we can call the latter environmental capital) can substitute for each other, at least within some limits.

In this context, it is essential to evolve techniques for planning and decision-making with a view to working out a viable programme for sustainable development. The tools of benefit-costs analysis and project appraisal need to be so recast as to combine the traditional economic efficiency criterion with the criterion of sustainable development. The problem of discounting the future streams of benefits and costs and the choice of appropriate discount rate assume especial significance in this regard. The concept of benefits and costs will have to be redefined to take account of the effect of a project on environment and sustainability of development in the long-run.

Gives the levels of development of States on the basis of the following determinants: (1) Per capita net State domestic product, (2) Unemployment rate, (3) Poverty ratio, (4) Per capita education expenditure, (5) Literacy rate, (6) Infant mortality rate, (7) Annual population growth rate, etc.

Adjudged on the basis of the statistical evidence, the five most backward States in India in terms of socio-economic development are Uttar Pradesh, Orissa, Bihar, Madhya Pradesh and Rajasthan. These States are extremely backward not only in terms of economic development but also by the levels of their per capita net State domestic product. It can also be said that states with higher per capita income tend to do well in terms of overall socio-economic development as well. Kerala, however, is an exception to this rule and proves that a high success rate in social development is possible with higher levels of expenditure in the social sectors even when the levels of per capita income in a State is low.

The region's natural resources used as goods are ground-water for drinking and irrigation and timber for paper and pulp. The ecosystems provide services of outdoor recreation and nature conservation while they assimilate surplus ammonium and nitrate from nature. Land is the most important resource in the region and any model that deals with the problems of land use and changes in the quality of land is of considerable interest.

Land pressure in various districts of the region is fairly high, particularly in small districts, given the available technology and the production constraints in such semi-arid parts of the region. Land pressure is particularly important in case of overstocking.

The critical success factors in coping with the problems of land pressure are the following:

— Controlling population growth in the areas concerned;

— Ensuring balanced livestock development;

— Controlling land alienation, mainly in smaller districts; and

— Controlling technological developments and related policies regarding boreholes.

Ecologically sustainable economic development has become a policy issue of major significance. Conceptualizing and analyzing sustainable development is clearly important at the regional level. The openness of a spatial system evokes the question of environmental sacrifices in space and time. When the issue of the substitutability of environmental decay is at stake, the related concept of weak and strong sustainability requires further exploration on the basis of a thorough investigation of underlying welfare concepts and associated collective welfare function.

In order to obtain a homostatic balance of resources in space and time, much attention has to be given to regional resource accounting. Efficiency, equity and externality aspects of resource use can then be given due emphasis, while attempts at valuing unpriced resources may provide a sound basis for project appraisal. Geographic information systems may be helpful to visualize all relevant policy aspects. In many cases, governments in an attempt to cope with environmental deterioration, have misjudged the causes of such decay and have even aggravated the original conditions. Thus, a closer analysis of the costs and remedies regarding both signal and response failures would be desirable. In the context of sustainable regional development, critical sucess factors refer to major focal points for policy intervention. Identification of such factors may induce proactive sustainability of policies. In sustainable regional development planning, where regions are open, critical success factors may also be found outside the specific region.

10

Urban-Industrial Challenge

With approximately 27 per cent of its population living in urban areas, India is one of the least urban countries, but with an urban population of 217 million (1991) it is also a country with one of the largest urban populations. India's towns and cities could, by themselves, make up the third largest nation of the world.

Urban India consists of close to 3500 towns varying in size from the smallest district towns with a population of 5,000 to the large urban agglomerations exceeding 10 million people. Nearly two-thirds of the urban population is concentrated in 317 'Class I' towns, or cities with a population of over 100,000 of which half lives in 23 metropolitan areas with populations exceeding 1 million. The four largest cities—Bombay, Calcutta, Delhi and Madras—between them account for one sixth of the urban total. the Class I towns are the fastest growing urban areas in India. Greater Bombay, with apopulation of 12.57 million, and Calcutta with 10.86 million, are among the largest metropolitan areas in the world.

While over the past four decades the popultion of India has more than doubled, during the same period the urban population has more than quadrupled. The growth has come as much from net migration as from natural increase (about 40 per cent each), with the balance due to reclassification and inclusion of new towns.

The National Commission on Urbanization (1988) states that "these urban centres have also generated tha most brutal and inhuman living conditions, with large sections of the citizens living in squatter settlements. The overcrowding in the slums and the desperate lack of water and sanitation leads not only to severe health problems but to abject degradation of human life." It further remarks that "in the decades to come, who knows how much political tension and physical viloence will be triggered off by the flrgrant display of wealth which coexists with the rising expectations of the poor and with the appalling conditions of congestion and pollution which form their environment?"

The estimate of proportion of urban people living in slums varies from about 20 per cent to 30 per cent. Looked at by class of town, the highest percentage of people living in slum areas is in the cities with a million plus population and the least in towns with less than 100,000 population. The growth rate of the slum population, largely through continuing in migration, is significantly faster than that of other segments of the urban population. While this phenomenon is in no way unique to India, it is the sheer size of the problem in India that is staggering.

About 27 per cent of the urban population lives below the poverty line, 30-40 per cent of the population of the larger metropolitan areas live in slums, 27 per cent does not have access to water-borne sanitation. Indian cities also have very high levels of air and water pollution. As a result, the environment that the rural migrant has to live in, is as harsh a choice between environment and development as one can pose.

And yet the choice is made. It is made by over 13,500 people each day who move from rural to urban environments and the several million who continue to live in the highly degraded areas of urban India. The urban slum is their 'gateway'. It is the 'solution' rather than the 'problem' of urban living. It is both a low cost housing solution and a low cost transportation solution, as the slum is usually close to the place of work. But it makes nevertheless for squalid surroundings. It is a price that is paid, and paid consciously—because the option, where it even exists, is worse. Urban poverty is preferred to rural poverty.

Air pollution is a problem in some urban areas. Heavy vehicles cause 47 per cent of the pollution while accounting for 8 per cent of the total number of vehicles on Indian roads. The production of automobiles in India has increase from 1,891 in 1955 to 116,564 in 1988 Two and three wheelers constituting 63 per cent of the number of vehicles cause 13 per cent of the total pollution. While this pollution does cause localized problems, the number of vehicles is so small that it has negligible impact at the global level. Efficient public transport options, which will cut down on both fossil fuel consumption and pollution need to be explored.

The noise levels in many of the Indian cities is much above the safe limit. This is due to diverse factors which include industrial manufacturing activities, excessive use of vehicle horns, and unregulated use of loudspeakers at social, political and religious events. Awareness must be created in this regard.

The question that is difficult to understand is not so much why the poor decide to stay in slums, but rather how much remains to be done about improving conditions in these areas. The Report of the National Commission on Urbanization feels that "For whatever reason, resource allocation in the urban field seems to follow a problem rather than anticipate it." Furthermore, "the inefficiency of our cities and towns is being perpetuated by obsolete, rigid and irrational laws, regulatory provisions and norms. The urban centres, with their concentration of diverse activities, should be generators of wealth; instead, they have degenerated into parasites looking elsewhere for support."

The family Welfare Programme has helped in containing the growth rate of population. Total Fertility Rate has declined from 4.5 in 1981 to 3.5 in 1993 as per the estimates of Sample Registration System (SRS). The Crude Birth Rate has decreased from 33.9 per provisional estimates of the SRS. The Crude Death Rate has also declined from 12.5 to 9 per thousand population over the same period. The Infant MOrtality Rate dropped from 110 per thousand live births in 1981 to 74 in 1995. The annual average exponential population growth rate has come down marginally from 2.22 per cent during 1971-81 to 2.14 per cent during 1981-91. The population, however, continues to grow as the decline in birth rate has not been as rapid as the decline in the death rate.

There are, however, inter-State differences in the achievements of the Family Welfare Programme. At one end of the spectrum are the States like Kerala, Tamil Nadu and Goa which have already achieved replacement level of fertility. At the other end, are the large States like Uttar Pradesh, Madhya Pradesh, Rajasthan and Bihar where fertility levels and bjirth rates continue to be higher than the national average. Therefore, decline in the rate of growth of population for the country as a whole depends upon how the large northern States perform in the family welfare programmes in the future. Unless effective steps are taken to bring about significant improvements in the programme, the performance in containing the growth of population at the All India level may not change significantly.

Recognising the close relationship between high birth rates and high rnfant mortality, high priority has been accorded to the Maternal and Child Health (MCH) programme since 1985. In order to achieves the main objective of MCH, (i.e. to improve the health status of women and children and to reduce maternal, infant and child morbidity and mortality rates), the Universal Immunisation Programme (UIP) was launched in 1985. From the year 1992-93 the UIP has been strengthened and expanded into the Child Survival and Safe Motherhood (CSSM) programme. Under this programme, apart from strengthening the existing MCH, initiative has been taken to expand the pilot projects on Acute Respiratory Infection Control and Traditional Birth Attendants training. For this, a provision of Rs.350 crore has been made in the 1996-97 budget as against Rs.220 crore in 1995-96 (BE).

From 1.4.1996, the Family Welfare Programme is being implemented on the basis of the "Target Free Approach" (TFA). This approach envisages replacement of the system of setting contraceptive targets from the top by a system of decentralised participatory planning at the Primary Health Centre level.

Pursuant to the World Health Organisation (WHO) goal to eradicate poliomyelitis (polio, a major crippling childhood disease) by the year 2000 A.D., the Pulse Polio Immunization (PPI) was launched in 1995-96. About 87 million children aged 0-3 years were administered as supplemented dose of oral polio vaccine on 9.12.1995 and 93 million on 20.1.1996, irrespective of their routine immunisation status. Since PPI received an overwhelming response from the public, the exercise was repeated on 7.12.1996 and 18,1.1997 covering about 120 million children in the age group of 0-5 years.

A Special School Health Check-up Scheme for Primary School Children was carried out in 27 States/ UTs in July 1996, and in the remaining 5 States between August and October 1996. The objectives of this Scheme were to detect common health related problems among primary school children; to conduct screening of children for appropriate referral and check up; to generate health awareness in the community; and to ensure arrangements for follow up and treatment at higher level medical facilities. Reports from 441 districts show 75.9 per cent coverage of schools and 84.9 per cent coverage of enrolled children.

In order to foster community involvement in the Family Welfare Programme, two new schemes have been started on a pilot basis. Under one of these, one revenue village in every district, among villages with a population of 500 or more, will be given an award of Rs. 2 lakh for achieving a reduction in the Crude Birth rate, Infant Mortality Rate and Child Mortality Rate. The second schemes aims to integrate family welfare and health care into the ongoing National Wastershed Development Project for Rainfed Areas (NWDPRA) of the Ministry of Agriculture. Under this scheme, the watershed level community based management structures, known as the 'Mitra Krishak Mandal' (MKM) will conduct surveys and prepare watershed level family welfare and health care plans. An amount of Rs. 5000 will be given to each village in the watershed areas, for specified activities like emergency obstetric care and purchase of essential medicines.

The Prenatal Diagnostic Techniques (Regulation and Preventation of Misuse) Act, 1994, has been brought into force from 1st January, 1996. This Act makes it illegal to use prenatal diagnostic techniques like amniocentesis for determining the sex of the foetus, a practice that often leads to abortion of female foetuses. Statutory machinery for implementation of the Act has been established.

Uttar Pradesh continued to be the largest state, population wise with 16.44 per cent people of the country living there (13,91,12,287) followed by Bihar with 10.21 per cent (8,63,74,465) and Maharashtra with 9.33 per cent (7,89,37,187). West Bengal occupied fourth place accounting for 8.04 per cent (6,80,77,965) of the country's population followed by Andhra Pradesh with 7.86 per cent (6,65,08,008). Ranking of the states and union territories according to population size is in table 2.

Bombay metropolis continued to be the most populated city of the country with urban population of 12.60 million, Calcutta taking the second place having 11.02 million. Delhi ranks third with a population (urban) of 8.42 million followed by Madras 5.42 million.

Population factors

One of the important indices of population concentration is the density of population. It is defined as the number of persons per square kilometre. The population density has gone up from 216 in 1981 to 267 persons in 1991 (excluding Assam and J&K). In 1901 it was 77 persons per sq km followed by Chandigarh (5,632). Lakshadweep which has the smallest population size is the fourth most densely populated area with a density of 1,616 persons per sq km. Arunachal Pradesh is the most sparsely populated area of the country with 10 persons per sq km.

The 10 heavily populated districts of the country are Calcutta, Madras, Greater Bombay, Hyderabad, Delhi, Chandigarh, Mahe, Howrah, Kanpur City and Bangalore. All of them have density of above 2,000 persons per square kilometre and 5.01 per cent of the country's population lives in these districts. The average density of these districts is 6,888.

In any study of the population, analysis of the sex composition plays a vital role. The sex composition of the population is affected by the differentials in the mortality conditions of males and females, sex selective migration and the sex ration at birth.

Sex ratio is defined as the number of females per 1000 males. In India, it has generally been adverse to women. The ratio has also declined over the years except in 1981 when it slightly improved to 934 from 927. In 1991, there has been a fall by seven points to 927 per thousand males. But Kerala represented a different spectrum. The state has a higher number of females than males, 1,036 females for thousand males.

In the Indian context, a sex ratio of 950 and above can be considered as favourable to females. The states and union terrtories coming under this category besides Kerala are Himachal Pradesh (976), Andhra Pradesh (972), Goa (967), Karnataka (960), Manipur (958), Orissa, (971), Tamil Nadu (974),

Dadra and Nagar Haveli (952), Daman and Diu (969) and Pondicherry (979). Chandigarh accounted for the lowest number of females per thousand males with 790.

Socio-economic dynamics

Overall economic growth in terms of Gross Domestic Product (GDP) at constant factor cost improved from 0.8% in 1991-92 to 6.3% in 1994-95 and 7% in 1995-96 aided by a growth rate of 2.4% by agriculture and allied sectors, 11.7% by industry and construction sector and 7% by services. Overall economic growth during the first four year of the 8th Plan (1992-97) averaged 5.9% per annum compared with the planned target of 5.6%.

The domestic savings rate measured in terms of gross domestic savings as a proportion of GDP at current market prices increased from an average rate of 21.3% in

1992-93 and 1993-94 to 24.4% in 1994-95. The rate of domestic investment measured in terms of gross domestic capital formation as a proportion of GDP at current market prices increased from 21.6% in 1993-94 to 25.2% in 1994-95.

Industrial production which was virtually stagnant in 1991-92 increased by 9.4% and 12.1% in 1995-96 supported by a growth rate of 6.9% in mining, 13.6% in manufacturing and 8.1% in electricity generation. As per the latest information available, industrial growth deceleration to 8.5% in April-June 1996 due to deceleration of growth rates in all the sub-sectors (3.6% in mining, 10.4% manufacturing and 2.2% in electricity generation). As per growth rates by use-based classification, capital goods sector recorded a growth rate of 14.2%, intermediate goods 11.9%, consumer durables 11.1% and consumer non-durables 8.6% in April-June 1996. However, the growth rate of basic goods sub-sector having a weight of 39.4% in the overall industrial production was only 4% in April-June 1996.

Seven infrastructural sectors, namely, electricity, coal, steel, cement, crude oil and petroleum product & fertilizer with a combined weight of 31% in the Index of Industrial Production (IIP) recorded a growth rate of 7.8% in 1995-96. But their growth rate decelerated to 3.2% in April-August 1996 due to poor performance of electricity generation (growth rate of only 2.4%) and crude oil production (decline of production by 10.4%).

The outlook of agricultural production in 1996-97 is excellent with foodgrains output likely to reach 197 million tonnes compared with 185 million tonnes in 1995-96. This is primarily due to this year's rainfall distribution being the best in the past five years. The late withdrawal of monsoon has further ensured bright prospects for rabi production this year.

The estimate of foodgrains production in 1995-96 has been 'scaled down to 185 million tonnes representing a sharp decline of nearly 6 million tonnes over the prec * eeding year. The shortfall was substantial (about 3 million tonnes) in wheat output, besides short-fall of production of rice and coarse cereals. Consequently wheat procurement dropped steeply to 8.2 million tonnes compared to 12.3 million tonnes in the preceding year. Public stock (Central Pool) of foodgrains was about 22.1 million tonnes as on September 1, 1996.

There are 23 districts in Assam of which Cachar, Karimganj and Hailakandi are the three plain districts and Karbi Anglong and North Cachar Hills are the two hill districts in its southern part. Karbi Anglong is known as the biggest district in southern Assam covering an area of 10,434 sq. kms in contrast to Hailakandi being the smallest district with the area of 378 sq. kms. The two hill districts cover 68% of the total area in South Assam. Out of 33 lakh population, 75% of it live in the three plain districts and the district Cachar alone gives shelter to 36.7% of its total population.

Over the years there has been consistent rise of both population and density in South Assam. The density of populaltion has increased from 75 per sq. km. in 1960–61 to 98 per sq. km. in 1970–71 and further to 149 per sq. km. in 1990–91 as against the corresponding figures of 286 persons in all Assam and 267 persons at the all India level. In contrast Karimganj has been observed to be the most thickly populated district in South Assam with the highest density of 457 persons per sq. km.

Out of 33 lakh population in South Assam, 15.89 lakh are living in the Cachar district alone as against 0.69 lakh in N.C. Hlls. The percentage of female population to total population is varying from district to district from the lowest of 46.16% to the highest of 48.61%. It is estimated that 76% of the total female population are living in the plain districts and percentage of female has been higher in rural areas than that of the urban areas in all the five districts in South Assam.

Urbanization is one of the important indcators of development in an economy. South Assam's economy being a part of the Indian economy is no exception to this. It is found that about 3.2 lakh population in South Assam are living in the urban areas. Among these urbanites 37.4% are living in the Cachar district and 22.1% in Karbi Anglong. It is estimated that 67% of the total urbanites are lliving in the plain districts only. The extent of urbanization is found to be too less in Kailakandi and N.C. Hills in comparison to other three districts in South Assam.

According to 1960-61 census reports, there were only one lakh of urban population in South Assam. However, there has been slow but a continuous rise in their number over different census periods. The number has increased from 1.51 lakh in 1970–71 to 3.19 lakh in 1990–91. In other words, the percentage of urban population to total population has increased from 6.04% to only 9.64% in 1990–91. The figure of 9.64% is comparatively too low to the al India average of 25.7% and all Assam average of 11.1%. The highest growth rate of urban population of 22.87% is observed in the N.C. Hills district. Growth of urban population has been observed to be relatively higher in the hill districts than that of the plain districts.

Literacy being another important indicator of socio–economic development reflects the relative position of the region in the country. It is estimated that 14.5 lakh of people in South Assam are literate of which 40.4% are living in the Cacher district alone. Only a measure 4.8% of the total literates live in N.C. Hills. It also reveals that 79% of the total literate in South Assam live in the three plain districts. There has been slow but a steady rise in the growth of literacy in the region. During 1960–61 the lliteracy rate was at the level of 26.7%. This was increased to 28.5% in 1970–71 and further to 43.9% in 1990–91. Comparing this literacy rate of 43.9% in South Assam with the corresponding rate of 42.5% in Assam and that of 52.2% in India it can be said that not only South Assam but also the whole of the Assam state is lagging behind in this respect. Moreover, within South Assam the lowest literacy rate of 35.9% is observed in the Karbi Anglong district as against 48.3% in Cachar.

Surprisingly female literacy is much better in this part of the state in Assam. It is estimated that 5.6 lakh females are literates. The percentage of female literacy is relatively at a higher level of 38.4% as against the corresponding rates of 35.2% in Assam and that of 24.8% at the all India level. However, it is in much worse a positon compared to Nagaland and Mizoram where the rates are 45.5% and 64.1% respectively. As far as different districts are concerned, there is no significant variation in the female literacy rates in South Assam.

The Central Statistical Organisation (CSO) conducted the first economic census in 1977 to bridge the data gaps in the unorganised sectors of non-agricultural economy. The economic census was aimed at providing basic information on distribution of non-agricultural enterprises and to provide a frame for follow-up surveys for collection of detailed information about the structure of enterprises, investments, input, output, emploument, etc. The first economic census was followed by two sample surveys-one in 1978-79 relating to unorganised manufacturing and the second in 979-80 devoted to trade, transport, hotels and restaurants, storage and warehousing and services.

The second Economic Census was conducted in 1980 during the houselisting operations of 1981 Population Census with increased scope and coverage. It covered all enterprises (establishments and own-account enterprises) in the non-agricultural sector excluding crop production and plantation. Based on the information thrown up by this Census, three follow-up surveys were carried out, one in 1983-84 on hotels and restaurants, transport, storage and warehousing and services; second in 1984-85 on unorganised manufacturing and third in 1985-86 on wholesale and retail trade. The frame of 1980 Census was updated during 1987-88 in 64 towns. On the basis of Economic Census 1980 and updated frame, four sample surveys were conducted.

The third Economic Census 1990 was conducted along with the houselisting operations of 1991 Population Census in all states/union territories except Jammu and Kashmir. The data processing of Economic Census 1990 was undertaken in a decentralised manner by state/ union territories. Some of the states/union territories utilised the services of Regional Computer Centres at Calcutta and Chandigarh. The all India results of Economic Census 1990 brought out shortly by the CSO for which processing and tabulation has been done by the Computer Centre, Department of SAtatistics. On the basis of the frame thrown up by Economic Census 1990, a follow-up survey covering sectors of mining and quarrying and storage and warehousing was conducted during 1992-93 and another survey on hotels and restaurants and transport was conducted during January to September, 1994.

According to 1980 Economic Census, there were 18.4 million enterprises in the country (excluding Assam) employing 53.6 million persons. Among these, these were 16.9 million enterprises (58.4 per cent in rural areas) engaged in non-agricultural activitties employing 50.7 million persons (43.3 per cent in rural areas). As per of the results of Economic Census 1990, there were 25 million enterprises out of which 22.7 million were in the non-agricultural sector. The total number of persons usually working were of the order of 72.1 million out of which 40.2 million were hired workers. A total of 17.7 million enterprises operated without any hired labour on a regular basis and were mainly run by the households themselves.

Ministry of Finance is responsible for administration of finances of the Government. It is concerned with all economic and financial matters affecting the country as a whole including mobilisation of resources for development and other purposes. It regulates expenditure of Government including transfer of resources to the states. This Ministry comprises three departments, namely, (i) Economic Affairs, (ii) Expenditure and (iii) Revenue.

The Department of Economic Affairs consists of seven main divisions namely, (i) Economic, (ii) Banking, (iii) Insurance, (iv) Budget, (v) Investment, (vi) External Finance and (vii) Currency and Coinage. This Department inter alia monitors current economic trends and advises Government on all matters of internal and external economic management inciuding working of commercial banks, term-lending institutions, investments regulations, external assistance, etc. Preparation of the Budget of the Union of India as well as the state governments and union territory administrations with legislature when under President's rule and their presentation to Parliament is also the responsibility of this Department.

The Department of Expenditure comprises eight main divisions, namely, (i) Plan finance Division, (ii)

Establishment Division, (iii) Cost Accounts Branch, (iv) Controller General of Accounts, (v) Finance Commission Division, (vi) Implementation Cell, (vii) Integrated Finance Division and (viii) Staff Inspection Unit.

Department of Revenue exercises control in respect of revenue matters relating to direct and indirect Union taxes through two statutory boards namely, Central Board of Direct Taxes and the Central Board of Excise and Customs. This Department is also entrusted with the administration and enforcement of controls and regulatory measures provided in the enactments concerning Central sales tax, stamp duties, gold control, foreign exchange and other relevant fiscal statutes. Control over production and disposal of opium and its products is also vested with this Department.

Industrial production grew by 9.7 per cent in the first seven months of 1996—97, 1.9 percentage points slower than the 11.7 per cent growth in the first seven months of the previous year, which was the highest in 25 years. The growth of 9.5 to 10.5 per cent would still be the second highest growth rate in 25 years. It says, "the good performance of industrial production in 1996—97 is due entirely to the manufacturing sector, which has maintained its high growth." During the first seven months of the year the rate of growth of the manufacturing sector was 12.1 per cent, virtually the same as 12.3 per cent in 1995—96.

The Survey attributes the slowing of industrial production to the dramatic fall in the rate of growth of electricity production and a slowing down of growth in the mining sector, mainly because of the 10 per cent decline in crude oil production. During the first seven months of the year, electricity production has grown only by 3.4 per cent compared to 10.1 per cent in the corresponding period of 1995—96. If despite slowdown of electricity generation, manufacturing has recorded good growth, one possible reason could be captive generation, which is increasingly being used as a backup to public supply, the Survey adds. This hypothesis is supported by the growth of about 22 per cent in the volume of diesel imports.

Another noteworthy aspect of industrial production in 1996—97 has been acceleration in the rate of growth of capital goods production to 16.5 per cent from 15 per cent in the first seven months of the previous year. In contrast capital goods inports have declined by six per cent in the first seven months of the year. This according to the Survey, shows the increased competitiveness of the domestic capital goods industry.

The Survey also refers to the deceleration in the growth rate in the production of consumer durables, such as cars, to 9.8 per cent in the first seven months of 1996—97, compared to 30.2 per cent in the first seven months of the previous year. The delisensing of investment in consumer durable and decontrol of imports of parts of these goods, contributed to boom in investment and production in the sector. The decline in growth during 1996—97 suggests that the pent—up demand in the domestic economy has been met. Further growth will depend on increased cost competitiveness, which requires fuller exploitation of the comparative advantage that India has in the production of labour—intensive parts. Some analysts, however, seen in the sudden saturation of the demand a falacy in the general belief of the size of the middle class with good purchasing power, estimated at 200 million.

The Survey rates as poor the overall performance of the core and infrastructure sectors during the first 8 months of 1996—97 (April—November). Six industries, namely electricity generation, coal, steel, crude oil, petroleum products and cement, with a combined weight of 28.8 per cent in the Index of Industrial Production (IIP), averaged a growth of 4.1 poer cent in April—November, 1995. It says the previous Surveys had emphasised the need to accelerate, widen and deepen reforms of th non—tradable infrastructure and energy sectors, to avert an impending mismatch between economic growth and provision of these services. The new government, it says has repeatedly stressed its firm determination to reform the infrastructure and energy sectors and has take a number of policy decisions and new initiatives.

The Survey says continuing restraint on money supply growth is among the factors that have kept the prices in check. Despite the recent rising trend inthe growth of WPI, the average inflation for 1996—97 is expected to be at least one percentage point less than the average inflation in the previous year. There was complete change in the sectoral pattern of price changes du;ring 1996—97. The annual rate of inflation accelerated sharply in the "fuel, power, light and lubricants" and primary articles, while decelerating in the "manufactures" group. The annual rate of price increase in the fuel—power group went up to 17.4 per cent in January 1997 from 1.1 per cent a year ago because of administered price increase, while that of primary articles to 11.7 per cent from 2.6 per cent. The rate of growth in prices of manufactured goods declined to 3.6 poer cent from 6.9 per cent in the previous year. The rise in prices of primary goods has largely been due to rise in prices of cereals and fruits and vegetables.

Money supply growth has been higher in 1996—97 than in 1995—96, the Survey says, adding "Upto the fornight ended January 17, 1997, broad money (M3) grew by 10.6 per cent as against 8.2 per cent growth in the corresponding period of 1995—96. The average call money rate declined from a high of 13.75 per cent at the beginning of the currently financial year to a range of 5 to 11 per cent in September 1996 and ruled between 10 and 11 per cent in December 1996, before falling to low single digits in January 1997. The reversal of the 1997—96 excess demand for funds for investment in 1996–97 has led to a general softening of interest rates during the year. The cut—off yields on 91—day treasury bills has come down from 12.4 per cent in the first week of July to around 7.5 per cent at the end of January 1997.

Control over fiscal deficit was identified by the Update to the Economic Survey, presented by the United Front Government last year as one of the three challenges for economicpolicy. The Budget for 1996—97 envisaged a reduction of the fiscal dificit by 0.8 per cent of GDP to 5 per cent from 5.8 per cent in 1995—96 (RE). The primary deficit is also budgeted to fall from 1.1 poer cent of GDP to 0.2 per cent, while the revenue deficit to 2.5 per cent of GDP from 3 per cent in 1995—96.

The reduction in fiscal deficit has been attempted through an increase in revenues coupled with a reduction in expenditure. Revenue receipts (net) are budgeted to increase by 18.3 per cent during 1996—97 (BE). Despite a larger outgo on account of interest payments, subsidies and provision for revision of salaries and pension, total revenue expenditure is budgeted to grow at a lower rate of 12.7 per cent compared to 17.5 per cent in the previously year (RE). This deceleration in the growth of revenue expenditure has led to a decline in revenue expenditure to GDP ratio from 13.1 per cent in 1995—96 to 12.9 per cent in 1996—97 (BE). This favourable outcome, the Survey claims, is largely on account of containment of non—interest, non—plan expenditure growth at 9.3 per cent during 1996—97, about half the growth of 18.6 per cent in 1995—96 (RE). Consequently, non–interest revenue expenditure as a proportion of GDP is budgeted to fall to 8.1 per cent from 8.3 per cent in 1996—97 (RE). The revenue deficit is budgeted to fall by 0.5 per cent point of GDP. One may, however, note that the comparison of Budget estimates (BE) with Revenue Estimates (RE) is not very realistic.

Attainment of industrialisation over the last 48 years has been striking feature of Indian economic development process which was launched as a conscious and deliberate policy in the early fifties. In pursuance of this policy, large investment has been made in building up capacity over a wide spectrum of industries. Industrial production has made rapid strides in terms of variety, quality and quantity. There has been a substantial diversification of industrial base during this period with the consequent ability to produce a very broad range of industrial goods. Self-reliance has been achieved in basic and capital good. Indigenous capabilities have now been established to the point of virtual self-sufficiency so that further expansion in various sectors such as mining, irrigation, power chemicals, transport and communication can be based primarily on indigenous equipment. Process of industrialisation has also fostered entrepreneurship and development of a wide variety of technical, managerial and operative skills. Today, the country is in a position to provide consultancy services as well as managers, technicians and skilled workers for setting up industrial projects aborad.

The Industrial Policy Resolution of 1948 marked the beginning of the evolution of Indian Industrial Policy. The resolution not only defined the broad contours of the policy, it delineated the role of the State in the industrial development both as an entrepreneur and as an authority.

Successive policy resolutions also reiterated this basic tilt in favour of the public sector. The Industrial Policy Resolution of 1956 gave the public sector a strategic role in the economy. It categorised industries which would be the exclusive responsibility of state or would progressively come under state control and others. Earmarking the pre-eminent position to the public sector, it envisaged private sector co-existing with the State and thus attempted to give the policy framework flexibility.

The Industrial Policy initiatives undertaken by Government since July 1991 have been designed to build on the past industrial achievements and to accelerate the process of making Indian industry internatinally competitive. It recognises the strength and maturity of the industry and attempts to provide the competitive stimulus for higher growth. The thrust of these initiatives has been to increase domestic and external competition through extensive application of market mechanism and facilitating forging of dynamic relationships with foreign investors and suppliers of technology. The process of reform has been continuous.

As on 31 March 1993 there were 245 central public sector undertakings, comprising of eight in the construction sector, 72 in services and remaining 165 in the manufacturing. The number of CPSUs as indicated above exclude nine companies, six insurance companies and three financial institutions with Central Government investment but without direct responsibility of management.

The total capital employed in the 245 CPSUs increased from Rs. 1,179.91 billion in 1991-92 to Rs. 1,399.33 billion in 1992-93. The overall rate of return on capital employed in the PSUs also increased from 2.0 per cent in 1991-92 to 2.43 per cent in 1992-93.

The number of small scale units as at the end of 31 March 1994 were 2.38 million comprising of 1.77 million registered units and 0.61 un-registered. The overall production in the small scale sector during 1993-94 has been estimated to have reached Rs. 2,416.5 billion. The total value of exports of these units has been Rs. 177.85 billion in 1992-93.

Agriculture

The rate of agricultural growth of the order of around 3.2 per cent per annum during the fifties was derived from acreage increases to the extent of 70 per cent. In the sixties, the rate of growth which was only 2.1 per cent in this sector and did not neutralize even the rate of increase of population in that decade, could be derived from acreage increase to the extent of 30 per cent only. The scope for any further increase in acreage for increasing agricultural peoduction has exhausted in the seventies and the entire increase in farm production had to come from improvement in per acre productivity. This has required high level of capital–intensive effort in the development of the agricultural sector.

According to a competent study, the capital output ratio in Indian agriculture has already touched the figure of four and is close to the same scale as is required in industry. For the same reason, the fact has to be reckoned with that absorption of labour in agriculture through a significant rise in yields on land has tended to be a comparatively limited and expensive process and this process alone cannot be relied upon to solve the growing unemployment problem. The running controversy on priorities as between agriculture and industry, in particular heavy industry, is thus futile and misleading in the context of the realities of Indian economic situation and its growth prospects. The idea that India enjoys a comparative advantage in agricultural output inIndia is now crucially dependent on growth of inputs from industry. The need is thus not to fforeclose available resources in the economy for the so called development needs of the agricultural sector but to mop up a substained part of the surpluses and incremental incomes generating in the agricultural sector to meet the investment requirements of infrastructural development, including heavy and intermediate goods industries,to inputs for agriculture at a rapid and accelerating pace.

If much credit is taken for achieving self—sufficiency in food grains relative to effective domestic demand, there is now much brave talk of making India one of the few "grain powers" in the world even while large number of Indian people still do not have access to adequate food. Agriculture in India will have to go a long way yet before it can feed the Indian people. It is too early to talk of India becoming a "grain power." But the official policy has already veered to the postion that the government would not come in the way of the farmers exporting their produce and these exports would not be banned "merely" for bringing supplies and prices down for the domestic consumers. The upshot has been that while good grains have been exported, two million tonnes of wheat are being imported in the current year, 1996—97 to meet even the effective demand in the domestic market. The danger inherent in this position is not imaginary.

The widening disparities in incomes and levels of living combined with growing concentration of land and the swelling ranks of landless rural labourers are manifest. It is not amiss either to consider the pricing of agricultural produce, more especially food grains—the primary wage goods—and examine its influence on the general price trend and structure of relative prices in the Indian economy. The Agricultural Priçes Commission, to start with, recommended a particular set of prices based on its studies of the cost of production, fair return to the farmer and fair prices for the consumer. It has been a practice, by and large, to improve upon the prices recommended by the APC in order to provide additional incentives to the surplus farmers to increase production for the market. After the launching of the so—called economic reforms in 1991, however, the baalance between the claims of the surplus farmer and the consumer has been tilting sharply in favour of the former and the inflationary impact of "incentive prices" for good grains and other agricultural produce has been ignored. Subsidised farming by way of what are called "incentive prices" for farm produce and subsidised inputs for agriculture like chemical fertilizers, private irrigation facilities like tubewells and pumpsets, power andcomparative soft—term credit, was conceived in the wake of the disastrous drought years of 1964-65 as the means of stimulating agricultural production for the market and securing control over a substantial part of the marketable surpluses so produced.

There were probably compelling reasons under the given ownership pattern in cultivable land for adopting this strategy when shortages of agricultural commodities, especially of food grains, ad emerged as an endemic problem of the economy—its stability and further growth. But the concomitant of this development has been the growing commercialization of agriculture and emergence within it to prominence of that segment of farmers with their commercial interests which produce and control agricultural surpluses. In the course of time, however, as shortage in cereals or other crops are overcome relative, of course, to effective market demand at the present low-level of purchasing power in the economy, the system of subsidised production and marketing in agriculture has become in essence a mechanism to ensure to the surplus producer a monopoly to all the gains arising from incrreases in production and productivity.

Among the vast numbers of Indian farmers, only a small fraction, and more than 10 per cent of the total, commanding the best cultivable land produces for the market on any scale. They also monopolise the subsidised supply of inputs and credit and benefits of infrastructural facilities such as irrigation and power created by public investment.

Agricultural crop production in 1996—97 is expected to show good recovery from the slower growth in 1995—96. Growth is projected at 3 per cent after a fall of 0.4 per cent in 1995—96. The sharp decline in foodgrains production by 3.4 per cent, which was responsible for the slow growth in 1995—96, is expected to be reversed by an increased of 3.3 per cent in 1996—97. Foodgrains production is expected to recovery is primarily due to coarse cereals, as well as an anticipated rise in wheat production which suffered a sharp setback in 1995—96.

As the agricultureal year runs from July to June, the estimates for 1995—96 were only firmed up after the end of the financial year. A large downward revision (of 3 million tonnes) was made in the estimate of wheat production for 1995—96. The revision was unexpected and unexplained, because average rainfall in 1995—96 was quite normal. The revision, late in calendar year 1996, also created severe problems for the management of the food economy.

Commercial crop production has done extremely well in 1996—97 with oilseeds and cotton expected to reach record levels of 24.1 million tonnes and 14.3 million tonnes, respectively. Jute and mesta have also shown a growth of 3.4 per cent this year. Sugarcane output is, however, unlikely to maintain the record level of 283 million tonnes attained in 1995—96.

Industrial production (as measured by the index of industrial production–IIP), grew by 9.8 per cent in the first seven months of 1996—97, 1.9 percentage points slower than the 11.7 per cent growth in the in the corresponding period of 1995—96. The good performance of industrial production in 1996—97 is due entirely to the manufacturing sector, which has maintained its high growth.

The slowing of industrial production is clearly attributable to the dramatic fall in the rate of growth of electricity production and a slowing of growth in the mining sector mainly because of the 10 per cent decline in crude oil production. During the first seven months of 1996—97, electricity production (as measured by the index) has grown by only 3.4 per cent compared to the 10.1 per cent growth in the corresponding period of 1995—96. It is somewhat surprising that manufacturing sector growth has been barely affected by the slow growth in electricity production. One possibility is that captive electricity generation, which is increasingly used as a back—up to public supply, has substituted for the lack of generation by electricity boards. The high growth of diesel imports, about 22 per cent by volume in the first seven months of 1996—97 (with total refinery throughput growing in the normal range of around 4 per cent), is consistent with this hypothesis. At present, electricity statistics incorporate little or no data on captive power generation.

Another noteworthy aspect of industrial growth this year is the acceleration in the rate of growth of capital goods production to 16.6 per cent in the first seven months of this year from 15 per cent in the first seven months of last year. This has off—set the decline in the rate of growth of consumer goods and basic goos. In contrast, capital goods imports have declined by 6 per cent in the first seven months of 1996—97. This shows the increased competitiveness of the domestic capital goods industry.

The overall performance of the core and infrastructure sectors during the first 8 months of 1996—97 (April—November) has been poor. Six industries namely, electricity generation, coal, steel, crude oil, petroleum products and cement, with a combined weight of 28.8 per cent in the Index of Industrial Production (IIP), averaged a growth of 4.1 per cent in April—November, 1996, less than half the 8.9 per cent, in April—November, 1995. The deceleration in the growth rate of these infrastructure industries is mainly due to a decline in crude oil production and power generation. Hydro power generation declined by 7.7 per cent, and thermal power generation grew by only 6.4 per cent in the April—November, 1996 as compared to 14.6 per cent in the April—March, 1995—96. Coal, cement and refineries' throughput have grown faster in April—November, 1996—97 compared to the corresponding period of 1995—96. Growth of sectors such as railways, ports and telecommunications, which do not appear in the IIP, also slowed. The rate of growth of railways' revenue earning goods traffic decelerated marginally from 7 per cent during 1995—96 to 6.3 per cent for April–November 1996. Growth of cargo handled at major ports and new telephone connections provided decelerated more sharply to 4.7 per cent in April—November, 1996 (from 9.1 per cent in 1995—96) and 8.3 per cent in April—November, 1996 (from 23.3 per cent in 1995–96), respectively. The slower growth in cargo handled by ports in probably the result of a deceleration in the growth of external trade. The telecomunications slowdown, however, suggests that the pace of implementation of telecommunications reform needs to be accelerated and its scope widened to include Department of Telecommunications as a service provider. Given the parlous financial state of many public utilities, particularly the State Electricity Boards, the possibility of crises worsens with each passing year. The new government has repeatedly stressed its firm determination to reform the infrastructure and energy sectors. In line with this commitment, a number of policy decisions have been taken and new initiatives launched.

High Yielding Variety Programme was started in 1966-67 as a major plan of agriculture strategy for increasing production of foodgrains in the country. Cropwise details are shown in table 3. The programme is supported through a number of Centrally-sponsored schemes and thrust has been shifted from single crop to cropping system approach since 1994-95. Identifying potential areas, the country has been grouped in three major cereal based cropping systems viz., (i) Integrated Cereal Development Programme in Rice Based Cropping System Areas (ICDP-Rice); (ii) Integrated Cereal Development Programme in Wheat Based Cropping System Areas (ICDP-Wheat); and (iii) Integrated Cereal Development Programme in Coarse Cereal Based Cropping System Areas (ICDP-Coarse Cereal).

These thrust programmes are designed to increase the productivity and production of foodgrains through adoption of latest scientific production technology. Minikit demonstration programme aims at popularising newly released varietity and getting the newly released evolved varieties tested under field conditions. For this a large number of seed minikits containing 0.25 kg to 10 kg seed are distributed at a nominal cost to farmers. State level training programmes are being organised at agricultural universities and ICAR research institutes in collaboration with concerned state agriculture departments to disseminate the latest crop production technology to the district/block level extension officers.

About 990 lakh hecare area in the country is rainfed accounting for 70 per cent of the net sown area of 1,410.6 lakh hectare. Crops grown and cropping practices followed in these areas entirely depend on the rainfall which is often erratic and unpredictable. Bulk of the crops like rice, jawar, bajara, other millets, pulses, oilseeds and cotton are grown in this area under rainfed conditions. Farmers in these areas, particularly, small and marginal, are still practising subsistence farming and are in the vertex of vicious circle. Wide fluctuations in production occur in these areas year after year. Increasing and stabilising agricultural production in these areas is, therefore, of crucial importance.

Government has given high priority for the development of dryland areas and, therefore, several programmes and projects have been launched for utilisation of potential of these areas for: (i) realising the projected requirement of about 240 mt of annual food production by 2000 AD and to smoothen out fluctuation in annual production; (ii) reducing regional disparities between irrigated and vast rainfed areas; (iii) restoring ecological balance by greening rainfed areas through appropriate mixture of trees, shrubs and grasses; and (iv) generating employment for rural masses and reducing large-scale migration from rural areas to already congested cities and towns. Holistic approach for integrated farming system development on watershed basis in rainfed areas would be main pursuit of the development activities under the National Watershed Development Project for Rainfed Areas (NWDPRA) in the Eighth Plan.

Allied sectors

The gross value of output from livestock sector (at current prices) is estimated to account for 26 per cent of the total value of output from Agriculture sector. This excludes the contribution of animal draught power. Animal husbandary is an important source of self employment and subsidiary occupation in rural and semi-urban areas and more so for people living in the drought prone, hilly, tribal and other poorly developed areas, where crop production on its own may not sustain them fully. As revealed by NSS, 1987-88 was 4.15 per cent as against 1.1 per cent for the agriculture sectore as a whole. The recent Land and Livestock Holding Survey (NSS, forth-eitghth round) further reveals that during eighties there was a substantial growth of dairy farming in the country.

The ratio of in-milk bovine stock to 100 households rose from 37 in 1981-82 to 46 in 1991-92. It also highlighted that the rise in ratio during eighties was most pronounced in the states with relvatively high average in milk stock, like Punjab, Haryana and Fajasthan. On the other hand, there was little improvement in the ratio in Kerala, Orissa and Tamil Nadu. The marginal and small holdings constitute the core of the milk production sector accounting for about 66 per cent of the in-milk bovine stock (1991-92 estimate).

In 1995-96, the country produced 66 million tonnes of milk. This represents an average annual growth of 4.5 per cent since 1990-91.

Poultry Farming has become an important activity providing additional income to the weaker sections of the population in rural and semi-urban areas. Poultry farming has made good progess due to research and developmental efforts of the Government and the organised private sector. Egg production is expected to have increased to about 27 billion during 1995-96. Land and Livestock Holding Survey (NSS, forty eighth round, October, 1996) point out that there has been a rapid growth in poultry farming during 1970s and 1980s. The poultry stock per hundred households rose steadily from 107 in 1971-72 to 195 in 1991-92. In 1991-92, the marginal category of farm households (constituting 48 per cent of the households) alone accounted for 55 per cent of poultry stock.

Under the cattle insurance policy, cover is provided for the sum insured or the market value of the animal at the time of death, whichever is less. Animals are normally insured upto 100 per cent of their market value. General Insurance Corporation (GIC) implements various cattle insurance programmes through its four companies under their "Market Agreement on Cattle Insurance". Buffaloes, calves/heifers, stud bulls, bullocks etc. of specified age groups are insured against death due to accidents inclusive of natural causes like fire, lighting, floods, storm, earthquakes, famine diseases, surgical operation, riot, strike and civil commotion and risk of breeding an calving. Insurance policy can also be extended to cover permanent total disability on payment of extra premium. Cattle purchase under poverty allevation programmes are insured under Master Policy. The animals are insured at concessional rate and part of the premium is subsidised by the Government. Under the Cattle Insurance Scheme, at present, about 10 per cent of the total cattle population is covered. The projected target for insuring cattle during 1996-97 was 88 lakhs out of which 48 lakhs was for 'scheme' animals and 40 likhs for 'non-scheme' animals. The position regarding number of cattel covered, premium collected and claims paid during the past 5 years. After taking into account management expenses and incentives, the scheme is presently operating on no-profit-no-loss basis. The scheme is thus operated by the Insurance Companies on their own risk.

India is the seventh largest producer of fish in the world and, perhaps, second in Inland fish production. Fishery sector plays a vital role in sustaining a fairly large proportion of population along the long 8129 kms. coast line. The contribution of fisheries to the net domestic product has increased from Rs. 1479 crore in 1984-85 to Rs. 9826 crore in 1994-95 at current in 1994-95 at current prices showing about six and a half times increase in ten years. The trend of fish production and exports. The target for fish production in 1996-97 is 51.40 lakh tonnes comprising 28.57 lakh tonnes from marine and 22.83 lakh tonnes from Inland waters. An area of 3.86 lakh hactares has been brought under scientific fish culture and 5.04 lakh farmers have been trained in improved practices upto 1995-96 through active support provided under Fish Farmers Development Agencies. Development of brackish water aquaculture through Brakish Water Fish Farmers Development Agencies have been established in the coastal states for providing a package of technical, financial and extension support for shrimp farming. A shrimp and fish culture project is under implementation with the World Bank assistance in 5 states.

Agriculture census: research and education

The Department of Agriculture and Cooperation has been conducting agricultural census in each of the Plan period since 1970-71 in collaboration with states and union territories on the recommendation of Food and Agriculture Organisation (FAO) of the United Nations. The censuses in 1970-71 and 1980-81 were organised as part of the World Agricultural Census Programme sponsored by the FAO. They were conducted on complete enumeration basis in states where the land records are maintained. In other states information was collected from 20 per cent villages on enquiry method. The other two censuses with agricultural years 1976-77 and 1985-86 as reference periods were conducted on a census-cum-sample basis to reduce the burden in collection and processing of primary data and also to keep costs low. The Fifth Agricultural Census with reference period 1990-91 has also been taken up on a census-cum-sample basis and the field work is completed in most of the *states/UTs. The data on number and area the states/UTs except Assam and Bihar. All the tables generated from the data relating to Agricultural Census 1990-91 have also been received from 22 states/UTs and the tabulation work in the remaining states/UTs is in progress.

Agricultural census seeks to collect information on distribution of holdings and area operated along with the related characteristics such as tenancy and terms of leasing, and use and cropping pattern, irrigation and source of irrigation, etc., by different size classes. The data is utilised for formulation of poverty alleviation programmes in generral and relief to small and marginal farmers in particular. As part of the agricultural census scheme, an input survey was also conducted for the first time in 1976-77 with a two per cent sample of villages as the first stage of selection. The second and third input surveys with reference periods 1981-82 and 1986-87 were also conducted as part of agricultural censuses 1980-81 and 1985-86 respectively in seven per cent of the total villages in the country. An All India bulletin on input survey, 1986-87 containing detailed results has also been prepared. The fourth input survey with reference period 1991-92 is in progress in seven per cent sample of villages in the country. The field work of Input Survey 1991-92 has been completed in all the states/UTs except Assam and Bihar and tabulation work is also in progress in those states/UTs where the field work has been completed.

The results relating to number and area of operational holdings of agricultural Census 1990-91, have been finalised for All India (in the case of Assam and Bihar, the data of Agricultural Census 1985-86 have been taken). According to the results of the Agricultural Census 1990-91 the total number of operational holdings in the country has increased from 972 lakh in 1985-86 to 1,053 lakh in 1990-91. Operated area on the other hand had risen only marginally, i.e., by about 0.6 per cent. Rise in number of holdings without corresponding increase in area clearly showed pressure of population on land with average size of holding declining from 1.69 hectare in 1985-86 to 1.57 hectare in 1990-91.

Holdings operated by the scheduled casted and scheduled tribes households increased both in number as well as area operated during 1990-91 as compared to 1985-86. In the case of scheduled castes there has been an increase of 9.2 per cent in the number of holdings while the increase in the area operated by them was 3.6 per cent from 1985-86 to 1990-91. On the other hand the scheduled tribes holdings increased by 11.6 per cent while the area operated by them increased by 3.8 per cent during 1990-91 as compared to 1985-86. According to the Agricultural Census 1990-91, the area operated by scheduled caste holdings accounted for 7.9 per cent while the area operated by scheduled tribes clearly accounted for 10.8 per cent of the total operated area. This clearly shows that there has been an improvement in the status of these social groups in the operation of land which may be attributed to various land reforms and other measures taken by the Government.

The Department of Agricultural Research and Education set up in 1973 in the Ministry of Agriculture is responsible for coordinating research and educational activities in agriculture, animal husbandary and fisheries.

Besides, it helps to bring about inter-departmental and inter-institutional collaboration with national and international agencies engaged in the same and allied fields. The Department provides government support, service and linkage to the Indian Council of Agricultural Research (ICAR).

Indian Council of Agricultural Research (ICAR), the main organisation of the Department of Agricultural Research and Education (DARE) of the Ministry of Agriculture has played pivotal role in developing agricultural technologies, input materials and critical scientific mass leading to self sufficiency in food. The ICAR is an autonomous apex body at national level which promotes science and technology programmes in the areas of agricultural research, education and extension education. The Council is directly involved in undertaking fundamental as well as applied reasearches in the traditional and frontier areas to offer solution to problems relating to the conservation and management of resources and productivity of crops, animals, fisheries etc. The activities of the ICAR organised into eight subject matter divisions, namely, Division of Crop Sciences, Horticulture, Soil Agronomy and Agro-forestry, Agricultural Engineering, Animal Sciences, Fisheries, Agricultural Extension and Agricultural Education.

The research is carried out through a chain of 45 institutes, four bureaux, nine project directorates (PD), 30 national research centres (NRCs) and 79 All India Coordinated Research Projects (AICRPs) located throughout the country, mostly at 27 state agricultural universities (SAUs) at their 200 zonal research stations. As part of promotional activity, the Council is also helping the SAUs in improving their infrastructural facilities as well as regional research capabilities.

The whole country has been divided into 120 distinct agro-climatic zones and in each of them, a multi-disciplinary regional research station has been established under on-going national agricultural research project. These stations carry out research on multi-dimensional problems of local importance and on factors acting as constraints to the enhancement of agricultural production in a given zone.

For transfer of new improved agricultural technologies developed, the ICAR has created integrated programme of Krishi Vigyan Kendras (KVKs), (183 on-going and 78 newly sanctioned). To train the trainers, there are eight trainers training centres (TTCs). Four of the ICAR institutes have Deemed-to-be University (DUs) status offering graduate and post-graduate education. SAUs allied field making the country self-sufficient in agricultural human resource. ICAR channelises Central assistance to SAUs for strengthening, promoting agriculture education, research and extension.

The educational programmes at the national level are by and large being conducted through 28 agricultural universities located in various states. This includes the North Eastern Hill University (NEHU), Manipur. Four of ICAR's institutes, viz. Indian Agricultural Research Institute, New Delhi, Indian Veterinary Research Institute, Izatnagar. National Dairy Research Institute, Karnal and Central Institute of Fishery Education, Bombay, also perform educational functions and offer post-graduate and basic programmes in the capacity of well-recognised deemed university and award degrees.

Under the SAUs, there are 61 agricultural colleges, 30 veterinary colleges, 16 agricultural engineering colleges, 18 home science colleges, nine fisheries colleges, eight dairy technology colleges, 13 colleges of forestry, eight colleges of horticulture and one college each in the field of sericulture, food science and technology. At present, the admission capacity at the under-graduate and post-graduate levels are 9.715 and 4,500 respectively excluding the capacity of admission in the colleges of central university.

Urban fringe

Urban fringe has been existing since the emergence of urban civilisation. However, its importance in the planning process has been realised only in recent times, particularly in the wake of the Industrial Revolution. No doubt, the concept of fringe is prevalent more in metropolitan and big cities than in small cities and towns.

It is now established that industrialisation and urbanisation are inter-related and irreversible processes. These are two sides of the same coin. A small town grows into a big town, a big town intoa city, and then it acquires the status of a metropolis and a mega city. Rapid urbanisation in the country has been accompanied by the emergence of urban fringe and slums in the cities. The existing areas of these cities are put under much pressure, causing excessive clustering and haphazard urban growth. The study on Management of Urban Fringe Land Development in selected Metropolitan cities undertaken by TCPO indicates that too much pressure on urban land during the last two decades has resulted into a decline in the per capita availability of urban land. As of now, a significant percentage 30% to 50% of population in metropolitan cities live in the slum areas in most deplorable and sub-standard conditions.

The emergence of urban fringe depends on various factors like growth of industrial, commercial and institutional activities in the fringe area, the availability of transportation facilities, proximity to the city, the existing spatial capacity of the city to absorb growing population, increasing economic activities and the basic infrastructural facilities being provided in the fringe areas, as well as in the city, etc. Therefore, it is difficult to assign a spatial boundary to define urban fringe.

According to Lewis Keeble the urban fringe is defined "as the land surrounding the town which is not considered as a part of it but whose use is influenced directly by the town". Richard Mayers considers the urban fringe "as the zone between the country and the city while to Andrews the rural urban fringe outward from the economic city in which there is an intermininglng of charteristically agriculture and urban land uses." George Wherewein defines the fringe "as the area of transition between well recognised urban land uses and the area devoted to agriculture".

As such there is no exact definition for urban fringe land. It seems it is not possible also. This is because no one can exactly say as to what distance ithe fringe land should extend from the city boundary. One may say that fringe land should include those areas which fall on the fringe of the city, that is the areas falling just out side the boundary of the city. But the question is upto what distance one should go? Some people define fringe areas as those areas which are not contiguous to the existing built up areas of the city, but those which are likely to become contiguous if provided with the right injection of investment towards the right injection of investmnet towards the development of physical and social infrastructure. The structure plan for the Madras Metropolitan Areas has defined urban fringe as those areas that are experiencing considerable pressure form the process of urbanisation.

During initial staes, the urban fringe land would be mostly under agricultural use. However, once migration of population form nearby areas into the fringe land starts, the available land in taken over for housing, commercial, institutional and industial uses.

During recent years, the trend towards rural-to-urban migration as well as urban-to-urban migraton is on the increase and the mobility characteristics are particularly strong towards metropolitan cities. Statistics show populaltion increase annually at national level—2%, at Urban level—3% and in metropolitan cities level—9%. As such, the existing areas of these cities are put under much pressure, causing excessive clustering and haphazard urban growth. According to 1991 census (provisional figures), about 65% of the total urban population live in Class-I cities and 50.6 per cent of urban population live in 23 metropolitan cities alone. Even though the rate of growth to over 40% in 12 metropolitan cities during 1971-81 has been less than the growth of urban population of 46%, the absolute addition of about 12 million people representing 24% of the total addition to urban population is distinctly very high. By the year 2000, India's urban population is excepted to be 325 million, twice the 1981 level, and more than half of India's population growth will occur in urban areas only.

It could be seen from this data that the pressure on land in urban areas had increased manifold during the last two decades resulting in further decline in the availability of per capita urban land. Further, nearly 30 to 50 per cent of the urban population in these cities has been living in slum areas with poor and sub-standard living conditions, with civic amenities far from satisfactory. The density of population in slums is also very high. Hence, the imbalance between the rapid growth or urban population in the metropolitan cities and relatively slow process of development of additional land for housing, commercial and other purposes has given rise to the following major problems in the metropolitan cities:

— Acute shortage of serviced land for residential, commercial and industrial purposes, resulting in urban sprawl and invasion on urban fringe.

— Continuous increase in density and loss of open spaces, more demand for land for housing and transportation have resulted in large conversion of land in the fringe.

— High land values due to ever-increasing gap between demand and supply of land for various uses.

— Increasing pressure on physical and social infrastructure due to massive spill-over, population pressure/economic activities etc.

— Acute shortage of housing, resulting in unauthorised construction, squatter settlements, up-coming of slums and even invasion of villages by the spill over population/economic activities etc.

— Inadequate finances/investment in urban infrastructure led to the concomitant problems of unplanned urban development on the green-belt leading to serious environmental/ecological problems.

— Fast urbanisation, coupled with sky rocketing land prices has deprived the poor/low income families to have access to shelter or even serviced land. Hence, not only the weaker section of the society but lower, middle income group of society but lower, middle income group of society have also started on public/private land, generally on the urban fringe. The Land Acquisition of land have further acted as a major constraint in smooth and expeditious a acquisition of land and making it available for urban development.

The TCPO's study on Management of Urban Fringe Land Development in selected Metropolitan Cities of India namely Madras, Hyderabad, Pune, Indore, Lucknow, and Jaipur was taken up to analyse the efficacy of existing policies and programmes in making serviced land available at affordable prices to the poor for utilisation of land, availability of vacant land, unutilised land for meeting future demand etc. The study has gone into the spatial problems of inner city, density pattern, migration, of various infrastructural facilities like water supply, transport, sewerage, drainage, electricity, roads and other physical amenities in the cities. An attempt has been made in the study to analyse the effects on the management of green-belt, environment and land use transformation, provision of water and transportation for land development. The findings of study are briefly given below:

— The fringe areas of Madras and Jaipur are inhabitated by mostly middle and higher income groups, whereas fringe areas of Hyderabad, Pune, Lucknow and Indore are dominated by poor or low-income people.

— The people living in urban fringe of these six cities are employed in private sector/informal sector. A significant proportion of the total population of these areas are also found to be self employed.

— In case of Madres and Hyderabad, a significant proportion of persons (50-70%) are employed locally. Hosever, in respect of other smaller cities, the majority of the earning members commute to the main city for work or for other purposes.

— Public transport service seems to be the most important mode of transport for work journeys performed by the households of the urban fringe areas. Public transport facilities appear to be good in the fringe areas of Hyderabad, Madras and Pune, wherwas private transport is playing important role in Jaipur, Lucknow and Indore.

— A good proportion of the households who settled in the fringe areas of Madras, Hyderabad and Jaipur have come from the main cities, whereas the households settled in the fringe areas of Pune, Lucknow and Indore have migrated from nearby rural areas.

— Growth of these urban fringe areas has taken place only around mid-1980s.

— Majority of the households in urban fringe areas of these metropolitan cities have their own houses. It shows that the priority of these households has been to have houses of their own .

— Construction in all these urban fringe areas is unauthorised. This may be due to the impression among the people that these construction or pucca houses would be regularised on the intervention of some social or political pressures later on.

— The majority of the households lack municipal or protected water supply and depend on open wells located within their premises. These households are also deprived of sewerage and drainage facilities. Majority of them have water-borne latrines connected to septic tanks.

— Fringe areas of these metropolitan cities lack adequate basic facilities like education/medicines etc. They have to depend for them on the main cities.

— The reasons for living in the fringe areas are the high cost of urban land within city, the city life being unaffordable for the poor.

— Majority of the households of the fringe areas wanted to have domestic water connections and drainage facilities in their localities.

— Land price in the fringe areas started rising around mid-1980s. The price level between 1980-85 was steady. A sharp rise in the price of land, however, occured after 1985. The Urban Land Ceiling and Regulation Act, 1976, instead of being helpful in preventing speculative transactions relating to scarce and precious land, has added to the misery of land-speculation. Thousands of hectares of surplus land that the government proposed to aquire nder the Act was caught in the never ending rigmarole of court litigations. In two decades of its existence, the government has been able to acquire barely 15,321 hectares of the total 2.21 lakh hectares declared surplus across the country.

In we give the percentage distribution of agricultural labour households according to their annual per capita consumer expenditure in 1956-57. The distributions are given separately for the six population zones of the country.

We have earlier accepted minimum desirable consumption in rural area to be Rs. 15 per capita per month or Rs. 180 per capita per annum at 1960-61 prices. At 1956-57 prices, this is approximately equal to Rs. 150 per capita annum. Hence it will be seen that about 57 per cent of the agricultural labour households lived below the minimum. The incidence of poverty among the agricultural labour households is again somewhat different in different regions. In Central India, 68.7 per cent of the agricultural labour households and in North India and South India, about 60.0 per cent of the agricultural labour households lived below the minimum.

It is obvious therefore that the incidence of poverty is much more common among all rural households. To judge what part of rural poverty is due to agricultural labour households, we should find the proportion of agricultural labour households among rural households living at different levels of per capita annual consumer expenditure. In we give the relevant data.

It will be seen that among rural households living at less than Rs. 100 per capita per annum, which, as we saw, corresponds to the rock-bottom of physical existence, agricultural labour households constituted more than 40 per cent. In South India, half of the rural households living at this level were agricultural labour households. Among rural households with annual per capita consumer expenditure between 101-150, agricultural labour households constituted nearly one-third. In South India, they constituted over 40 per cent of the rural households living at this level.

Among the rural households with annual per capita expenditure between Rs. 151-200, the proportion of agricultural labour households is no larger than in the general rural population. Among rural households with annual per capita consumer expenditure of more than Rs. 200, the proportion of agricultural labour households is naturally small.

Thus the rural poverty at the lowest level is largely accounted for by the agricultural labour households. Nevertheless, even at this level, they do not account for more than half the poor. The remaining rural poor are presumably small cultivators.

In we give the percentage distribution of small landowners (possessing cultivated land) according to their per capita monthly expenditure in 1955-56. It will be seen that the distribution, by consumer expenditure, of households with less than 0.5 acre of cultivated land is quite similar to that of the agricultural labour households. Indeed, these households would be classified as agricultural labour households because their main source of income would be from hired labour on other farms.

With landholdings of between 0.5 and 1.5 acres, the situation is only slightly better. Nearly 75 per cent of the households with these size holdings lived below Rs. 13 per capita per month which, in 1955-56, would be approximately the equivalent of Rs. 15 per capita per month in 1960-61.

With larger landholdings the situation naturally improves. However, even with cultivated landholdings between 3.50-4.99 acres, nearly 60 per cent of the households still lived below the minimum of Rs. 13 per capita per month.

In spite of these rather old and fragmentary data, it is clear that the rural poor consist predomnantly of agricultural labour households and small landholders with cultivated holdings of less than 5.0 acres and particularly less than 2.5 acres. The two groups would also include village artisans progressively thrown out of their traditional employment. The urban poor are only an overflow of the rural poor into the urban area. Fundamentally, they belong to the same class as the rural poor. However, as they live long enough in urban poverty, they acquire characteristics of their own. Little is known of their life and labour in the growing cities.

The National Sample Survey (NSS) offers more direct and independent estimates of private consumer expenditure. These are based on direct inquiries made from a random sample of households. The NSS estimate of per capita private consumer expenditure in 1960-61 is Rs. 278.8. The difference between this estimate and the one obtained above (Rs. 276.3) is small. Indeed, considering the entirely independent sources of data from which the two estimates are built up, the agreement between the two is remarkably close. We may therefore neglect the difference between the two.

An advantage of the NSS estimates of private consumer expenditure is that they are available for the rural and urban populations separately. In 1960-61, out of the total of 434 million population, 356 million lived in rural areas and 78 million lived in urban areas. According to the NSS estimates, the per capita private consumer expenditure of the rural population was Rs. 261.2 while that of the urban population was Rs. 359.2. Thus, the per capita consumer expenditure of the urban population was about 37.7 per cent higher than that of the rural population. This does not however mean that the urban population on an average was so much better off than the rural population. The prices of consumer goods and services are usually higher in the urban area than in the rural area. This must be allowed for before judging the relative levels of living in the urban and the rural areas.

Another advantage of the NSS estimates of private consumer expenditure is that they enable us to obtain a distribution of the rural and urban populations according to per capita consumer expenditure. In we give the distribution of the rural and urban populations according to the monthly per capita consumer expenditure in 1960-61. For each monthly expenditure class, the average annual per capita expenditure is also shown for convenience of reference.

Thus, according to the National Sample Survey, the per capita rural consumption in 1960-61 was Rs. 261.2 per annum; and nearly two-thirds (more than 63.25 per cent) of the rural population lived below this average.

Similarly, the per capita urban consumption in 1960-61 was Rs. 359.2 per annum; and nearly two-thirds (more than 64.51 per cent) of the urban population lived below this average. Of course, this is in the nature of the distribution and it only means that the country is poor. But sizable sections of the population are much poorer. Thus, in 1960-61, 6.38 per cent of the rural population had per capita consumer expenditure of less than Rs. 8 per month which is 27 paise per day. Another 11.95 per cent had per capita consumer expenditure less than Rs. 11 per month which is 37 paise per day. Another 9.88 per cent had per capita consumer expenditure less than Rs. 13 per month which is 43 paise per day. Yet another 9.82 per cent of the population had per capita consumer expediture less than Rs. 15 per month which is 50 paise per day. The four classes mentioned above constituted a little under 40 per cent (38.03) of the rural population. In 1960-61, they lived with less than 50 paise per day per capita.

The situation in the urban areas was in fact a little worse. Apparently, only 21.69 per cent of the urban population had per capita consumer expenditure of less than Rs. 15 per month or 50 paise per day. However, as we shall presently see, the cost of urban living at this level is at least 50 per cent more so that the equivalent consumer expenditure in urban area would be Rs. 22.5 per month or 75 paise per day. It will be seen that in 1960-61, about 50 per cent of the urban population lived below this level.

People not familiar with these sections of the population, say the 40 per cent poorest rural population and the 50 per cent poorest urban population, have wondered how men at all subsist at these levels. Therefore, when somebody occasionally brings these facts to public notice, some of them are shocked and are righteously indignant; others simply do not believe.

Nevertheless, such are the facts of poverty in this country.

It will therefore be worthwhile examining, even if briefly, the standard and quality of living at this level. A simple index to judge the standard of living is the distribution of the total consumer expenditure between major items such as food, fuel, clothing, etc. The poor must devote a large part of their expenditure to food so that little is left for anything else. In we give the distribution of the rural consumer expenditure between major items of expenditure at different levels of total expenditure are given in.

It will be noticed that, in 1960-61, the poorest households having per capita monthly expenditure less than Rs. 8 constituted 6.38 per cent of the rural population and 2.15 per cent of the urban population. Their annual per capita expenditure was less than Rs. 80 (Rs. 79.3 in rural area and Rs. 77.6 in urban area). More than 90 per cent of this small expenditure is devoted to food and fuel for cooking. In rural area, 64.42 per cent of the total expenditure at this level is spent on foodgrains and substitutes such as tapioca; another 18.25 per cent is spent on other items of food and 8.74 per cent is spent on fuel and light. The distribùtion of urban consumer expenditure at this level is quite similar. Evidently, this is the rock bottom of physical existence and there is little room for variation.

If we leave out this rock bottom, the pattern of consumer expenditure begings to show marked differences between rural and urban living. As we move up from the poorest to the somewhat better, the proportion of expenditure on food and especially on foodgrains declines in both rural and urban areas; but it declines much more rapidly in the urban than in the rural case. For rural households with per capita monthly expenditure of Rs. 18-21 or annual per capita expenditure of Rs. 237.3, which is a little below the average (Rs. 261.2), about half (50.31 per cent) of the total expenditure is spent on foodgrains and substitutes, and about a quarter (24.10 per cent) on the other items of food. At this level, about 75.0 per cent of the expenditure is spent on food and if we add to it the expendirture on fuel and light (6.67 per cent), more than 80.0 per cent is spent on sheer physical existence.

In urban area, the proportion spent on foodgrains and substitutes declines rather rapidly and is partly made up by increased proportion of expenditure on other items of food. For households with monthly per capita expenditure of Rs. 24-28, or annual per capita expenditure of Rs. 315.4, which is a little below the average (Rs. 359.2), about a third (32.72 per cent) of the total expenditure is spent on foodgrains and substitutes and another one-third (34.56 per cent) on other items of food. Their expenditure on fuel and light accounts for nearly 7.0 per cent. Hence, even in urban areas, the households living a little below the average seem to spend almost 75.0 per cent of their total expenditure on bare physical existence.

A distinguished study group set up by the Government of India in July 1962 has deliberated on the question of what should be regarded the nationally desirable minimum level of consumer expenditure. The study group recommended that a per capita monthly consumer expenditure of Rs. 20 (at 1960-61 prices) should be deemed the national minimum. The basis of this determination is not known. Apparently, the study group also did not make a distinction between rural and urban living costs. In our computation above, we have regarded that level of consumer expenditure desirable which secures a diet adequate at léast in respect of calories. In

1960-61, this was Rs. 170 per capita per annum for rural households and Rs. 271 per capita per annum for urban households. It will be noticed that the rural minimum determined by us is considerably below that proposed by the study group while the urban minimum determined by us is a little above that proposed by the study group. In deference, we propose to revise the rural minimum slightly upwards to Rs. 180 per annum or Rs. 15 per month. We may also round off the urban minimum to Rs. 270 per annum or Rs. 22.5 per month. With these minima, it seems that, in 1960-61, about 40 per cent of the rural population and about 50 per cent of the urban population lived below the desirable minimum.

The cost of minimum living varies not only between rural and urban areas but also between ural or urban areas of different States. As we shall presently see, the level of per capita consumer expenditure at which a diet with 2,250 calories is attained differs considerably from State to state. This is partly due to differences in prices and partly due to differnces in consumer preferences in the sense that consumers in some States seem to attach a higher priority to food than do consumers in some other States.

The results of the National Sample Survey for 1960-61 are not published in sufficient detail to bring out these differences between States. However, the results for 1961-62 are available in sufficient detail. They give State-wise data on quantities of various items of food consumed at various per capita consumer expenditure levels. It is therefore possible to find for each State the level of consumer expenditure at which a diet with 2,250 calories is reached and the proportion of the population having consumer expenditure below this level. The results for the rural population are shown in.

In this shown, for each State, the monthly per capita expenditure class in which a diet with 2,250 calories is reached (column 2). In subsequent columns of the are shown the per capita total annual consumer expenditure (column 3), the calorie equivalent of daily diet (column 4), and the proportion of the population lying below this level (column 5). For computing this proportion, we have taken into account half the population lying in the monthly per capita expenditure class mentioned in column 2 together with the population falling in the lower classes. It will be seen that, in different States, the food consumption reaches the desired *level also varies greatly from State to State. Some of the differences are worth noting.

In Jammu-Kashmir, Punjab, Gujarat, Mysore, Bihar and Orissa, the desired calorie-level is achieved at about the same level of total consumer expenditure (Rs. 13-15 per capita per month). Nevertheless, the proportion of population lying below this level varies from 43.88 per cent in Orissa and 37.88 per cent in Bihar to 19.09 per cent in Gujarat and less than 14.0 per cent in Punjab and Jammu-Kashmir. In West Bengal, the desired calorie-level is reached at a slightly higher expenditure level (Rs. 15-18 per capita per month) and the proportion lying below this level is 44.09 per cent which is close to the situation in Orissa. In Assam, the desired calorie-level is reached at an even higher expenditure level (Rs. 18-21 per month per capita) and the proportion of population lying below the desired level is also somewhat higher, namely 47.57 per cent. In Madras, Maharashtra and Andhra Pradesh, the desired calorie-level is reached at about the same expenditure level (Rs. 18-21 per month per capita), but the proportion of population lying below this level is much greater in these States–55.19 per cent in Tamil Nadu, 61.04 per cent in Maharashtra and 62.14 per cent in Andhra Pradesh.

At the other end are Uttar Pradesh, Madhya Pradesh and Rajasthan. In these States, the desired calorie-level is achieved at much lower expenditure levels (Rs. 11-13 per capita per month in Uttar Pradesh and Madhya Pradesh, and Rs. 8-11 in Rajasthan) and the proportion of population lying below this level is also much smaller (25.79 per cent in Madhya Pradesh, 18.13 per cent in Uttar Pradesh and 13.29 in Rajasthan).

The case of Kerala is extreme and peculiar. Here the desired calorie-level is reached not until the total expenditure is as high as Rs. 34-43 per capita per month. Consequently, 90.75 per cent of the rural population of the State appear to have diets below the desired level. This may be true. It happens because, in Kerala, tapioca is widely used as a subsitute for foodgrains and, weight for weight, tapioca has a calorie value only one-third that of foodgrains. It is possible therefore that in Kerala 90 per cent of the rural population in fact lives on diet inadequate even in respect of calories. Alternatively, it is possible that the National Sample Survey has underestimated certain items of food such as banana, coconut, and fish entering into the diets of these people and that consequently the extent of malnutrition in Kerala has been somewhat exaggerated in the above figures.

If we apply the State-wise estimates of the proportion of the rural population living on inadequate diets to the State-wise rural population in 1960-61, it seems that, in that year, 135 million rural people, which is about 38 per cent of the total rural population, lived on diets inadequate even in respect of calories.

As in the case of the rural population so in the case of the urban population, the level of consumer expenditure at which the diet reaches adequacy in respect of calories varies greatly from State to State. The relevant data derived from the National Sample Survey for 1961-62 are given in. It is clear that the level of consumer expenditure at which the diet reaches adequacy in calories and the proportion of the urban population living below this level vary greatly from State to State. But everywhere the incidence of poverty is much greater in the urban areas than in the rural areas.

If we apply the State-wise estimates of the proportion of the urban population living on inadequate diets to the State-wise urban population in 1960-61, it seems that, in year, 135 million rural people, which is about 38 per cent of the total rural population, lived on diets inadequate even in respect of calories.

As in the case of the rural population so in the case of the urban population, the level of consumer expenditure at which the diet reaches adequacy in respect of calories varies greatly from State to State. The relevant data derived from the National Sample Survey for 1961-62 are given in. It is clear that the level of consumer expenditure at which the diet reaches adequacy in calories and the proportion of the urban population living below this level vary greatly from State of State. But everywhere the incidence of poverty is much greater in the urban areas than in the rural areas.

If was apply the State-wise estimates of the proportion of the urban population living on inadequate diets to the State-wise urban population in 1960-61, it seems that, in that year, 42 million urban people, which is about 54 per cent of the total urban population, lived on diets inadequate even in respect of calories. Adding this number to the estimate of rual population living on inadequate diets, namely 135 million, it seems that in 1960-61, between 175 million to 180 million people in the country lived on diets inadequate even in respect of calories. This briefly is the measure of the extent of poverty prevailing in the country at the beginning of the last decade.

An area of priority in the Ninth Plan is to improve project implementation and delivery mechanisms and to ensure that the intended benefits actually reach the people. Further, several social sector programmes are formulated without addressing the isssue of sustainability of benefits and most programmes run with ever-increasing government budgets and thus pre—empt resources which could find better alternative uses. The Ninth Plan must introduce necessary correctives to reverse many of the unsustainable trends in the implementation of poverty alleviation programmes. Just allotting higher outlay for rural development will mean nothing unless a major streamlining takes palce in the implementation and delivery systems.

The existion schemes whose delivery costs are disproportionately high or which fail to make the desired impact should be considered for reorientation and discontinuation. It is necessary to shelve such schemes whose delivery cost exceeds, say 15 to 20 oer cent of the total cost of operating the programme. Monitoring and evaluation of programmes have to be made equally effective and purposeful. Therefore, the Centre, States and the grass roots level organizations/institutions would need to be involved to ensure the effectiveness of the system. It is encouraging that the Planning Commission would bring out compendium of evaluation studies and give wider publicity of the findings of research studies conducted and sponsored by it. This would be helpful for a meaningful public debate on issues involved.

An overall increase in the level of real wages of the unorgainzed workers will also help empowering them to be able to secure maximum advantage from the other developmental programmes of the government. The very concepts of democratic decentralozation and empowerment of the people imply a steady reducation in the paternalistic role of the State and increased emphasis on empowerment of the people themselves. It is hoped that during the Ninth Plan there will be much more attention on bringing about awareness among the unorganized workers as also on providing effective redressal mechanisms to enforce their rights. The approach document of the Plan rightly observes that one of the most important weaknesses of the Indian social sector programmes has been is inabiligy to inform the target benefiviaries about the schemes that are available and to which they have a rightful clain. The Ninth Plan will, hopefully, stress the creation and deployment of an effective information dissemination system,and the necessary redressal mechanism for making the demands effective.

Finally, of course, there is no unique way to describe an ideal gorwth process. It can be hoped that the Ninth Plan will lay down foundations for a more progressive process of planning than has been the case so far. Growth involves a dynamic interaction of linked changes. The economic endocrine gland has to be clear as to how much other matters mingt have advanced. As such, it can also be argued that little attention is required to any particular rate of economic growth so long as it is positive.

Wouldn't it then make little sense to worry whether a baby will end up five or six feet tall when the real anxiety should be whether the baby can be safely brought through the problems of infancy, childhood and adolescence? The slower rate of growth, once under way, can pick-up speed and, of course, can slow down too. But the higher gorwth rate has the prospect of slowing down only. It is desirable to have a steady growth as it has more possibility of ending up with the fastest rate of growth of the economy just as the movement on a highway gives to the motorest the highest speed. The crux of planning is to find the turnpike and reach it. Also gorwth is no longer the guarantor of trickle down effects. To what extent these plan promises are taken care of in the Ninth Plan, can be anybody's guess.

Against the per capita net availability of 501.9 gms of cereals the estimated consumption of cereals was of the order of 394 gms i.e. 78.6 per cent of the net availability. similarly in the case of pulses, per capita consumption was 28.05 gms. i.e. 75.8 per cent of net availability. Inequality in the consumption of foods among different income groups gets masked in the overall consumption estimates. Among the poor, nearly 80 per cent of consumption expenditure goes for food items. Recent surveys indicate:

— Percapita cereal consumption has declined over the years resulting in the aggregate energy intake of 1859 k.cal per capita as against 2200 k.cal recommended.

— 47.7 per cent of households have calorie inadequacy and 19.8 per cent of households have protein inadequacy. 19.5 per cent of households have both calorie and protein inadequacy.

— The exetent of moderate and severe growth retardation in preschool children varied from 34 per cent in Kerala to 72 per cent in Gujarat.

— 47 per cent of adults have body mass index value below 18.5 indicating large scale prevalance of chronic energy deficiency in the community.

— Haemoglobin levels among pregnant mothers reveal that as many as 87.5 per cent of mothers were anaemic.

— About 30 per cent of infants born had low birth weight.

— 167 million people are considered to be at risk for iodine deficiency disorders and 54 million have goitre.

— Preventable blindness due to Vitamin A deficiency still large.

Looking back the distance travelled and counting on various milestones towards food security, the country can be proud of some of the achievements so far. Yet the final milestone looks to be a long march. Shrinking arable land resources, soil degradation and depletion of nutrients from the soil, poor water management and unsustainable use of ground water, loss of momentum in the growth of food output, inefficient biological utilisation of the nutrients consumed due to poor environment and growing population are some of the problems the country faces in the march towards the final milestone of a hunger-free nation. The over-exploitation of the aquifer is also leading to the leaching of high levels of arsenic from natural underground sources into thousands of village wells in West Bengal. As estimated 200,000 people already have arsenic-induced skin lesions.

It is estimated that there are about 20 million species of poants, out of which 50,000 are edible. However, we are not using more than 200 plants as food, 80 per cent of our food supply however comes only from about eight species. We are today laying much emphgasis on developing new varieties of these few plants. We should enlarge the food basket by including the excluded. Many nutritious grains fall under the classification "coarse grains". It is time we start referring to them as "nutritious grains". They are rich in micronutrients like Fe and Ca.

Seeing that between 75.0 and 80.0 per cent of the total expenditure at levels a little below the average is spent on food and its preparation, we might briefly examine the nutritional adequacy or otherwise of food at this level. In we show the per capita daily consumption of foodgrains and substitutes at different levels of expenditure. As is to be expected, the consumption of foodgrains increases as we move from the poorest to the somewhat better. This occurs much more rapidly in rural area than in the urban area. In rural area, the per capita daily cosumption of foodgrains and substitutes reaches 616 grams for households with per capita monthly expenditure of Rs. 13-15 or per capita annual expenditure of Rs. 170.8. Calculating at the rate of 3.3 calories per gram of foodgrains (including substitutes), 616 grams of foodgrains give 2,033 calories per capita per day. As we have seen, this takes up nearly 60.0 per cent of the total consumer expenditure of these households. They spend another about 20.0 per cent on other items of food such as edible oil, ghee and butter, sugar and gur, and a little milk, meat and fish. The quantities of these items are rather small and they yield about 200 calories per capita per day. Thus the entire food at this level seems to give about 2,250 calories per capita per day. Nutritional experts regard this as adequate under Indian conditions of climate, etc. It means that, in 1960-61, an annual per capita consumer expenditure of Rs. 170 was essential to give a diet adequate at least in respect of calories. At consumer expenditure below this level, the diet was inadequate even in respect of calories. With reference to the population lying in monthly per capita expenditure classes Rs. 0-8, 8-11, 11-13 and half the population lying in the class Rs. 13-15 had per capita expenditure below this level. These classes add up to 33.123 per cent of the total rural population. Thus, in 1960-61, about one-third of the rural population lived on diets inadequate even in respect of calories.

In 1993-94, the Planning Commission stated that only 18.96 per cent of the Indian people were below the poverty line. Now we are told that it is 40 per cent. A couple of shocking statistics, recently released by the National Council of Applied Economic Research (NCAER) provide a horrifying picture of where we are. The first figure is that 39 per cent of India's population of nearly one billion remain under the poverty line, a number that has not changed in a decade. In real terms, this means a very large number of Indians have an earning capacity of a couple of chapatis. According to another survey by the NCAER, 37 per cent lof the country's rural population are landless and therefore unable to grow their own crop to put off hunger.

The second figure, less publicised but avilable from international agencies, is that food grains production is 1991 million tonnes in 1994-95 to 185 million tonnes in 1995-96 and in the case of wheat from 65.5 million tonnes to 62.6 million tonnes in same period. Unsurprisingly the worst shortfalls are in the politically volatile States of Uttar Pradesh and Bihar and yet the naked face of hunger continues to be maskedby the hypocrisy that India is a food grain exporter.

Apart from the rising poulation, agro-economists put forward a number of reasons for fall in food grain production, among them soil exhaustion and the larger number of landless that are concentrated in the States of UP, Bihar and eastern India. What they don't spell out is the endemic political instability and coruption these States, and the interminable cycle of fodder scams and caste wars, that are pushing the poor deeper into the poverty trap.

Economic reports do not point out that the agricultural ministry for many years has been managed by ministers, who only represent the narrow interests of wealthy landed farmers like themselves, and have no truck with the poor landless peasants.

The Ninth Plan will be an heir to the same hypocrisy despite agriculture being put on the top by all then nine objectives of the Plan.

J. Gaur, a retired officer of Rajasthan government has a telling story about his visit to one of the villages of Dungarpur district. He was shocked to know from one of the poor schoolboys that he was served the family had ten members. This speaks volumes about our rural development and family planning programmes. The population clock outside the Capital's (Delhi) All-India Institute of Medical Sciences is galloping ahead but, for India's shoddy family planning programme, time has stood still. The latest census data is proof, if any were needed, that we are sitting on a population time bomb. By 2040, India will be the world's most populous nation. In a situation where over 18 million—or six Singapores—are being added to the population every year, it can be of little comfort to learn that curde birth rates have declined from 34.7 per cent in 1991 or indeed that fertility levels have shown a negligible decrease of two per cent in that period. If the population has to stabilize at even a staggering 100 crore by 2001-2005, the average birth rate has to be reduced to two children per woman. But so far, only Kerala and Tamil Nadu have achieved this with Madhya Pradesh stated to do so only after 2060, Rajasthan by 2048, Bihar by 2039 and Uttar Pradesh by 2100. The government has confined itself to making tall claims about running a family planning campaign which is so "people oriented" that all targets have been removed. The truth is that it is Central run and almost totally dependent on female sterilisation ignoring the variety of options which are available.

The desired goal of population as mentioned as one of the objectives of the Ninth Plan could be achieved only through the willing co-operation of the population and specially of the rural people. The magic words are 'literacy' and 'healthcare'.

There is no "political will" as is evident from the fact that no political party has cared to emphasize the need for some concrete steps to restrict population growth in their election manifestoes. There is no mention of family planning even in the Common Minimum Programme of the United Front government.

It should be a matter of deep concern for every thinking Indian that after 45 years of the so-called planning, the country does not have a comprehensive education policy. This is despite the constitutional objective to provite universal primary education and eradication of funding, enormous sums have been wasted on subsidies and populist schemes from which money is easily diverted into the pockets of corrupt politicians and officials. Even in education, priorities have been misplaced. While primary and vocational education, which would improve the skills of the work force, have been neglected, money has been spent on creating an army of inadequately unemployable at various levels. The crying need of the hour is not elaborate plans but the 'political will' to act and innovate.

The late S.K. Dey, a Minister of State in Nehru's Cabinet once visited Tamil Nadu. He met the late Kumarappa at Gandhi Niketan and with some pride of achievenment he claimed that the Community Development Programe was a grand success. Kumarappa was sharp to retort : "What is your scale for measuring the success of your projects? S.K. Dey answered by giving elaborate statistics of the miles of roads constructed, number of wells dug, school-buildings built, dispensaries opened, fertilizers distributed, improved seeds introduced, the manure pits constructed, and all the usual figures. Kumarappa looked doubtfully at S.K. Dey and said in a derisive voice, "this is your scale" and laughed. Pricked by Kumarappa's remarks, Dey asked, "what then is your scale of success?" Kumarappa in a very emphatic tone said: "Mr Dey, before I cover an area with the Community Development Programme, I would select some six poor persons, count their ribs and if after three years (or five years) of implementing the C.D. Programme, there is some flesh to cover these ribs, thn I will call it a success". Dey was dismayed and implicitly accepted that his approach was defective. Kumarappa continued to say thay S.K. Dey was "trying to throw a silk shirt on a hungry person". The essentials of development are brought out in this one sentence. In other words, villages have developed and not the villagers.

Kalia a poor villager at the time of India's Independence thought, he was poor. He was told he was not poor but needy. Then as to be called needy was self-defeating, he was addressed as deprived which was again changed to underprivileged. This term was also later changed to disadvantaged. Kalia said : "I have no dime or rupee yet but a rich vocabulary". He further said : "I have no idea of Five Year Plan". He was about 20 years of age at the time of India's Independence. Now he is about 70 years of age. In the last two-and -a-half decades, he was not able to eat chapatis with pulses. His earnings are so meagre that he is unable to afford prices to buy pulses for his family consisting of six members.

The life and vitality of human beings depend crucially on certain vitamins and minerals that help in the efficient functioning of the brain, immune system, reproduction and energy metabolism. The body needs only small amounts of these nutrients, but it cannot synthesize them. They must be provided through diet. Deficiencies of even the small amounts required cause learning disabilities, impair work capacity and bring illness and death. Micronutrient malnutrition (silent hunger) is most devastating for pre—school children and pregnant women but is also debilitating for all ages. And it is debilitating the national economy as well. The most important and well studied micro-nutrient deficiencies are vitamin A, Iodine and Iron. Virtually every developing country has deficiencies in the micro nutrients large enough to constitute a public health problem. Many developing countries have multiple deficiencies. Taken together micronutrient deficiencies affect a far greater number of people in the world than Protein-Energy malnutrition. 1.6 billion people live in areas where soils lack sufficient iodine, 655 million suffer from goitre, 26 million have had brain damage and 5.7 million cretinism. Two billion pre-school children suffer from iron deficinet anaemia. 254 million pre-school children are affected by subclinical, severe and moderate deficiencies of Vitamin A.

In India, 167 millions are exposed to the risk of Iodine deficiency of which 54 million have goitre. Surveys conducted by DGHS indicate that 186 districts are IDD endemic area with goitre rates over 10 per cent. As regards Iron deficiency anaemia, multicentre study conducted by ICMR reveal that 87.5 per cent were anaemic. Deficiency of Vitamin A has long been known to be the largest preventable cause of blindness.

The main intervention strategies against micronutrient malnutrition are:

- Diet supplementation of vulnerable population.
- Dietary improvements.
- Fortification of common foods.

The richest sources of micronutrients are green leafy vegetable and fruits. India is rich in vegetable crops, some of which have good carotene content. Future programmes with respect to horticultural products must be directed towards identifying and propagating high micro-nutrient concentration varieties. People know when they are hungry but they have no natural hunger for vitamin. A, Iron, Iodine and other micronutrients. They do not know they need them and they often do not know what foods provide them.

Deficiency in soil nutrients reflect in the plants grown in the soil. One—half of all soils in all developing countries are deficient or low in available micronutrients. Soil depletion of S, Fe, Mn, Zn and Cu are due to intensive and indiscriminate irrigation and heavy use of high analysis chemical fertilisers. This gets reflected in the plants grown in these soils. Hence, in the national soil health care programme, we should ensure that both the macro-and micro-nutrient needs of soils are addressed.

The term Green Revolution was coined by Dr. William Gadd of USA in 1968, when our farmers brought about a quantum jump in wheat production by taking to semi-dwarf, non-lodging varieties with great enthusiasm and when similar progress appeared feasible in rice. Punjab took the lead because of the scientific and educational backstopping given by the Punjab Agricultural University on the one hand and on the other, by the presence of the essential pre-requisites for progress such as land consolidation and leveling, rural communication, rural electrification and above all, owner cultivation.

Twenty eight years after the term "Green Revolution" was coined, we are in a position to draw a balance sheet and chalk out a strategy for the future.

Apart from erasing the "begging bowl" image of India, the most important gain has been the saving of forests and land, thanks to the productivity improvement associated with high yielding varieties. This year, Indian farmers harvested over 60 million tonnes of wheat, as compared to 6 million tonnes at the time of our Independence in 1947. Punjab farmers have raised the average yield of wheat to over 40 quintals per hectare. Likewise, Tamil Nadu farmers have raised the average yield of rice to over 50 quintals per hectare. If the yield improvement associated with the Green Revolution in wheat and rice had not taken place, we will need another 70 million hectares to produce the wheat and rice we now harvest. Thus, the productivity inmprovement associated with the Green Revolution is best described as forest and land saving agriculture. The productivity improvement has taken place not only in wheat and rice but also in relation to milk and eggs. Only in the case of pulses, we are lagging behind.

The population of India is growing at a rate of 1.8 per cent per year. If this trend continues, our population will double itself in less than 40 years. Only Kerala, Tamil Nadu, Goa and Mizoram have so far achieved a demographic transition to low birth and death rates. Besides population increase, improved purchasing power among the poor will enhance the demand for food, since undernutrition and poverty go together. In contrast, per capita availability of arable land is shrinking. Water efficiency is still on the whole low and water disputes are growing. In addition to the gradual decline in per capita availability of land and water, various forms of biotic and abiotic stresses are spreading.

There is still a widespread mismatch between production and post-harvest technologies. In perishable commotities like fruits, vegetables, flowers, meat and other animal products, this mismatch is often severe, affecting the inyterests of both producers and consumers. This is why foreign experts frequently refer to the setting in of a fatigue of the Green Revolution. Lester Brown and Hal Kane in their book "Full House" released last year predict that at the current rate of population growth and environmental degradation coupled with an improvement in the consumption capacity of the poor, India will have to import annually over 40 million tonnes of food grains by the year 2030. This is four times the quantity we imported in 1966 i.e. before the onset of the Green Revolution. We should examine this issue seriously and should not allow complacency overtake the farm sector, just because we now have over 30 million tonnes of food grains available with Government.

Industrial countries are responsible for much of the global environmental problems such as potential changes in temperature, precipitation, sea level and incidence of ultraviolet-B radiation. While further agricultural intensification in industrialised countries will be ecologically disastrous, the failure to achieve agricultural intensification and diversification in developing countries where farming provides most of the jobs-will be socially disastrous. This is because, agriculture including crop and animal husbandary, forestry and agro-forestry, fisheries and agro-industries provides livelihood to over 70 per cent of our population. The smaller the farm, the greater is the need for higher marketable surplus for increasing income.

Eleven million new livelihoods will have to be created every year in India and these have to come largely from the farm and rural industries sectors. Importing food and other agricultural commodities will hence have the same impact as importing unemployment. Thus, what we need now is an environmentally sustainable and socially equitable green revolution or what may be termed as ever-green revolution.

Those who advocate going back to the old methods of farming ignore the fact that just a century ago when the population of undivided India was 281 million, famines claimed 30 million lives between 1870 and 1900. The famine eradication strategy of India comprising the following steps is perhaps the most important achievement of independent India:

- Enhanced production and productivity.
- Better distribution through the public distribution system.
- Adequate grain reserves.
- Purchasing power enhancement through various employment generation and guarantee schemes.
- Special intervention programmes for children, pregnant and nursing mothers and old and infirm persons.

While famines have been prevented, widespread under-nutrition prevails among the economically underprivileged. Since non-food factors like health care, environmental hygiene and literacy play an important role in promoting sustainable food security of the level of the individual, we should redefine security.

Steps for achieveing sustainable food security are as under:

First sustained physical access to food will involve a transition from chemical and machnery intensive to ecological farming technologies.

Second, the emphasis on economic access underlines the need for promo9ting sustainable livelihoods through multiple income-earning opportunities.

Third, environmental access involves on the one hand attention to soil health care, water harvesting management and the conservation of forest and biodiversity, and on the other to sanitation, environment hygiene, primary health care and primary education.

If the political vision to implement this mission is forthcoming, population stabilisation can be more readily achieved. The prediction of Margins de Condorcet made in 1975 that population will stabilise itself, if children are born for happiness and not just for existence, will then come true.

The emphasis on the individual is important, since the household is not often a homogenous unit. Women and girl children tend to suffer more from under-nutrition than men and boys. UNDP's 1995 Human Development Report contains distressing data on the growing feminisation of poverty. To give operational content to such a concept of food security, we should initiate a Hunger-Free Area Programme (HFAP) consisting of the following components:

- Ensuring sustainable availability of food production over population growth through the development and dissemination of ecotechnologies, supported by appropriate packages of services and public policies. Ecotechnology involves the blending of the ecological prudence and technologies of the past, with the best in frontier technologies, particularly biotechnology, information technology, space technology, renewablre energy technology and management technology. Without ecotechnological empowerment, farm men and women will not be able to produce more food and other agricultural commodities on an environmentally sustainable basis from less land, water and energy resources.
- Sustain the productivity of the natural resource base, by conserving and improving the ecological foundations essential for continuous advances in crop and animal productivity.

- Ensure adequacy of household incomes through promotional social security, such as accessing assets, employment and organisational and marketing empowerment. Agricultural programmes should concurrently aim at more food, more jobs and more income. Integrated attention to farm and non-farm employment and value-addition to primary agricultural commodities will be necessary to enhance income and rural livelihood security.

- Provide entitlement to food through protective social security measures to the vulnerable groups, such as employment guarantee and food for nutrition programmes.

- Introduce a National Food and Livelihood Security Act for the purpose of paying integrated attention to:

— Conservation of lands, water, forests, biodiversity and the protection of the atmosphere.

— Enchancing productivity through ecotechnologies.

— Improving distribution in order to eliminate endemic hunger.

— Maintenance of adequate food security reserves.

— Strengthneing the techno-infrastructure for better post-harvest technology and expanding the coverage of sanitary and phytosanitary measures, and

— Efficient research, education, extension, marketing systems both to take full advantage of emerging opportunities in international trade and to ensure that research and extension designed to promote public good receive adequate support.

The major problems that confront India are poverty and unemployment. And both are interrelated. There is a lot of controversy regarding the estimates of poverty in the country. Estimates of Tendulkar and Jain show that rural poverty has increased from 37.5 per cent in 1990-91 to 39.7 per cent in 1993-94. On the other hand, urban poverty has declined from 35 per cent in 1990-91 to 30.9 per cent in 1993. The upshot of the argument is that even in 1993-94, around 40 per cent of the rural population (around 250 million) and 31 per cent of the urban population were below the poverty line, or food insecure in terms of not having enough calories.

The continuance of poverty at such a colossal level has created great distortions in the economy. There are several reasons why poverty has persisted in rural areas. One obvious factor which has hurt the poor is the sharp increase in the prices of food grains. During the last five or six years, procurement prices of food grains have increased considerably recultural labourers. Secondly, the rural poor appear to have been left out of the gains of increased productivity in the agricultural sector. Thirdly, the rate of growth in employment in rural areas (both males and females), during the period 1987-88 to 1993-94 was significantly lower as comparesd to the urban areas as shown in.

According to the 50th Round of the NSSO, while 'Open' unemployment at a little over 6.0 per cent, remained more or less unchanged. And casualization increased with a corresponding decline in self-employment, both in rural and urban areas. Casual wage employment increased from 31.2 per cent in 1987-88 to 33.5 per cent in 1993-94, while self-employment declined from 53.6 per cent to 51.9 per cent. Regular salaried employment also declined from 15.2 per cent to 14.7 per cent.

The census figures have given an alarming new for Indian planners again. The data paint a dismal picture both with regard to increase in population and unemployment. By 2040, India is set to become the world's most populous country with a population of 126 crores. And as far as unemployment situation is concerned, one-third of the populztion—300 million were estimated to be without work in 1994.

This implies that unless some effective steps are taken to control population, the rate of employment will increase in future.

The approach paper, however, recognizes that a sustained and long-lasting solution to gthe problem of poverty depends on the creation of adequate employment opportunities through a broad based programme of development and economic growth. Therefore, in the Ninth Plan, a great deal of emphasis has been given to agriculture and rural development. And agriculture has been delinked from rural development in order to emphasize the development of irrigation, watershed development, animal husbandry schemes, social forestry and so on.

This study is concerned with the problem of poverty in India. It is a problem of low national income and its unequal distribution; of slow pace of development and inequitable distribution of the small gains of development. Before one discusses how to meet the threat this problem poses, one should know its dimensions and understand the process through which it seems to be deepening. We shall therefore begin with a brief review of the situation at the beginning of the sixties, that is, in 1960-61.

National income (Net National Product at Factor Cost) per capita, that is per person, is a useful summary measure to judge the well being of a people. The National Income of the Indian Union, excluding Portuguese and French territories, in 1960-61 was Rs.

13,308 crores. The corresponding population in that year (October 1, 1960) was 43.4 crores. Hece the National Income per capita in that year works out to be Rs. 306.7.

A more direct measure of the level of living of a people is per capita Private Consumer Expenditure. To arrive at this, we begin with Net Domestic Product which is only slightly different from the Net National Product and the distinction between the two need not detain us here. The whole of the Net Domestic Product is not expended domestically. A part of the goods and services produced at home is exported. On the other hand, a number or goods and services are imported. If we deduct from the Net Domestic Product the exports and add to it the imports, we get the Net Domestic Expenditure.

Again, the whole of the Net Domestic Expenditure is not Private consumer Expenditure. A part of it goes into net investment or what is called Net Domestic Capital Formation. This adds to the productive capacity of the economy and hence leads to higher national product in future. But in a given year, it does not form part of consumption. Another part of Net Domestic Expenditure is consumption by Government. This consists partly of expenditure on administration and partly of expenditure on social welfare such as education and public health. The latter is what is often termed socialised consumption and it adds to the welfare of the people. But presently it constitutes a small part of the total consumer expenditure. We may therefore neglect it. We therefore deduct from the Net Domestic Expenditure, firstly the Net Domestic Capital Formation and secondly the consumption Expenditure of Government. We thus arrive at the Private Consumer Expenditure. When this is divided by the population, we get the per capita private consumer expenditure. This provides a simple measure of the well being or standard of living of the people.

For the year 1960-61, the computation appears as under:

Thus, in 1960-61, the consumer expenditure in India amounted to Rs. 276.3 per capita per annum or 75.7 paise per day per person. This sums up the average level of living prevailing in 1960-61.

Sustainable food security

The commitment of the international community to ensure food and nutrition security to every child, woman and man on our planet has been reiterated at several international conferences held during this decade.

Despite such high level political reaffirmation of the need to achieve speedily the goal of "Food for All", over 800 million human beings now suffer from hunger and malnutrition. Hidden hunger, arising from the deficiency of the essential micronutrients is widespread. Endemic hunger is now more due to the lack of adequate income at the household level than due to the lack of food in the market. Both poverty as well as non-food factors such as environmental hygiene, sanitation and lack of safe drinking water are becoming major contributors of food insecurity at the level of communities and individuals. A majority of the food insecure live in Asia.

There is also increasing concern about the earth's capacity to produce adequate food for the growing population. The increase in human population, now mostly confined to the developing countries, coupled with enhanced purchasing power leading to greater capability to buy food and increasing urbanisation will lead to a higher growth rate in demand for food as well as more diversified food products in the coming millennium. Thus, on the one hand, there will be need for intensification and diversification of agriculture, particularly in the developing countries, on the other, the ecological foundations essential for sustainable advances in crop and animal productivity are getting eroded. This situation has led to the ringing of alarm bells by experts concerning the earth's capacity to produce adequate food to meet growing needs. Lester Brown has concluded; "Constraints imposed by the earth's natural systems, the environmental degradation of land and water resources and the diminshing backlog of yield-raising agricultural technologies are slowing the growth in world food production, raising questions about the earth's population carrying capacity. The earth's capacity to produce enough food to satisfy expanding demand is now emerging as the overriding environmental issue as the world approaches the 21st Century".

The year 1998 will mark the bicentenary of Malthus's essay on population. The onward march of science and technology, supported by appropriate public policies, has so far helped humankind to keep Malthusian forebodings on the population-food supply equation at bay. It is, however, becoming increasingly clear that without concerted national and global action to arrest environmental degradation, promote economic and gender equity and check population growth, the Malthusian spectre may still come true in the next century. The Food and Agriculture Organisation of the United Nations (FAO) therefore, organised a World Food Summit in Rome from November 13 to 17, 1996.

At this Summit, a Rome Declaration on World Food Security and a World Food Summit Plan of Action were adopted.

The Declaration makes a commitment to reduce the number of undernourished people to half their present level no later than 2015. It also states:

"We will pusue participatory and sustainable food, agriculture, fisheries, forestry and rural development policies and practices in high and low potential areas which are essential to adequate and reliable food supplies".

"We will strive to ensure that food, agricultural trade and overall trade policies are conducive to fostering food security for all through a fair and market-oriented world trade system".

The Plan of Action includes the following seven commitments:

- Create an enabling political, social and economic environment designed to create the best conditions for the eradication of poverty, and for durable peace.
- Implement policies aimed at eradicating poverty and inequality and improving physical and economic access to sufficient, nutritionally adequate and safe food and its effective utilization.
- Pursue participatory and sustainable food, agriculture, fisheries, forestry and rural development policies and practices in high and low potential areas.
- Ensure that food, agricultural trade and overall trade policies are conducive to fostering food security for all.
- Prevent and be prepared for national disasters and man-made emergencies.
- Promote optimal allocation and use of public and private investments to foster human resources, sustianable food agriculture, fisheries and forestry systems, and rural development, in nigh and low potential areas.

- Implement, monitor and follow-up the Rome Plan of Action at all levels in cooperation with the international community.

The above plan of action integrates the principles of (a) conservation of the ecological foundations essential for sustainable advances in agricultural productivity and production, (b) sustainable production through ecotechnologies and (c) equity in acces to food through an appropriate blend of national and international action in the area of entitlements and employment. The Science Academies Summit held in Madras in July, 96, recommneded that all nations may provide an overall public policy support to action at these three levels through the enactment of a National Food and Livelihood Security Act designed to achieve the following objectives:

- That every individual has the physical, economic, social and enviormental access to balanced diet that includes the necessary macro-and micronutrients, safe drinking water, sanitation, environmental hygiene, primary health care and education so as to lead a healthy and productive life.
- That food originates from efficient and environmentally benign production technologies that conserve and enhance the natural resource base of crops, animal husbandry, forestry, inland and marine fisheries.

The Chief Minister of Tamil Nadu, India in his budget speech delivered on July 17, 1996 made the following announcement.

Feed the people who are hungary Educate the people to uplift the World"

To fulfil this dream of Mahakavi Bharatiyar, this Government will launch a new "Hunger Free Area

Programme" with an aim to eradicate poverty induced hunger. A number of schemes are already under implementation to alleviate poverty and to cater to the nutrition requirements of different groups of the population. Gaps in this coverage will be identified which can then be specifically targeted under the Hunger Free Area programme. Preovision has been made in the Budget for preparing a detailed strategy to implement this programme in association with Dr. M.S. Swaminathan.

Studies at MSSRF have shown that by adding a horizontal dimension to numerous vertically structured programmes and by promoting a coalition of all concerned with ending hunger and deprivation, it is now possible to provide opportunities for a healthy and productive life for all.

The problem of food and nutrition security at the level of the individual has to be viewed in 3 dimensions. First,, inadequate purchasing power leads to calorie-protein under-nutrition. Second, the lack of the needed quantity and variety of micronutrients and vitamins in the diet leads to several nutritional disorders including blingness caused by Vitamin A deficiency. This kind of problem is referred to as "hidden hunger", a problem which affects today more than 2 billion people in the world. Third, lack of environmental hygiene and sanitation leads to a low biological absorption and retention of food, due to intestinal infection and diarrohea. Thus, both food and non-food factors assume importance in determining the nutrition secu;rity of an individual. Concurrent action at all these levels is necessary in a Hunger-Free Area Programme. The various steps involved in this process are described below:

— Identify the basic underlying reasons for chronic under and malnutrition.

— Collate information on available programmes and opportunities for the sustainable end of hunger.

— Articulate the steps needed to provide the 'missing elements' in achieving the end of hunger.

— Mobilise local level community action and commiotment for achieving the end of endemic hunger by the end of the Ninth Five Year Plan and enlist mass media support for this purpose.

— Assess the extent of (i) Financial resources required (ii) Technical resources for technological empowerment necessary (iii) Managerial and Organisational resources needed.

— Foster the organization of a Grassroots level Coalition for Ending Hunger in each HFAP area comprising representatives of

- Elected representatives of the people.
- Government agencies.
- Civil society-non-governmental organizations, voluntary agencies, services organizations like Rotary clubs, Lions clubs, etc.
- Academia-Research, Training Instituitons and Universities.
- Corporate Sector.
- Financial Institutions and
- Mass Media.

The Coalition for Ending Hunger will be responsible for designing, implementing and monitoring the Hunger Free Area programme.

The challenge lies in converting HFAP from a concept into an operational programme. In such a programme, emphasis will have to be placed during the remaining years of this century on generating additional livelihood opportunities for those living below the poverty line in villages and towns. The increasing feminisation of poverty demands that priority attention be given to women and girl children. Based on these considerations, the following operational framework is suggested for a National Hunger-Free Area Programme.

This phase will relate tot he analysis of gaps and constraints. Under the Gap Analysis Programme, an inventory will be made of all the entitlements currently available to those living below the poverty line both through the Central and State Government programmes. The inventory will be suitably classified so as to differentiate social security and nutrition intervention programmes from those relating to employment generation.

Once the Entitlements Database is compiled detailed study based on random sampling techniques will be conducted in about 100 villages of a district to assess the extent to which the entitlements have actually reached the intended families. Within families, special studies will be conducted to ascertain the extent of male-female differences in access to entitlements. The gap between what the poor are entitled to and what they are actually receiving will be grouped according to gender and economic status (I.E., those having assets like land or livestock or fish pond or tress and those who do not own any productive asset).

Once the GAP Analysis is completed, a careful identification of the reasons for the gap and the contrainsts faced by the pooring getting their entitlements will be made. Such a gap and constraints analysis will be the starting how direct and imdirect opverty elimination programmes can be made to reach the unreached organisationfunctioning in the villages including under the GAP Analysis would be made together with an assessment of their effectiveness in serving as bridges between Government agencies and the poor. Discussions will be held with both voluntary organizations and men and women members of elected Panchayats and Nagarpalikas on how the gap can be ended and how the delivery systems of poverty in thier efficiency and impact.

This phase-II will be a strategic planning phase giving particular attention to the following:

(a) Steps needed to fill the gap between entitlements and actual delivery.

(b) Opportunities for mobilising human, financial resources in the concerned areas for improving the efficiency of delilvery of on-going programmes and for initiating new programmes to meet the unmet minimum needs of the population.

(c) Identification of methods of achieving synergy and convergence among all the programmes, whether governmental or non-governmental.

(d) Articulation of new livelihood opportunities based on both farm and non-farm occupations.

(e) Introduction of organisational and management methods which will ensure the oversight and effective participation of the primary stake holders in the implementation of programmes designed to strengthen the security of their livelihoods, and

(f) Identification of young women and men in the concerned villages for forming a Corps of Hunger Fighters. The young hunger fighters would undertake responsibilities such as creating awareness of entitlements, improving delivery systems and promoting environmental hygiene and garbage and sewage recycling.

The hunger fighters would be given a small honorarium for meeting their travel and other expenses and for compensating them for thier time. The members of the Corps of Hunger Fighters will be drawn from those who have a social or economic stake in living in their respective villages. There will be equal number of women and men in such a corps.

As a result of the work done during phases 1 and 2, awareness of the possibilities for ending hunger and deprivation, analaysis of methods of achieving the desired goals and an implementable action plan would have emerged. The Action Programme, to be effective, must emerge from discussions with the poor families and on the basis of their suggestions. The phase will therefore be opportune to establish a broad based local level Coalition for Ending Hunger and Deprivation. Such a Coalition for Ending Hunger could consist of representatives of local self-government institutions, government agencies responsible for fighting poverty and hunger, academic community, the civil society, corporate sector, women's and youth organisations, financial institutions and the mass media. Such a coalition will assign specific tasks to each member of the coalition in the areas of awareness generation, resource mobilisation task implementation, monitoring and evaluation. The Coalition will aim to add a horizontal dimension zto vertically structured government programmes. Coalition members will also help to develop methods of achieving gender equality and eliminating social evils like dowery and alcoholism.

During ths period, HFAP will be converted from a desirable concept to anb implementable local level action plan. Intensive efforts will be made to sensitise all sections of the community to the uncommon opportunities now available for achieving a sustainable end to hunger. The poor themselves will play an active role in both the planning and implementation phase. Many of the members of the grassroots level Corps of Hunger Fighters will come from landless labour families. The Corps of Hunger Fighters will include elected members of Panchayats and Nagarpalikas, so that they are able to serve as links between the elected bodies and the people. There should be a minimum of two members of the corps drawn form every village/town, so that they are able to play a role in improving environmental hygiene and sanitation as well as the health and nutrition secutity of the families living in their village/town.

Ours is a land of the young. Nearly 400 million women and men are below the age of 21. The nation's future depends upon the opportunity they get for a productive and healthy life. Youth can be attracted and retained in farming only if farming becomes and economically rewarding. This is where ecological agriculture, which is knowledge intensive, can prove to be a double advantage.

Our society is characterised by cultural, religious, linguistic and political pluralism. Political pluralism at the level of the central government provides an opportunity for elevating issues relating to hunger elimination and poverty alleviation to a level of overriding priority, transcending political frontiers and placing them at the top of the political agenda. The Government of Tamil Nadu has taken the first bold step in this directon by deciding to initiate a cencerted attempt to eliminate poverty-induced hunger. We should work for spreading the Hunger-Free Area programme throughout the country before we enter the next century.

Integrating environemntal considerations into development planning is not an easy task. Unless concern is backed by an ability to take ameliorative action, little can be achieved. India has been very conscious of this and has, over the past few decades, taken important steps to increase its capacity to handle environmental issues.

The initiatives have come equally from the Government, NGO's and individuals. Many collaborative and joint programmes exist today between the Government and the NGO's.

Environment and development problems are complex and there cannot be generalized and simplified solutions. Answers have to be found which are ecologically, economically and socio-culturally consistent in the particular milie. Given the size and diversity of a country like India, this task becomes extremely difficult.

Expertise is requied in framing appropriate policies and legislation, in planning, in creating mechanisms for implementation, in * education and public awareness. India also needs to be above to bring its perspective to global forums and participate in evolving international treaties, protocols and conventions. Most importantly, with the increasing emphasis on decentralized decision—making and the stress on micro-planning, this capacity-building is taking on a greater urgency. Capability is required to enable decisions to be made in a decentralized manner—decisions which are not imported solutions, but are appropriate to the particular situation.

Addressing the plenary session of the UN Conference on Human Environment in Stockholm in 1972, Prime Minister Indira Gandhi and said, "Even though our industrial development is in its infancy and at its most difficult stage, we are taking various steps to deal with the incipient environmental imbalances, more so because of our concern for the human species, whic is also imperilled." It was at her initiative that a National Council Environmental Planning and Coordination (NECPC) was set up in 1972 to identify and investigate the problems of preserving or improving the human environment in the country, and to propose solution to environmental problems.

Another Empowered Committee, the Tiwari Committee, was set up in 1980 to review and recommend legislative measures and administrative machinery for ensuring environmental protection. On the recommendation of this Committee, the Department of Environment was set up in 1980 as the focal agency in the administrative structure of the Central Government for planning, promotion and coordination of environmental programmes. This department became part of the new Ministry of Environment and Forest in 1985.

The Ministry is the apex body under the Government of India for planning, promotion and coordination of environmental and forestry programmes. Its activities include conservation and survey of flora and fauna, prevention and control of pollution, afforestation and regeneration of degraded areas, impact assessment, forest conservation and research, and education and information. The National Wastelands Development Board and the Ganga Project Directorate are major components of the Ministry.

Most of the states have also set up their own Departments of Environment, Pollution Control Boards and other associated bodies. Various other ministries and departments, including those of Urban Development, Oceanography, Non-Conventional Energy Sources etc., at the state and central levels, are also concerned with different aspects of the environment Greater coordination among these various agencies—government and non-government-would strengthen environmental efforts. State Governments are in the process of involving themselves seriously in environmental planning.

The Directory of Environmental NGOs, brought out by the World Wide Fund for Nature - India (WWF-I) in 1989, lists about 850 NGOs working in this field, but there are porbably at least four times this number. Their involvement is clearly seen. As the Secretary General of WWF-I says, "India's impressively large body of NGOs is becoming active on the environmental front because fo the increasingly clear nexus between meaningful, equitable, sustainable economic growth and the conservation of the environment...For instance, the National Environmental Awareness Campaign promoted by the Ministry has successfully encouraged many NGOs whose primary concerns are rural development, appropriate technology, civil rights, women's development, tribal welfare etc. The interaction between NGOs and State Governments is largely confined to functional matters (clearance, information, advice etc.) whereas for financial and technical support various central departments and agencies have to be relied upon. However now there is a concerted effort by the Government to use their expertise for their own programmes."

NGOs range from clubs which encourage and assist in adventure travel, exploration, and dissemination of knowledge about an ecosystem to agencies which deal with various issues like creating gainful employment, wastelands development, afforestation, rehabilitation of tribals, and with preparation of educational materials and aids. They may be as small as groups of two or three persons, or as large as organizations with an eight-thousand-strong membership.

One of the most important signs of environmental

awareness in India is the rise of people's movements which are challenging existing socio-political structures and development models, and are showing alternative paths. These have led not only to action at the grassroot level, but are also helping to shape developmental policies.

Environmental degradation

There are a host of human interventions including development activities which have resulted in considerable environmental degration. Major human interventions in forests are deforestation, commercial logging, setting up protected area, partial closure of forests, etc which are described below:

- There is increasing deforestation due to commercial exploitation, building of dams, mining and construction activities. Of the world's estimated 8.4 billion hectares of forests in 1990, tropical forests covered 1.76 billion ha. During 1981-90, tropical forests were lost at the rate of 0.8 per cent (15.4 million ha) a year, as per estimates of the World Resources Institute. The net annual deforestation during 1981-90 exceeded two per cent in 10 tropical countries of Asia and Africa.
- Commercial logging for industrial activities is increasing rapidly. Eighty-four per cent of such logging took place in closed tropical broadleaf forests in primary (undisturbed forests) during the 1980s. Logging activity is a causal factor for forest degradation and is reflected in rough wood production which increased by 19 per cent between 1979-81 to 1989-91. Globally, almost 50 per cent of such rough wood is used for industrial purposes, the rest for heating and cooking.
- Setting up of protected areas for conservation purposes has led to complications and conflict-

situation with indigenous communities and also denial of many of their rights and privileges.

- Closure of parts of forests for setting up of industries or agro-based activities for private, semi-private lands, construction of railways, roads and new settlements has led to shrinkage of forest cover and increased hardship for local communities in their day-to-day existence.
- Interventions for adhering to international agreements have also alienated many local communities and some of their practices, eg, tribal hunting of wild animals which goes against biodiversity agreements.
- Policies of economic liberalization, privatization and globalization have both, directly and indirectly, led to reduction of forest cover and cuts in subsidies and grants affecting food subsidies and other welfare schemes involving poor and marginalized communities.

Human rights are a extensive as human life and, whether or not enshrined in national constitutions or bills of right or in international covenants to which nations are signatory, first order rights are inherent and inalienable. As Jefferson said, "the God that gave us life, gave us liberty at the same time". These rights are not gifted and cannot be taken away except by due process of law. To act otherwise is to violate Human Rights. There are, however, a whole series of rights, other than the basic or fundamental freedoms, which are statutory or derive from subscription to international or regional covenants.

Human Rights may be broadly classified as civil and political (so-called civil liberties and democratic rights), and social, economic and cultural. The latter include rights to development, the rights of women and children, a whole new family of environmental rights, rights to education and health, and to employment and to enjoy the fruits of labour. Both sets of rights are growing. Thus, freedom of speech and expression has developed to encompass the right to information. Privacy is now increasingly protected. There will be refinements and new situations will bring forth new rights such as now, in some societies, of pays, and may be for victims of AIDS.

A comparison of South Asian constitutions will probably indicate a broad similarity in the basic rights enunciated. Interpretations and implementation might vary. Derogations are permitted in emergency situations and these instances have been extensive in all parts of South Asia and have sometimes continued long after the proximate cause, perhaps well justified in some cases, has passed. The Indian Emergency (1975-77) and martial law or emergency regimes in Pakistan, Nepal, Bangladesh and Sri Lanka can also be cited. Many statutes contain preventive laws (preventive detention in India), and special laws may be invoked in given circumstances such as declaring certain areas to be disturbed and applying therein summary procedures (such as the Armed Forces Special Powers Act in India).

The South Asian nations are members of the United Nations and have variously subscribed to a number of international instruments including the international Covenants on Civil and Political Rights/Economic and Social Rights, the Geneva Conventions, ILO conventions and so forth. However, retification has not always followed speedily or at all. For instance, India took a long time to ratify the Convention on the Rights of the Child and has yet to ratify the Convention Against Torture. The record of the other South Asian governments would probably reveal similar lags or omissions which need to be overcome. Even where ratifications has taken place it is not certain whether governments have cared to create public awareness about national adherence to these conventions and to explain their implications or to examine whether national laws need to be upgraded, expanded or created to give them an enforceable statutory basis. This is an exercise national governments should be asked to undertake and could be the subjects of a report of SAARC.

While human rights are proclaimed, newly-independent nations have sometimes been prone to stress sovereign or national rights, the rights of the state, over individual human rights. This was true worldwide until the second world war and in some ways continue to be so even in the more industrially advanced and politically older or mature societies because of the fears and compulsions of the cold war. With the end of the East-West divide, the West has given more emphasis to human rights and democratic governance and has come to attach trade and aid conditionalities for "good performance". While this may be justified at one level, the question that arises, as it does in the domestic domain, is who will police the policeman? Also, how far observing is the human rights record of smaller and weaker countries. Such conditionalities are also creeping into the field of environment, the rights of so-called indigenous people, a misnomer when applied to South Asian societies, and so on.

Development, gender, minority, regional and environmental rights, among others, are of great importance to South Asia where poverty, gender inequalities, disparities, illiteracy, bonded labour and child labour are widespread. Poverty robs the individual of dignity and, often, children of their childhood. While, therefore, development rights are vitally important, there are no hierarchy of rights. All rights, political, civil cultural, social and economic, are indivisible and mutually reinforcing. This is a normative value that South Asia must accept and proclaim so that one right is not used to supersede and thereby deny another.

South Asia has a number of human rights organisations, statutory and voluntary. In India, for scheduled castes and tribes and statutory bodies such as the Press Council, the Minorities Commission, the National Commission for Women, and the Commissioner for Linguistic Minorities. A statutory Human Rights Commission has been brought into being by ordinance and incorporates many improvements in relation to an earlier Bill. Pakistan has a very active non-governmental Human Rights Commission whose reports merit wider distribution in the region. The Human Rights Organisation of Nepal (HURON) played an important part in securing the change-over from the panchayati system to the vigorous multi-party democracy that was established in 1991. Bangladesh has a Coordinating Council for Human Rights (CCHRB) which aims to publish annual reports.

All the countries of South Asia are in transition and there is much ferment: violence, terrorism, ethnic discords, the rise of religious fundamentalisms, basic rights, but the exploitation of religion for partisan political ends, can be dangerous as India has discovered. Likewise caste. With the process of nation-building still underway, individual and state rights tend to clash. A more careful study of events and trends and a sharing of experience could promote clarity and wisdom in dealing with highly complex and volatile situations.

Human rights violations regrettably occur everywhere around the globe in greater or lesser measure. What matters, however, is that violation, aberrant action and derogations are brought to light by the media, the law enforcement agencies and human rights groups or by the community at large and the guilty are brought to book. While human rights mechanisms need to be strengthened or even created where necessary, human rights problems most often begin where due process and the criminal justice system break down. This then leads to false cases, torture, custodial death, extortion, rape, corruption, et al. The public preception of a breakdown in the local criminal justice system led to the Bhagalpur blindings in Bihar in the 1980s when there was widespread public approval of known criminals being blinded while in detention for fear that they would otherwise be bailed out or released and continue with their depredations.

The restoration of the efficacy, integrity and speed of the criminal justice system (including the working of the police and jails) is perhaps the single most important item that should be on the South Asian human rights agenda. For prevention is better than cure. Political interference with the police, the politicisation of crime and the criminalisation of politics have played havoc. Dealing with human rights violations then becomes a case of trying to shut the stable door after the horse has bolted. The understaffing of courts, mounting arrears and costs, and dilatory procedures are discrediting the rule of law.

Yet the judiciary has been innovative. In India, for example, public interest litigation has opened new doors, overriding former impediments of locus standi in relations to the cause of action and treating a single case as a class action. Judicial verdicts have also amplified Article 21, the Right to Life, to embrace "rights to livelihood, health, education, shelter, dignity, minimum wage, environment" (Upendra Baxi).

Environmental issues have come to the fore in South Asia with poverty, population and livestock pressures leading to deforestation, erosion of common property resources and environmental degradation generally. The land can no longer support burgeoning numbers and the region is spawning its share of inadvertent cities and threatens to (and does) explode with crime and violence. Water and energy shortages confront us and industrial, pollution and development blight are increasingly visible, though yet in the early stages. The warning signals are there.

South Asia's environmental problems are largely related to the economics of survival, poverty in a broad sense being the worst polluter. Population control and ensuring an early demographic transition are of the highest importance. Primary education and health and improving the status of women hold the key as Sri Lanka, and Kerala and Goa in India have well demonstrated. The pace of development must be hastened and the fruits of development more equitably shared. There have to be alternative sources of fodder and fuel, improved land-use patterns, better land and water management and greater emphasis on biofertilisers and integrated pest management so as to avoid incremental toxicity entering the food chain. Rivers are becoming sewers. The Ganga Action Plan, now being extended to the Yamuna, Damodar, Gomati and other rivers, represents the largest river clean-up operation ever undertaken anywhere. Conservation, substainability and maintenance of bio-diversity have become key ideas.

South Asia is setting new pollution standards and seeking to upgrade technology and maintenance systems, but there is a long way to go. Environmental groups are active and environmental awareness is spreading. Indian courts have ordered the closure of polluting industries for failure to ensure minimal emission of effluent standards despite being allowed resonable time, access to credit, and technical assistance to upgrade their technology. Environmental tribunals are contemplated.

Two problems will have to be confronted. One is internal pressure from local groups and communities to adopt alternative strategies of development: decentralised, low-energy, appropriate technology, small-is-beautiful, back-to-nature systems. While the opposition to ostentatious consumption, crass consumerism and waste is widel'y shared, there will be reservations about nostalgia, romanticising the past, overlooking the tremendous growth of population which is likely to double or triple again before it stabilises in South Asia, and ignoring the demand for minimal life styles and national infra-structure in a globalised setting. There has to be a practical via media. At the other end of the scale, the North would like to globalise tropical forests and bio-diversity and points to population growth as a looming ecological threat, leading to green house warming, a possible sea-rise, and destablising climate changes. This ignores the unsustainable life styles of the North and its massive contribution to global warming since the industrial revolution, but more particularly, in the past few decades. Global conferencing and the Rio meet have brought about some convergence, but maybe not nearly enough.

South Asia, as a clearly demacrated monsoonal geopolitical entity, should concert action on both the regional and global planes. The Himalayan-Karakoram barrier constitutes a critical watershed the greening of which should be worth something as a global carbon sink and oxygen bank. Debt-for-nature swaps and debt forgiveness by the North, linked to environmental improvement and technological upgradation in South

Asia, should be jointly explored. The natural disaster study undertaken by SAARC (1989-91) marks a beginning towards collective action on environmental issues and optimal harnessing of shared natural resources such as rivers and bio-diversity.

There could be joint studies and research programmes in South Asia to meet the challenge of global warming and sea-rise effects, to fight locusts and study seismicity.

On the human rights plane, it is perhaps not widely known that a South Asian Forum for Human Rights was formally set up in Kathmandu in February, 1993, a spinoff from a suggestion mooted at the World Human Rights Congress in Delhi in 1990. This is a non-governmental body that plans to promote networking and interaction among human rights groups in the region. All the SAARC nations other than the Maldives are represented. It is still at an embryonic stage but could grow. The setting up of SAARC observer groups to monitor elections in the region represents another initiative. Perhaps the time has come to moot the establishment of a human rights cell within SAARC or more informally to gather information, liaise and sensitise governments on issues and opportunities that call for concerted action.

Human rights and environmental issues are very much on the national, regional and international agenda today. These concerns have wide linkages and need to be properly understood and fully internalised in national and regional policies and instruments.

Disease control and health improvement

Given the existing conditions of poor environmental sanitation and the weakness of the public health system it may not be possible to completely prevent out breaks of communicable diseases in the near future. Nevertheless, early detection and prompt response could result in rapid containment and control of the outbreak, reduction in morbidity and mortality. The building up of the disease surveillance and response mechanisms have received considerable attention during the Eighth Plan period. It is felt disease surveillance and response must be based at district level ensure prompt response. This system needs to be given the necessary back up laboratory support and epidemiological expertise so that containment measures are based on suond data and are logical. This back up system should be evolved through strengthening and optimal utilisation of the facilities and expertise available in the National Institution's/medical colleges.

Increasing incidence of hospital acquired infections and accidental infection in health care providers and waste disposers renders it imperative that efforts are made to improve infection control and waste management through utilisaton of appropriate affordable technology at all levels of health care. Planning Commission and the Ministry of Health and Family Welfare Programme have initiated steps to take up specific pilot projects.

Increasing longevity, demographic transition resulting in rapidly rising numbers of aged population, urbanisation, increasing pollution, a change over from traditional diets, sedentary life style and increase in the stress of day to day living have led to the increase in life style related disorders and noncommunicable diseases. Noncommunicable diseases such as cardio-and cerebrovascular diseases resulting in heart attacks and strokes, diabetes and common malignancies are emerging as major public health problems in the country. Pilot projects for district based integrated noncummunicable disease control programmes carried out through the existing primary and secondary level facilities, using diabetes as a model, have been initiated in the Eighth Plan. The experience gained will be used to expand such programmes.

Rapidly growing population, urbanisation, changing agricultural, industrial and water resource management, increasing use of pesticides and fossil fuels have all resulted in perceptible deterioration in the quality of environment and attendant adverse health consequences. Pilot projects exploring the dimensions of the problem and aimed at seeking realistic solutions were initiated during the Eighth Plan period. Efforts are also under way to document extent of the problem of environmental pollution and its impact on health status of the population. Prevention and management of health consequences of environmental deterioration will receive increasing attention.

Over the last two decades occupational health has received considerable attention. Continuous monitoring of safety of work environment and workers' health status, both in the organised and unorganised sector with emphasis on gender specific and child labour related issues, documenting the magnitude and types of the occupational health problems, initiating appropriate preventive and remedial measures will be developed into a structured health programme are being taken up wherever possible.

Several major development activities in any field such as Agriculture, Industries, Urban and Rural Development have resulted in environment changes; some of these could have health implications. In order to minimise these it has been suggested that all large development projects should have Health Impact assesment and then necessary provision for health care of people involved in development activities and prevention and management of health consequences of developmental activities on the population living in the vicinity of the project should be incorporated and costed as part of the project. These suggestions are being considered by appropriate implementing agencies.

The past fifty years have witnessed the development of a vast health care infrastructure and manpower aimed at providing health care to the population. National Programmes have been evolved and implemented to control major public health problems. The investment in Public health has shown considerable increase over the plan periods. However there has not been any increase in the proportion of the Plan outlay allocated to health sector. There is an increase in the disease burden due to communicable and non-communicable disease caused by the growing population, newer diseases and changing life styles. There are evolving technologies for health care and increasing expectations of the population for health care. All these have resulted in the ever widening gap between what is possible and what is affordable. It is imperative that in the coming decades this gap is bridged and at the same time equity and excellence are ensured in health care services.

The family Welfare Programme has helped in containing the growth rate of population. Total Fertility Rate has declined from 4.5 in 1981 to 3.5 in 1993 as per the estimates of Sample Registration System (SRS). The Crude Birth Rate has decreased from 33.9 per provisional estimates of the SRS. The Crude Death Rate has also declined from 12.5 to 9 per thousand population over the same period. The Infant MOrtality Rate dropped from 110 per thousand live births in 1981 to 74 in 1995. The annual average exponential population growth rate has come down marginally from 2.22 per cent during 1971-81 to 2.14 per cent during 1981-91. The population, however, continues to grow as the decline in birth rate has not been as rapid as the decline in the death rate.

There are, however, inter-State differences in the achievements of the Family Welfare Programme. At one end of the spectrum are the States like Kerala, Tamil Nadu and Goa which have already achieved replacement level of fertility. At the other end, are the large States like Uttar Pradesh, Madhya Pradesh, Rajasthan and Bihar where fertility levels and bjirth rates continue to be higher than the national average. Therefore, decline in the rate of growth of population for the country as a whole depends upon how the large northern States perform in the family welfare programmes in the future. Unless effective steps are taken to bring about significant improvements in the programme, the performance in containing the growth of population at the All India level may not change significantly.

Recognising the close relationship between high birth rates and high rnfant mortality, high priority has been accorded to the Maternal and Child Health (MCH) programme since 1985. In order to achieves the main objective of MCH, (i.e. to improve the health status of women and children and to reduce maternal, infant and child morbidity and mortality rates), the Universal Immunisation Programme (UIP) was launched in 1985. From the year 1992-93 the UIP has been strengthened and expanded into the Child Survival and Safe Motherhood (CSSM) programme. Under this programme, apart from strengthening the existing MCH, initiative has been taken to expand the pilot projects on Acute Respiratory Infection Control and Traditional Birth Attendants training. For this, a provision of Rs.350 crore has been made in the 1996-97 budget as against Rs.220 crore in 1995-96 (BE).

From 1.4.1996, the Family Welfare Programme is being implemented on the basis of the "Target Free Approach" (TFA). This approach envisages replacement of the system of setting contraceptive targets from the top by a system of decentralised participatory planning at the Primary Health Centre level.

Pursuant to the World Health Organisation (WHO) goal to eradicate poliomyelitis by the year 2000 A.D., the Pulse Polio Immunization (PPI) was launched in 1995-96. About 87 million children aged 0-3 years were administered as supplemented dose of oral polio vaccine on 9.12.1995 and 93 million on 20.1.1996, irrespective of their routine immunisation status. Since PPI received an overwhelming response from the public, the exercise was repeated on 7.12.1996 and 18,1.1997 covering about 120 million children in the age group of 0-5 years.

A Special School Health Check-up Scheme for Primary School Children was carried out in 27 States/ UTs in July 1996, and in the remaining 5 States between August and October 1996. The objectives of this Scheme were to detect common health related problems among primary school children; to conduct screening of children for appropriate referral and check up; to generate health awareness in the community; and to ensure arrangements for follow up and treatment at higher level medical facilities. Reports from 441 districts show 75.9 per cent coverage of schools and 84.9 per cent coverage of enrolled children.

In order to foster community involvement in the Family Welfare Programme, two new schemes have been started on a pilot basis. Under one of these, one revenue village in every district, among villages with a population of 500 or more, will be given an award of Rs. 2 lakh for achieving a reduction in the Crude Birth rate, Infant Mortality Rate and Child Mortality Rate. The second schemes aims to integrate family welfare and health care into the ongoing National Wastershed Development Project for Rainfed Areas (NWDPRA) of the Ministry of Agriculture. Under this scheme, the watershed level community based management structures, known as the 'Mitra Krishak Mandal' (MKM) will conduct surveys and prepare watershed level family welfare and health care plans. An amount of Rs. 5000 will be given to each village in the watershed areas, for specified activities like emergency obstetric care and purchase of essential medicines.